The Gallant Six Hundred

The Gallant
Six Hundred

A Tragedy of Obsessions

John Harris

 Mason & Lipscomb PUBLISHERS   NEW YORK

To my wife,
who has been a refugee from
more battles in her married life
than any woman ought to be
called upon to endure

Contents

Illustrations follow page 128

Author's Preface

As the author of a recent book on Custer's last battle wrote in his preface, 'an attempt to tell again the much discussed story . . . requires a great deal of courage and at least an explanation.' Like that incident, the only cavalry battle of the Crimea is still surrounded by fierce debates and has been attended by more speculation and surmise than engagements of far greater magnitude. Like that incident also it has become to a large extent engulfed in legend.

My own interest in the Battle of Balaclava started in the Thirties when, as a young newspaperman, I met an old old man who had seen it take place as a drummer boy aged 12. He thought his age was eighty-odd but it turned out to be ten years more and he may well have been the last survivor of the Crimea.

It has been said often that the cavalry in the Crimea was badly led, but badly led troops could never have behaved as they did on the day of their ordeal. On starving horses, the Heavy Brigade went twice into action and the Light Brigade offered to go a second time if necessary and doubtless would have done if called upon. Their divisional commander, Lord Lucan, was no Murat but too many wrong impressions have grown up around him and around Louis Edward Nolan, the aide-de-camp who carried the fatal order to him. Much of what has been written about them has stemmed from Kinglake, who wrote what has become accepted as the official history of the campaign but, painstaking as Kinglake was, his work was called by some at the time 'romance rather than history,' and, with new material available, parts of his work are shown to be unreliable. He had undertaken it at Lady Raglan's request and it is difficult at times not to suspect him of cheating a little where Lord Raglan's reputation was concerned. Yet, with one or two exceptions, most historians since have followed him closely with regard to the cavalry; and in addition all too often letters have been quoted out of their chronological order and what was clearly mess chatter has been offered as fact.

Of every event, two—sometimes more—views can always be found. Sometimes it is a matter of pride, sometimes loyalty, sometimes self-esteem, and it is a historian's job to make a choice one way or the other. While I have not tried to defend anyone where his conduct is indefensible, I have felt I must separate Raglan's undoubted charm from his lack of skill as a general, and Lucan's skill as a divisional commander from his lack of charm as a man. He must have been far more able than has ever been allowed, but he has suffered far too much by being linked in obloquy with his brother-in-law, the unmanageable Lord Cardigan, and I have been surprised how many people—both of his period and of mine—have considered he has not received justice.

I am very much in debt to many people: The Reading Room staff of the National Army Museum, Mr. D. W. King and the Ministry of Defence Library, the Royal United Services Institute Library; the Sheffield City Libraries; Major-Generals H. Essame and G. N. Wood, who have often helped me with advice; Mr. Peter Howard of *The Sheffield Morning Telegraph*; Mr. R. R. Mellor, of the Library and Records Dept. of the Foreign and Commonwealth Office, for information on Sir John Blunt; the Army Museum's Ogilby Trust; the Marquess of Anglesey, the editor, and Leo Cooper, Ltd., the publishers of *Little Hodge*, for permission to quote from the letters of Col. E. C. Hodge; Michael Joseph Ltd., for permission to quote from *Henry Clifford: His Letters and Drawings from the Crimea*; Philip Warner, the author, and Arthur Barker, Ltd., the publishers of *The Crimean War—A Reappraisal*, for permission to quote from the letters of Captain Temple Goodman; Gerald Duckworth & Co. Ltd., the publishers, for permission to quote from *A Diary of the Crimea* by George Palmer Evelyn, edited by Cyril Falls; Major and Mrs. John Maxse, for permission to quote from the Maxse papers now in the West Sussex Record Office; Sir Francis Portal, Bt., for the loan of the letters of Captain Robert Portal; Colonel H. Moyse-Bartlett, author of *Louis Edward Nolan and His Influence on the British Cavalry*, for help and the offer of notes; the present Lord Lucan for the loan of books; the staff of the West Sussex County Library, who became almost as involved as I did, and many others. As any author writing on this subject must be, I am also indebted to Cecil Woodham-Smith's fine book *The Reason Why*.

J.H.

Chain of Command

Lord Raglan

| First Division (Duke of Cambridge) | Second Division (Sir G. de Lacy Evans) | Third Division (Sir Richard England) | Fourth Division (Sir George Cathcart) | Light Division (Sir George Brown) | Cavalry Division (Lord Lucan) |

Light Brigade (Lord Cardigan)

4th. and 13th. Light Dragoons
8th. and 11th. Hussars
17th. Lancers

Heavy Brigade (Sir James Y. Scarlett)

1st. Dragoons (The Royals)
2nd. Dragoons (Scots Greys)
6th. Dragoons (The Inniskillings)
4th. Dragoon Guards
5th. Dragoon Guards

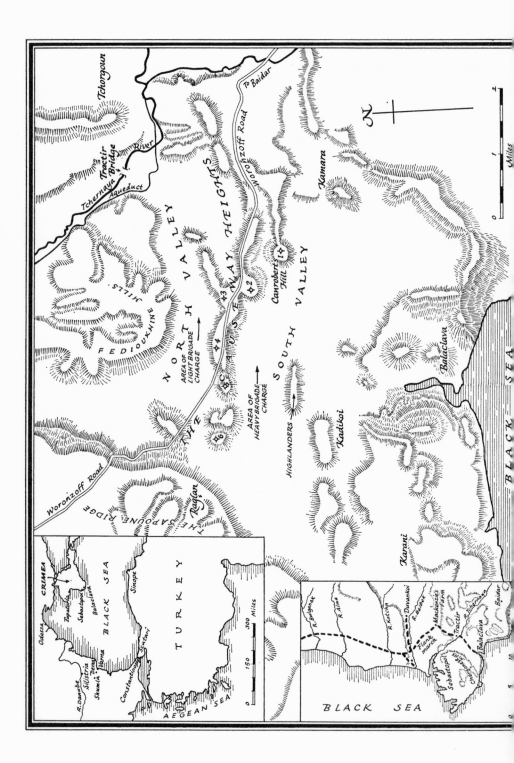

1 The sick man of Europe

MARCH, 1854, and England was at war again! After forty years of peace she was preparing to march side by side with her ancient enemy, France, against Russia, an old ally of the Napoleonic Wars.

Two years before, she had buried her greatest hero of that age, Wellington, the Great Duke, the victor of Waterloo, a soldier of such stature that by comparison everyone else had appeared to be dwarfs, and it had seemed then as if with his departure war had been put aside for ever in favour of the one thing Napoleon had so despised in the English character, her gift for commerce. Half London had seen the funeral procession as it had moved between the shuttered shops and the balconies swathed with black crêpe. Under a cold autumn sky which threw out the curve of St. Paul's, they had heard the thin rise and fall of brass punctuated by the thud of muffled drums and the high scream of Guards officers. The clatter of muskets against the stones had broken the silence and the Dead March had pealed loudly between the long lines of bearskins over the thump of the drums and the slow tramp of heavy boots. Behind the line of State coaches, the immense funeral car, dragged by a team of twelve horses loaned by a brewery company, had resembled some ponderous galley with its twisted bronze columns, its mourning canopy and silver-spangled pall, its figured bas-reliefs of weapons and victories. Alongside it had paced mounted field marshals, glittering with stars, and the groan of the wheels over the cobbles had sounded like the grind of ghostly artillery from Albuera, Bussaco, Salamanca, Vitoria and Waterloo. As it had reached the last short slope to the cathedral door, its size had almost been its undoing and George Higginson, a young Grenadier officer on duty at that point, had been startled to see half-a-dozen roughly clad figures carrying crowbars emerge from under the draperies

17

and begin to lever at the wheels. As the music had ceased the Garter King-at-Arms had intoned the titles of the dead man . . . 'Field Marshal the Duke of Wellington, Marquis of Douro, Duke of Ciudad Rodrigo, Duke of Vitoria, Marquis of Torres Vedras, Count Vimeiro, Knight of the Garter, General Commander of the Bath, Companion of the Golden Fleece, Lord High Constable of England . . .'

They had seemed at the time like signal guns saluting a dead age and the end of all conflict, but now, only two years later, here they were again, preparing to go into battle beside the nephew of the dead man's old adversary, another Napoleon, on behalf of some half-civilised bunch of Levantines who hitherto had been noted only for their gift for atrocities.

*

Russia had suddenly in the last year or two begun to look dangerous. She had her eye on Constantinople, but in the hands of Russia, Constantinople would have been a menace to half of Europe. It would have given Russia's Black Sea Fleet from the new naval base at Sebastopol access to the Mediterranean yet would also have proved a safe haven behind which it could shelter from any pursuit. It would have provided her with a route to the Balkans and made her influence felt throughout the Levant and the Holy Land as far as Egypt. Knowing this, Tsar Nicholas had been casting greedy eyes on the helpless country on his doorstep for some time. With her decaying systems, Turkey invited attack and, as Nicholas had said, was 'the sick man of Europe'. He felt Turkey was dying and that the nations of Europe should come to some agreement about dividing up the corpse. It was his idea that Britain should take Egypt and possibly Crete, while Russia's influence should cover Constantinople pending a settlement of the troubled Balkans which would place Roumania, Serbia and Bulgaria as independent states under Russian protection. Britain was unmoved.

However, Nicholas had one great advantage. As head of the Greek Orthodox Church, he was already titular religious leader of 14,000,000 of Turkey's Christian subjects, and in 1853 it dawned on him that he had a perfect excuse to make trouble in the Church of the Holy Sepulchre in Bethlehem, at that time part of the Turkish Empire. This church, according to tradition built on the site of the stable where Christ was born, had been the scene of violent clashes between monks of the Orthodox Church and monks of the Roman Catholic Church, protected by France since the time of the Crusades. The quarrel concerned the Catholics' right to the key to the main door of the church and the two doors which led from it to the Manger. As several Orthodox monks were killed, Nicholas was able to make it his reason to act and he sent Prince Mentschikoff, an imperious bully who had detested the Turks ever since he had been emasculated by a shot from a Turkish gun in the war of 1828, to threaten the Sultan. An ultimatum was sent in which it was insisted that the keys and the privileges should be restored at once to the Greek Church and that the Sultan should also acknowledge Nicholas's right to be protector of that Church throughout his territories. The Sultan gave way on the first demand but inevitably found the second impossible to accept.

The Great Powers did what they could to reduce the tension but, unfortunately, allowing themselves to become rattled by French demands for the safety of French civilians in the Middle East, the British government now foolishly ordered the fleet to the Dardanelles and Nicholas responded by ordering his troops into the Turkish principalities of Moldavia and Wallachia, now Roumania. This time the ultimatum went the other way and by 23 October Russia and Turkey were at war.

*

At first the Turks managed to startle the Russians by their ability and strength along the Danube, and still no one else was involved but on 30 November the Turkish Fleet, caught in harbour at Sinope by the Russians, was completely destroyed with the loss of 4,000 sailors. This perfectly legitimate act of war for some reason roused the English to an extraordinary fury and mobs began to parade the London streets, singing jingles about the Russian Bear, the Turkey, the Cock-a-doodle and the Lion. It was now clear to everyone that war was coming. On 21 January, 1854, the Russian *Court Gazette* 'teemed' with abuse of France and England, who were described as having invented for the Turks the word 'independence', a word hitherto unknown in that language and, though the Queen's speech at the opening of Parliament in February still clung to the hope for peace, it also sternly referred to the preparations for war and augmentations of the army and navy.

Augmentation, unfortunately, was easier said than done. Not only the death of the Duke of Wellington but the Prince Consort's magnum opus, the Great Exhibition of 1851, had led the country to imagine she was done with fighting. Britain was no longer a rural nation but a nation of cities and towns and great factories dependent on foreign trade, and the developments in industry had built huge new empires in Lancashire, Yorkshire and the Midlands, and a forceful new middle class had sprung up, arrogant in its wealth and convinced that in its dark cities lay the future of the nation. It had become so easy by the middle of the 19th century to believe that her future lay not in war but in her gift for trade that the Services had been allowed to run down, and the navy was the first to become aware of the fact. The demands of the Mediterranean Fleet had already exhausted its diminished resources and as the British Baltic Fleet prepared on 10 March to take up its station, despite the efforts that had been made there were no Baltic pilots, a great shortage of officers and—so it was said—no more than 300 real seamen in any ship. The final humiliation was that there was no ammunition either and it had to follow later.[1]

[1] For Notes on Sources see pages 287 to 292.

Seventeen days later, on 27 March, 1854, France declared war on Russia, and the following day Lord Aberdeen committed Britain once more to battle. It was to begin a period of disaster, indifference, carelessness and gross mismanagement, and for a very large proportion of the men involved, death in ill-planned, badly fought battles or from one of the many diseases that always plagued mid-Victorian armies.

2 Uneducated as soldiers

IT was clear at once that this new war was not to be just another skirmish against savages, which was all both the French and the British had experienced since Waterloo, but a clash of great European powers, and every soldier in the army wanted to be in on it, and from their offices beyond the broad parade grounds, in clubs and at dinners, regimental commanders immediately began to put forward their claims to be included in any force that was sent to the East. It was decided that this time it could not be left merely to the obscure line regiments who had previously always held the frontiers, and the decision was to bring home to the United Kingdom the tragedy of war as no struggle had done since Waterloo. For the first time since that campaign great families were involved as famous and fashionable regiments were named, and young men who had done little else but strut about in gorgeous uniforms suddenly found themselves hurrying round in search of equipment.

Some regiments had left for the East before war had been declared. On 14 February the 1st Battalion of the Coldstream Guards had left St. George's Barracks for Malta and as they had passed down the Strand omnibuses and cabs came to a halt and the occupants joined with the vast crowd in cheering them. The Grenadiers, after a disorderly night when someone left the gate open and allowed tearful wives to stream into the barracks,[1] marched from the Tower cheered by people still in their night clothes, followed a few days later by the 1st Battalion of the Scots Fusiliers, strengthened with volunteers from the 2nd. Considering that they were heading for the Middle East, their equipment was singularly unsuitable. They were wearing heavy uniforms and bearskins, but when Higginson, the Grenadier who had been startled to see workmen appear from beneath Wellington's funeral car, protested, he was told 'My dear fellow, you'll probably not go beyond Malta.'

Though the Guards had always been popular in London as a spectacle, on the whole the rest of the army had not been taken into the hearts of the population to quite the same degree. While truncheons had become more conspicuous by 1854 than sabres for keeping the peace, the army was still occasionally called out by magistrates to put down industrial riots, a fact which, while it did not endear it to the working classes, also curiously failed to make the new property- and factory-owners more affectionate. In addition, it was still really the army of Waterloo and the Peninsula—the difference being that it had no glory about its banners save those which had become a little tarnished with the passing of time.

Its methods of recruiting had set it apart from the rest of the nation. Enlisting until a few years earlier had been for 21 years or what amounted to the whole of a man's life and the soldier had been a creature apart, living in vast barrack blocks on the outskirts of the towns. In the older ones, the conditions were often so bad the rate of mortality was sometimes higher than that of the civilian population outside, despite the fact that the soldiers were all strong young men who had been subjected to a fitness test.

Surrounded by squalid little houses and a multitude of beer-shops, they were often in close proximity to a small-arms or powder factory. The whole area proclaimed the army's occupation with notices and it often exploded at night in brawls as gunner turned against infantryman, or cavalryman against engineer. 'Up the Heavies and to hell with the Light Bobs' would always start a fight.

This was not universal, however. At Hillsborough, near Sheffield, a brand-new barracks had just been completed at the then enormous cost of £121,000, and plans were in existence for the addition of an infants' school, gymnasium and married quarters. This was unusual, however, and units posted to Sheffield counted themselves lucky. For the rest of the army, the last years of the Duke of Wellington's rule had done dreadful damage.

Always a reactionary, in his old age he had allowed most of his work to be done by others while he dozed at his desk, and in all promotions he considered first the families of the Beauforts, the Westmorlands and the Pakenhams, to which he was connected.

There was no medical service, other than the regimental hospitals which were efficient enough by the standards of the day, and no plans whatsoever for the building up of one, and the military organisation as a whole was in a complicated and inefficient state. There was a Secretary for War, who was only concerned with war after it had been declared, and a Secretary at War, who administered the army of the day. Under his supervision was the General Commanding-in-Chief of the Army, whose military headquarters were the Horse Guards. The Board of Ordnance, entirely separate, was controlled by the Master-General of the Ordnance, who also commanded the artillery and the engineers. The Commissariat Department was worked by the Treasury and the medical arrangements by the Army Medical Board. There was no land transport and no organisation to provide it, and the staff of the supply departments had been cut to a few clerks, who were so overwhelmed when war came that all the processes by which the troops were to receive food and clothing or be cared for when sick or wounded fell into confusion. Worst of all, there was no single head to co-ordinate the work and no clear line drawn by which any one department knew precisely what its duties covered; in many cases departments ignored their responsibilities simply because they felt they belonged to another department.

There were not even any reserves. Years of disinterest, maladministration and cheeseparing had brought Wellington's great machine to a perilous state of inefficiency. There was little or no field training, and the higher commanders had no practice whatsoever in handling formations bigger than a brigade, and even that not very often. It was an 'army of regiments', though there had been an attempt the year before to assemble for manoeuvres at Chobham. The deluging rain and the vast throng of representatives of Society and their ladies in the camps to view the proceedings, however, had rendered the whole thing absurd and the Russian observer's report to St. Petersburg had probably strengthened the Tsar's belief that he had nothing to fear.

The staff were probably the weakest unit in the army. A man was considered eccentric if he wished to go to Staff College and the excellent new institution at Sandhurst had been allowed to run down so that there were only six students there in 1854. As for the rest, their experience was non-existent and though rules were laid down for courses for the quartermaster-general's and adjutant-general's departments, everyone ignored them and relied instead on favouritism and 'interest'.[2] Field Marshal Lord Wolseley, then a young officer, said that he would not have trusted the staff with a subaltern's picket, and they were likened to the fountains in Trafalgar Square, which 'only played from eleven to five o'clock'. Too often—though there were many brilliant exceptions—they were Society dawdlers and were unfit for their positions, which they had acquired almost entirely by influence. Almost every member of the staff had a title of his own or was connected to someone who had.

It might well have been that great numbers of officers could have been brought in from the Indian Army where, at least, they had experience of active service, but to be fair the Indian Army had had more than its share of disasters. An expedition to Kabul 12 years before had been wiped out, one single survivor riding in to bring the news; there had been a poor showing at Mudki only six years before, and at Chilianwallah hesitation and bad leadership had almost brought a defeat. However, there were a few officers available who had returned to England for such reasons as family business or ill health and a few who had served in the British Legion in the Carlist Wars in Spain, and they were suddenly in great demand as advisers by men who stared at their own records of service and realised how threadbare they were.

Despite their low numbers, the regiments themselves were not in bad shape. Recruits had all too often come from the illiterate, dispossessed peasants of Ireland—out of 1,400 killed in the first battle in the Crimea, 750 proved to be Irish, while the Welch Fusiliers were Irish almost to a man. But things were changing and, with the length of service reduced and the older men disappearing, a new type of recruit was beginning to come forward. To a large extent this was due to the disappearance of the old savagery of service.

Contrary to popular belief, it was not Miss Florence Nightingale who reformed the British Army. The reform had started in 1846. Although the aristocracy considered it had a right to lead, it also considered it had a duty, and the spirit-breaking methods of the Prussians had always been strongly resisted by humanitarian officers. Though much has been heard of pipeclay and the lash, little has been said of those officers who tried to relieve the hardships of their men. By the time of the Crimean War the new ideas had taken firm root and there was a growing spirit of humanity. Abuses were being killed and at no time was flogging the mainstay of discipline. The authorities called for regular records of it and they show that in many cases there was no record at all.

In fact, good regiments had a social relationship between officers and men that was years ahead of its time, and provided schools and savings banks for those who wished to use them. In this the regimental officers were the prime movers, and often acted as teachers to coach promising soldiers, while Bible classes and temperance societies were started by men like 'Holy' Havelock.

The officers, in fact, were much better as individuals than they have been allowed to appear, though on the whole their skill was not high, but, as the purchasing of commissions had never been sacred, there was a surprising number of skilled men who had come up from the ranks. For the most part they were considerate, and the purchase system, by which they had received their commissions, had not produced a bad crop despite its faults.

Throwing up free-thinking men of impressive individualism who said what they wished simply because they knew that, since their promotion did not depend on toadying, they could afford to, oddly enough it also encouraged advancement because colonels lost their purchase price when they were raised to the rank of general and were therefore careful, if they were not dedicated, to sell out before they were upped by an unexpected rush of promotion. Privileged young men monotonously continued to justify their privileges by becoming not only good soldiers but sometimes even great ones.[3]

The complaints against the system did not come from the ranks who, on the whole, were more than satisfied with the men who commanded them. Even up to 1914 they preferred to be led by 'toffs', and they had no trust in men in the ranks with ideas above their station. On the whole, their satisfaction was justified and officers took an interest in their men to the extent of trying to place them at the end of their service in jobs on their own estates or the estates of relatives; letters from the army of the period are full of requests for 'something to be done' for this or that ageing man or NCO. Some went even further. Shocked at the inadequacy of Government married quarters, officers of the Guards raised £9,000 between them which they used to provide decent homes for 54 families which they rented at 2/6 a week.

As units the regiments worked well. The artillery and engineers, even if they sometimes regarded their particular branches in the nature of religions, were also thoroughly efficient and the cavalry still knew how to ride knee to knee, and that was something.

3 Everything old at the top

WITH the declaration of war now being posted up in provincial towns, as the country looked about it in a state of militant euphoria for leaders for its army, to its surprise all it could see was a row of ageing men who had been little more than boys at the time of their last action. These men who now stood first in line had seen nothing of war since 1815 and had by now grown rusty with desk work. It was a commentary on the sad state of the army that Fitzroy James Henry Somerset, first Baron Raglan, was the inevitable and only choice as commander. Although by 1854 he was 66 years of age, he had never commanded even a company of infantry in battle, but there was no other choice, because the few who had recent experience of fighting had not the requisite aristocratic background for the chief command.

Raglan was the youngest of the Duke of Beaufort's eleven children and his commission in the 4th Light Dragoons was bought for him while he was still only a 15-year-old schoolboy. He had served in the Peninsula on Wellington's staff and had shown himself a brave officer, but after the peace of 1814 he had joined the embassy in Paris. By this time a lieutenant-colonel in the Guards, in that year he married Wellington's niece and in Wellington's absence acted as Minister Plenipotentiary. It was a duty that suited him admirably. He was tactful, industrious and discreet and he spoke French fluently. He rejoined the Duke for the 100 Days campaign and lost his right arm to what must have been one of the last shots at Waterloo, but, after learning to write with his left hand, he returned to his post at the embassy in Paris and later served for a while with the embassy in Turkey and accompanied the Duke in his embassy to St. Petersburg. He had by now developed so strong a taste for diplomatic business, in fact, it affected his military attitudes, but when the Duke of Wellington became commander-in-chief he joined him as military secretary.

On Wellington's death, he had hoped to be made commander-in-chief himself but he was passed over in favour of Lord Hardinge who, although older in years, was junior in service, and became instead master-general of ordnance. He was not rich but he was also far from poor and, despite his one arm, enjoyed hunting and shooting and good living. Unashamedly reactionary and with few original ideas, he was little interested in music, painting or books, or in the sciences which were changing the whole way of English life, but he was a handsome man, in features not at all unlike his hero, the Duke. He also had the same impassiveness, the same beliefs, the same calm nobility, but unfortunately, these attitudes did not belong to the bustling mid-19th century and he would have been more at home in the days when war was little more than a formalised series of manœuvres. To be fair to him he knew his limitations, and for safety he modelled himself on the victor of Waterloo. He formed the same habit of understatement, the same dislike of military splendour, the same dislike of being cheered by his men, the same attitude to nepotism.

Unfortunately, unlike the Duke, he was a poor chooser of men and selected them more for their pleasant personalities than for their drive. Lord de Ros, his quartermaster-general—equivalent to a modern chief of staff—was noted for his good humour and eccentricities but was entirely without experience and apparently not interested in acquiring it. His adjutant-general, James Bucknall Estcourt, while possessing more industry, also had no experience but once again was blessed with a 'remarkably kind and courteous disposition', while his aides—among whom were five of his own nephews—with one or two exceptions, were of much the same type, pleasant young men well known in Society but almost entirely lacking in ability.

The French commander was a very different kettle of fish and it says much for Raglan's charm that the Frenchman tried to carry out his orders to 'march in step', despite his sometimes quaint ideas of how a war should be conducted. Given to resounding gestures, he had inevitably changed the prosaic name with which he had been saddled at birth to the more imposing Achille St. Arnaud. He was ambitious and vain, a little, wily, debauched-looking man already suffering from the angina which was to kill him. He had made his name in Algeria and when Napoleon III had been looking around for a ruthless resourceful soldier to help with the coup d'état which made him Emperor his eye fell on St. Arnaud. He had been rewarded with a baton and the command of the French expeditionary force. Sly, crafty and given to usurping the Allied command whenever he could, he was never the man to appeal to the cool, aloof Raglan, and was probably one of the reasons why Raglan so often referred to the enemy as 'the French'.

On paper, the appointments of Raglan's subordinate commanders appeared to make sense. The Light Division was given to Major-General Sir George Brown, who was even older than Raglan and a Peninsula veteran of Craufurd's famous Light Division. An exceedingly handsome man, always shaved to the bone, tightly stocked and spotless—'like a piece of well-washed china'—he had spent most of his military life in administration and was considered one of the most churlish officers in the army. The First Division—the Guards and the Highlanders—was commanded by the Duke of Cambridge, the Queen's cousin. This was a prestige appointment, for although he was well versed in the principles of military organisation and was one of the few men who had taken the trouble to study the deployment of regiments and brigades in one unit, the Duke was only 35 and his experience of war was nil.

The Second Division was commanded by Sir George de Lacy Evans, who had a brilliant record in the Peninsula, the American and Waterloo campaigns, and the more recent Carlist Wars in Spain. The Third Division was given to Sir Richard England, aged 61, who, as one authority puts it, was 'of no particular career'. Roger Fenton, the photographer, could only comment of him when he met him, 'He's not a bad rider.' The Fourth Division was led by Sir George Cathcart, who had been present with the Russians in the Leipzig campaign of 1813 and had been on Wellington's staff at Waterloo. His noble connections were his chief assets, though his reputation for energy and drive was such that he carried a secret commission to take over the chief command in the event of Lord Raglan's death. The chief engineer, Sir John Burgoyne, was a man of great personality and experience and despite his age—he was 72—he had tremendous energy. Almost to a man they were short-sighted.

There was a top-heaviness of age about the command, and George Maude, of the Royal Horse Artillery, said 'There is an old commander-in-chief, an old engineer, old brigadiers—in fact everything old at the top. This makes everything sluggish.'

This was not entirely true. The commander of the Cavalry Division, George Charles Bingham, third Earl of Lucan, at 54, was by no means old or sluggish and he did not need glasses.

The eldest son of the second earl, with the privileges of aristocracy he was proud and overbearing but far from stupid. He had joined the army at the age of 16 when a commission was bought for him in the 6th Regiment of Foot, but by means of purchase, within ten years, at the age of 26 he had attained the rank of lieutenant-colonel in command of the 17th. Lancers, one of the most famous regiments in the British Army. He had twice bought a step in promotion, and had appeared on the roster of five different regiments, and though by the standards of the day this was not unusual, Bingham's rise had been quicker than most. In 1826 he was a major, and the following year when the command of the Lancers became vacant he was said to have bought it for £25,000, £20,000 over the regulation price, but since an army agent told a commission in 1857 that the highest he had ever heard of for a cavalry command was £18,000 the sum paid was probably exaggerated in the press. The command, however, had been bought over the head of the senior major, Anthony Bacon, an officer with experience in the Peninsula and at Waterloo, who, realising his chances of ever obtaining command were gone, sold his commission and became a mercenary.

Despite the usurpation, Bingham did not, like so many who had bought commands, merely sit back and enjoy himself. He poured money into the regiment, which soon became known as 'Bingham's Dandies', and in return, according to Sir John Fortescue's regimental history, he brought it 'up to a very high state of efficiency'. He had come at a time 'when such a commander was especially valuable, for the slack period of the army . . . was telling heavily on the cavalry', and the drill had become impractical and obsolete. He was a keen soldier but in the long peace after Waterloo, there was little chance of earning distinction and in 1828 he obtained leave to join the Russian Army as a volunteer against the Turks in Bulgaria at Varna, Shumla and Widdin. He commanded a cavalry division under the walls of Adrianople in 1829 and returned to his regiment with the Order of St. Anne, a good reputation and a sound knowledge of both the Russians and the Turks. He had been indifferent to discomfort and had shown great physical courage, and the Russians had written of him 'Lord Bingham never let slip an opportunity to be in the fighting'. The British Ambassador to Russia had added that his conduct had been such as to draw the attention of the Tsar, who had chided him for too freely exposing his life. He had also brought back, from his close acquaintance with the Cossacks, some new and useful ideas about lance exercises, and probably knew more about the Russian Army than anyone else of his day. He had a high respect for their infantry, but a low—and as it turned out, a correct—opinion of their cavalry.

By now Bingham had brought his regiment to a high standard of skill and, unlike many other colonels, had gone to a great deal of trouble to master his profession, but with England well settled in her long peace, it seemed he was unlikely ever to use the skill he had acquired and he turned his interest instead to farming. He went in for new methods and, in 1837, gave up his command for half-pay and turned to the family estates in

32

Ireland, which were run down, poverty-stricken and backward. There were no industries in Ireland at this time, few large towns and few farms, and it was a country of smallholdings not big enough to support their owners or the people who rented them. For the most part the peasants lived in huts which they shared with their animals and their rents were rarely paid, and the country, dependent only on the potato, had been tottering on the edge of famine for generations. To Bingham, after his succession to the title in 1839 the Earl of Lucan, there was only one solution, consolidation—the bringing together of small units—which was already proving successful in industry. Lucan saw in it the answer to his problem and in this he was far ahead of most Irish landowners who were largely indifferent to the bankruptcy of their lands, preferring only to draw from them what they could and live in comfort in England. Unlike these men, Lucan reduced his own income and risked his capital, but, to his surprise, his schemes were not welcomed by the backward, suspicious people of Mayo, and his plans to evict the hundreds of tenants who were giving neither him nor them elbow room for improvement happened to come in the years of the potato famine. The crop had failed in 1845 and again in 1846 and since it had failed also in England and on the Continent, the prices of grain and other foods rose steeply. The disaster was unimaginable. The Irish people were starving, yet, since most of them had lived entirely off their own potatoes, there was no organisation for the buying and selling of food, and England did nothing.

Lucan surveyed the horror with the self-righteousness of a man who could afford to say 'I told you so'. By now, however, it seemed that half the population of Ireland was on relief and thousands of them were arriving in Liverpool and Glasgow, and when the Irish landlords were accused in Parliament the Earl of Lucan was one of the first targets. Though it was admitted that he was at least endeavouring to improve his estates and that he spent far more on them than he drew from them, the methods of his agents had been ruthless and with the emotionalism which is always a British trait his critics saw not what he had done, only the methods he had used.

By 1848 the famine was over and Lucan was pleased enough that intelligent men who could manage to eschew emotion had felt he was right to do what he had, but by 1854 he was restless again. He was 54 years old now and though his mop of black hair had disappeared his face had retained its alert aggressive look. There was no suggestion in it of the thickening of age or the slowing down of mental processes, and he still enjoyed perfect health. Tall, bald, with the sweeping whiskers of the period, according to Kinglake, he 'saw like a hawk and his energy was that of a much younger man. He was lithe and slender and still possessed the same fierce tearing energy, his face lighting when his interest was caught so that his eyes shone and his teeth showed even and white.' Moreover, also according to Kinglake, his intellectual abilities were still 'of a very high order'. When war came he pointed out his period with the Russians and offered his services in any capacity, but aware of his rustiness, he asked with reasonable modesty only if he might be given an infantry brigade. Instead, he was given the Cavalry Division.

It was suggested that his record in Ireland was the reason for the offer but it was more likely his service in the war of 1828-9 that concerned the men who chose him. He probably knew more than anyone of his rank of the territory where the British army expected to fight and he knew a great deal of the army the British were about to face. His reputation was good and, though his temper was known to be sharp, quick tempers in subordinates had never before proved a handicap to a commander-in-chief. Joachim Murat, the greatest cavalryman of all time, was often 'speechless' or 'choking' with rage and the other Napoleonic marshals couldn't stand him. At no time could his greatest admirer have called him modest or self-effacing but he had no self-doubts, was fearless, quick-thinking and, with a tearing energy, often quite impossible. Lucan had many of the same faults and he had commanded a division of cavalry—Russian cavalry at that!—and, by comparison with his contemporaries, his experience was fresh in his mind. (Though it was true he had not seen active service for 25 years, many of the successful generals of World War II had had no experience of combat for almost as long.) He also knew the Turks well and though he was impulsive, as one officer who had no reason to like him said of him, 'Damn the fellow, he's brave.' Controlled by a strong commander-in-chief, his faults might have been turned to excellent advantage.

4 The English Murat

SUCH was the state of the army, there could be only two brigades of cavalry and the command of the Heavy Brigade under Lucan was given to Sir James Yorke Scarlett, son of Lord Abinger, a stout florid man with no experience of war and suffering from the general complaint of myopia. However, he had a great ability to get the best out of men and, as commander of the 5th Dragoon Guards, had been universally popular. He was modest enough to select for his staff one of the experienced young officers from the Indian Army, Lieutenant James Alexander Elliot, grandson of the Earl of Minto, who happened to be in England and had hurried to make his experience available.

Scarlett's appointment seemed sound enough but in choosing the commander of the Light Brigade, the Horse Guards perpetrated what seemed to most people at the time a ghastly practical joke. They chose James Thomas Brudenell, seventh Earl of Cardigan, probably because he had also travelled in Russia, but what they did not allow for was that Cardigan was Lord Lucan's brother-in-law and that he and Lucan could not stand each other.

Cardigan was a self-important military fanatic who had lost no time in applying for a command. He was 57 years old and suffered from a chronic bronchitic condition, and an official comment on another officer made at a later date—'Personally I would not breed from this officer'—would probably have fitted him well. He was handsome and tall with blue eyes and fair hair in the best English style, with a long aristocratic nose and a proud bearing, but though he had dash and gallantry, he also had a mulish obstinacy and no great amount of sense.

He had been to Oxford but had left without taking any examinations and travelled in Russia, Sweden and Italy. He had already acquired a seat in the Commons with a pocket borough and had been involved in the divorce of an old friend, whose wife he had married, when, through the influence of the Duke of York, a cornetcy was bought for him in the 8th Hussars in 1824, at the age of 27. With a background of vast wealth and seven sisters, he did not enjoy being a subordinate, however, and within two years he had bought his way up to captain.

He had soon formed a high opinion of his own military capacities but these were chiefly concerned with the minutiae of dress, and he was difficult, self-assertive and quarrelsome. In 1832 he bought the command of the 15th Hussars for a sum said to be between £35,000 and £40,000 but, like Lucan's purchase price, it was probably a reporter's imaginative conception, as in the Crimea he claimed that there was £10,000 'on the point of his sword'. Though the 15th Hussars was a good regiment, he demanded perfection, but perhaps because he had never had to worry about the cost of his horses, he never troubled to acquire that most important of cavalry techniques, horsemastership, and his horses constantly suffered because he never knew how much they could stand.

His haughty manner and paranoiac behaviour led to constant quarrels with his officers and he began to believe they were conspiring against him, and by the end of 1833 he had brought one of them to a court martial. It did not do him much good because it soon became obvious he had given orders for officers' conversations to be taken down secretly, and had been in the habit of taunting them and cross-examining NCOs and men about them. He did not even perform well in court and when the court martial backfired, he was removed from command.

Brudenell was startled and took the matter to Lord Hill, the commander-in-chief, the Prime Minister, Lord John Russell, and finally to the Duke of Wellington. He was a man with a great gift for misunderstanding people and he came away from all these interviews believing they were on his side and by March, 1838, he was able to bring sufficient influence to bear on Lord Hill that he was gazetted lieutenant-colonel of the 11th Light Dragoons. It had cost him, the newspapers assserted, another £40,000.

His handling of the 11th was no better than his handling of the 15th. He joined them in India, in October, 1837, but by January, 1838, had discovered that the climate did not suit him and, when the regiment was ordered home, he was the first to leave. While on his way, he learned that his father had died and he had become the seventh Earl of Cardigan and the owner of vast estates.

He had not changed in the slightest, and as soon as the regiment reached England the trouble started all over again. He did not appear to like officers who had served in India, and, since there is little to say in Cardigan's favour, it is only fair to quote Sir William Mansfield, a commander-in-chief, India, later Lord Sandhurst, who said that Indian officers were not always as zealous or as smart as a commanding officer had a right to expect, and that their fibre and behaviour had often been sapped by heat, liquor, idleness and supercession. After ten years in India, he claimed, they were often physically and morally weaker, 'less amenable to discipline . . . more slothful, and . . . incapable of prolonged effort'. Cardigan let it be known that these were his sentiments also. He was soon involved in a dispute with the press, which was quick to point out that Lord Cardigan was 'none other' than the infamous Lord Brudenell, and the whole sorry story of the 15th was dragged up again.

In 1840, however, when Prince Albert arrived in England for his marriage to Queen Victoria, it was the 11th which met him at Dover and escorted him to London, and the Prince became colonel-in-chief and the regiment became hussars, with uniforms of the Prince's design. They wore jackets of blue edged with gold, furred pelisses, sealskin busbies with plumes, and cherry-coloured trousers which earned them the name of Cherry Bums—translated for polite society as Cherubims. Cardigan met most of the expense and provided £10 over and above the price the government allowed for the purchase of each horse. It was estimated he spent £10,000 a year on the regiment out of his own pocket.

He was again soon at loggerheads with his officers, however, and was involved in a duel in which he shot his opponent. Arrested but released on bail, he was immediately involved with another officer, Lieutenant William Charles Forrest, who later rose to be a general and colonel of the regiment. Forrest was a man of good humour, though, according to his next commanding officer—a much more easy-going man than Cardigan—inclined to laziness. He was a great hand with a pen and comes across the years as a man with a love of gossip and not a little malice who could make a good story better. The Times immediately took up cudgels on his behalf and Cardigan was booed in the street.

The continued courts martial were beginning at last to worry the army authorities. Letters were exchanged between Lord Hill and the Duke of Wellington and finally the adjutant-general, Sir John MacDonald, appeared in the mess of the 11th, where, behind locked doors, he upbraided not only the officers but also the Earl of Cardigan in a way that The Times said could only be looked on with indifference by 'the most stupid or most hardened of men'.

Cardigan's unpopularity was at its highest and he was booed at the theatre. One of the officers with whom he was in disagreement was summoned to an interview with Lord Raglan, at that time still Lord Fitzroy Somerset, military secretary at the Horse Guards, who, despite the dissimilarity of their manner and characters, was a personal friend of Lord Cardigan. Somerset used his well-known charm and, in a way that left Cardigan untouched, the matter was settled. It was no sooner disposed of, however, when Cardigan had to appear at the Old Bailey as a result of his duel. He elected, as was his right, to be tried by his peers in the House of Lords and vast sums of money were spent on a grotesque trial which found him—not unexpectedly—not guilty.

The Times again thundered its protests and a debate took place in the Commons. The trouble was not over, however, and

Cardigan, arrogant and mulish over details, continued to be a constant source of derision to the press and in Parliament. For sound military reasons, however, the Duke of Wellington decided against action being taken against him, and oddly enough the Queen, with whom Cardigan was on surprisingly good terms, also came down on his side. Nevertheless, such was the feeling against him, it was felt advisable that Prince Albert should cease to be colonel of his regiment.

Cardigan went his way completely unscathed. His marriage had failed and he was involved in several scandals and three times within eighteen months rebuked by Wellington, now commander-in-chief on Lord Hill's retirement. Yet, such was his colossal conceit, he asked more than once to be made Lord Lieutenant of Northamptonshire, considering that, with his holdings there and the fact that he was a staunch Tory, he had every right to that position, and when a vacancy occurred in the Order of the Garter, he even took the incredible step of applying—not once but three times—to be admitted.

To be fair to him, though his faults were legion, it is also true that he suffered a great deal from irresponsible newspapermen. But, relying far too much on the awe that sprang from his wealth and title, he entirely forgot the rising middle classes and there is no doubt that he brought the malice of the press on himself by his overbearing manners, because his was not the only regiment which had been involved in trouble. There had been several since Waterloo, and for all his 'arbitrary and narrow' manner, he did improve its drill, discipline and turn-out, and after his death it thought enough of him to change the time of the last trumpet of the day from 10 p.m. to the minute when he drew his last breath.

By the time he was given the command of the Light Brigade, Cardigan had quietened down considerably. His bronchitis troubled him and a bladder complaint forced him to take treatment, and he had even come to be regarded with a certain amount of rueful affection. Known as Jim the Bear, he was generous to his men and, since he always remained popular with them, it is hard to avoid the thought that Mansfield's strictures on 'Indian' officers were not unjust. His reputation, in fact, was higher than the troubles in the mess had seemed to suggest and though the more discerning among them failed to find any good reason for it, his men even considered him 'the English Murat'.[1]

This curious affection for Cardigan is hard to explain but deference to the hereditary nobility—Thackeray called it 'lordolatry' —was deep-rooted, and probably explains why he got away with so much so often. Despite the righteous indignation of those numerous wealthy and respectable men of the middle classes who had so many reasons for resenting their practical stigmatisation by the nobility as second-class citizens, the higher classes had never stood so high in relative rank, and for all their bluster the middle classes remained toadies at heart.

The aristocracy had an exclusive and caste-like air about it and boys began boasting about their social position as soon as they left the nursery. Their society was small and select and had not yet been affected by the industrial and commercial creations which began to flood into it later in the century, and peers had to be 'very bad or very peculiar indeed not to be accorded the conventional respectful treatment'.[2] Though Cardigan's sense was not admired, his ancestry, courage and panache were, but, with his fatal habit of getting ideas firmly set in his mind when they were quite incorrect, he was now allowed to get hold of another.

He was not at all happy at being placed in a subordinate position—especially under his brother-in-law—and, to placate him, he was given the assurance that his command was an independent one, so that he came away from the Horse Guards with the idea firmly in his head that he did not have to answer to Lord Lucan for anything.

5 Such ignorance they displayed

It is more than probable that Cardigan had got the idea of independent command into his head long before he visited the Horse Guards, and Raglan, with his always earnest desire not to upset anyone, was the last person in the world to knock it out. The appointment was announced in the middle of March and was immediately the gossip of London. Well-intentioned friends at once bombarded Lord Lucan with warnings, while the colonels of the regiments under his command viewed the proximity of the brothers-in-law with concern. Lord George Paget, colonel of the 4th Light Dragoons, a man of shrewdness and wit, had grave doubts about them being able to work together at all, and Colonel Edward Cooper Hodge, of the 4th Dragoon Guards, commented, 'They do not speak. How this will answer on service I do not know.'

Indeed, the diligent, dedicated, irascible, unpopular Lucan and the vain and self-important Cardigan were never likely to get on. Lucan regarded his brother-in-law as 'a feather-bed soldier' not fit to command an escort, while Cardigan was said to have taken offence against Lucan because his sister, Lady Lucan, had parted from her husband. The two men's paths had rarely crossed, however, because while Cardigan lived splendidly on his estates, in London, or on his yacht, Lucan, indifferent to discomfort, had continued to camp out in Ireland, often in disputes and often tediously right. He was well aware of the problems that faced him. He knew of Cardigan's narrow mind and his lack of sense. Indeed, he had been warned, it seemed, by everyone in London. But he had been considered a good commanding officer and he believed the cavalry would not let him down.

*

The earliest use of cavalry had been the provision of information about the enemy and Gustavus Adolphus of Sweden was among the first to employ them properly. Cromwell had learned a great deal from him but, what was more important, he had realised that cavalry needed a special spirit, an élan that was missing from the 'decayed servingmen and tapsters' he had first seen at Edgehill, and his men began to acquire that sense of superiority which has characterised cavalry of all ages and all nations and caused the other arms to envy and dislike them for their airs. By the 18th century they had begun to develop into heavy cavalry and light cavalry and mounted infantrymen who came to be known as dragoons. Heavy cavalry were used for shock action, big men on big horses, often wearing armour. Light cavalry were employed mainly on reconnaissance, though each, of course, could when necessary do the other's job. Dragoons used their horses simply to convey them to a given spot where they then fought as infantry.

In the Napoleonic Wars the British cavalry, forgetting Cromwell's method of charging at the trot, never had the high reputation of the French and it had always been a great source of annoyance with Wellington that while other commanders could rely on their cavalry to win them battles, he could only expect his to get him into scrapes. His attitude was that they were entirely lacking in discipline and, indeed, he had lost the greater part of the Union Brigade at Waterloo because the Earl of Uxbridge, instead of placing himself in a position to control them, had charged at their head. His words on the subject were forceful. His cavalry officers, he claimed, had acquired a trick of 'galloping at everything, and then galloping back as fast as they gallop at the enemy. They never . . . think of manoeuvring before an enemy— so little that one would think they cannot manoeuvre, excepting on Wimbledon Common, and . . . they never keep a reserve.' By 1854 they were expensive, aristocratic and splendid, though on the whole in their limited way they were also very efficient.

While the infantry as often as not had been recruited among

the illiterate Irish peasants or from the rookeries of the poor, the cavalry, with its better conditions, included large numbers of English yeomen and sons of farmers. The Irish were there, too, of course, sons of small squireens, but they were there for the horses, not to get a roof over their heads, and many men in the ranks were God-fearing, devout, well-behaved and intelligent, and they were proud of being cavalrymen. John Penn, a man with years of service in India with the 3rd Light Dragoons, had rushed immediately on his return to England to join the 17th Lancers, Bingham's Dandies, or the Death or Glory Boys, so as not to miss the fun; while Scarlett, appealing at Cahir Barracks, in Tipperary, for 15 volunteers from the 7th Dragoon Guards to bring his own regiment up to strength for the war, was delighted to see every available man step forward.

The training of these men had been largely left to the NCOs and the NCOs had responded magnificently. With rough fatherliness they had produced men who knew their drill backwards, could ride magnificently and were expert not only with their weapons but also at the complicated manoeuvres which were designed to place them rapidly in line for a devastating assault and a quick retirement to the flank for a rally. They had learned the exacting duties of outposts and pickets and that most useful of all assets—how to ride with their eyes ahead, keeping their dressing by instinct. In their ranks were saddlers and farriers who were pure craftsmen.[1]

Though there was a growing professionalism among them, the officers, as in the infantry, did not always measure up in skill. But, despite their sweeping whiskers and languid airs, they were keen riders to hounds and, bound by their common love of horses, they were usually considerate to their men and just as often popular. The men were respectful but by no means browbeaten and were not afraid to offer their pithy comments, and Private William Pennington, of Cardigan's regiment, the 11th Hussars, the son of a civil servant who was also principal of one of the most respected private schools in London, had a very warm feeling for them. A recruit in Dublin in the autumn of 1853, he found the rugged treatment he had heard of was quite the reverse, and put down some of the stories to the old hands' habit of trying to frighten recruits. When he queried the terrifying tales, he was listened to sympathetically and was told that the men who had alarmed him would be well and truly attended to. In the 17th Lancers there was a library and an excellent spirit of good comradeship, and Lord George Paget, colonel of the 4th Light Dragoons, was on excellent terms with his men, while no one could call the diminutive Hodge, of the 4th Dragoon Guards, a tyrant. Colonel Shewell, of the 8th Hussars, a very strict and religious man, was called 'the Old Woman', and John Douglas, who had taken over the 11th Hussars on Cardigan's appointment as brigadier, was a handsome man regarded with some pride by his soldiers. These officers were no slower than the infantry to attend to the social needs of their men. The 4th Light Dragoons had a trust fund for the welfare of soldiers' widows and children and in the 5th Dragoon Guards Scarlett and other officers contributed almost £500, a not inconsiderable sum in 1854, towards the care of those wives who were not to accompany the regiment abroad.

Unfortunately, reserves were so low that no regiment could produce more than two squadrons for the Army of the East and it took ten regiments to make up the two brigades. Even those squadrons which were to go had not sufficient horses and there was a great deal of hither and thither among the colonels. Hodge's chief concern was with getting rid of his 53 young and unreliable mounts and his older, overweight men, and when he was instructed to provide 250 horses and 295 men he had no idea where he was to find them. In the end horses were transferred from the King's Dragoon Guards, for which he gave back 20 of his young ones, faintly ashamed of what he had done because he considered them 'as great a set of brutes' as he ever saw.

The government was not unaware of the difficulties, however, and on 11 March the Duke of Newcastle, Secretary for War, had written to Lord Raglan suggesting that horses should be purchased in the Middle East for when the cavalry arrived. When he suggested for the mission Captain Louis Edward Nolan, of the 15th Hussars, who had recently arrived home from India, the last character in the drama took the stage.

*

Though of comparatively junior rank, Captain Nolan had been in the public eye a great deal in recent months. He had come to the notice of the Duke of Cambridge and other titled staff officers as a brilliant trainer of horses and instructor of riders. He had a great gift for languages and had served in the Austrian cavalry and studied the mounted arm in Russia, Sweden and Germany. A brilliant rider, he had written a book which showed his vast knowledge of horses, and another on cavalry tactics, though this was more suspect, as his knowledge of war was pure theory. Despite service in India during the wars there, his regiment had never heard a shot fired in anger, and, although on the strength of the 15th Hussars for 15 years, he had spent five in training or staff duties and another four on leave.

He was young, dashing and good-looking in a dark Italian style and there were already many legends in existence about him. He seemed a romantic, brilliant figure, who was reputed to come from an old military family and, after service in the Austrian Army, had been persuaded, because of his ability, to return to England by high-ranking officers from the Horse Guards. His father was described as a distinguished Irish officer who had been British vice-consul in Milan where he had taken a beautiful Italian wife. The truth, however, was a little different. Nolan's grandfather had been a trooper in the 13th Light Dragoons who had died of fever in the West Indies, while his orphaned father had been granted a commission in a foot regiment through the generosity of his grandfather's commanding officer. His service had been entirely on garrison duties and he had ended up in Milan on half-pay, acting as unpaid assistant to the consul. His wife came from Holborn and it is hard to suspect that he did not marry her for her property because he seems to have been a very sharp practitioner and an inveterate name-dropper with a gift for self-promotion, capable of self-delusion or even outright lies. The juggling he had done with the value of his commission to get his sons into the army was unbelievable.[2]

None of this was Captain Nolan's fault, of course, though he had acquired his father's ability to delude himself, and the reception given to his books had made him a little conceited. While he was uniformly kind, even-tempered and thoughtful to rankers, on military matters he was headstrong and impatient—even arrogant and intolerant—especially where senior officers were concerned.

To make eveything official he was placed on the staff of Brigadier-General Richard Airey, who had a brigade in the Light Division, and was furnished with letters of introduction, funds and an officer from the Commissariat Department, and by 8 April he was trying to buy horses at Shumla in Bulgaria, where he became friendly with an ex-officer of the Rifle Brigade, George Palmer Evelyn, who was in the East hoping to see some fun and beginning to wish he were back in harness.[3]

With Nolan looking after the problem of remounts, the struggle to make up regimental strength continued and Hodge busied himself teaching his officers how to pack valises, roll cloaks and put together a saddle. 'Such ignorance they displayed,' he mourned. 'Not one of them knew by sight the lower part of a breastplate.' But Hodge was easily depressed, and, not relishing the possibility of losing the money he had spent on purchasing his colonelcy, his orders left him with none of the excitement and exultation most men felt. 'Now begins a life or neither profit nor pleasure,' he wrote gloomily. 'I expect no more peace, comfort or happiness in the world.'

*

The line regiments were already heading for the coast. The uniform they wore was hardly one for a climate where the temperature could reach up to the hundreds, but believing, as the British invariably do, that the whole affair would be over by Christmas, it was not considered worth worrying about.

It was decided to march the mounted force across France to embark at Marseilles, a prospect which Hodge, listening to the whirr of grindstones as swords were sharpened, regarded with horror. The weather would be hot, there would be too much cheap brandy, the horses would be knocked up, and no one, except for two or three officers, could speak French! However, after keeping the railway and shipping authorities on the alert for weeks, Lord Hardinge, the commander-in-chief, changed his mind and the decision was made to Hodge's great relief to send the cavalry by sailing ship.

The fact that the hereditary nobility had once more walked into all the top jobs had not been missed and the middle classes, represented by the press, were quick to pounce on the announcement. Leaping to the attack, *The Daily News* quite rightly pointed out to Lord Hardinge that a voyage to the Middle East would take eight weeks by sail, during which time the horses would never be able to lie down or move about and would be put ashore with cramped and useless limbs.

They were looking for high-born, high-ranking people to castigate and it was inevitable that before long they should pick on Cardigan. When bulletins from the 11th Hussars stated that leather patches were being sewn on their cherry-coloured trousers to make them more able to withstand the rigours of active service, *The Times* chose to be sarcastic, and all the provincial papers seized on the case with glee. One of them hastened to say that 'cerise was a charming colour for a lady's bonnet ribbon but not for the pantaloons of a cavalry soldier', and blamed the Prince Consort 'for having clothed a regiment of light cavalry in the most unserviceable nether garments that can well be conceived'.[4]

The embarkation of the cavalry took place at various ports throughout the United Kingdom. Private Pennington was one of the first to leave, with the baggage party of 60 men and horses of the 11th Hussars. With the local people generous with whisky, they climbed on board ship with their officers, happy to have got away from the more serious discipline at headquarters. Behind them, long glittering processions wound down to the coast.

Officers took their wives with them, and there were several young brides. Captain Duberly, paymaster of the 8th Hussars, was accompanied by his wife, Fanny, a daring horsewoman who took her favourite mount with her. Captain Cresswell took his wife, too, as also did Captain Lord Errol, of the Rifle Brigade, whose wife was even accompanied by a French maid. Wives of NCOs and men were also allowed to accompany their regiments, though these were limited in numbers and led to heartbreak and not a little cunning. One woman of the Rifle Brigade dressed herself in uniform, shouldered a rifle and marched on board as a private soldier.

The arrival of the 17th Lancers in Portsmouth presented a curious spectacle in a purely naval town.[5] The place was full of Easter holidaymakers, and as the regiment reached the outskirts, to the cry of the gulls and tunes played by military bands, everyone swarmed into the narrow streets to see the flutter of pennons and the glitter of steel.

Bonneted ladies, on the docks beneath the towering masts and yardarms to watch the horses slung aboard, saw several hard knocks given by the plunging frightened animals, but one man, his head cut, told Colonel Lawrenson that it didn't matter as it was 'nothing like what he expected to receive before long'.

Little thought had been given by the Horse Guards to the arrangements and the 13th Light Dragoons had to embark in six different ships, all of them too small. In one of them, the *Mary Anne*, ballast broke loose and rolled under the horses, knocking several over. On the *Culloden*, horses had to be moved to get at water casks which were placed with other stores *under the horse holds*, and some of the barrels of peas they took out were dated 1828.

Those cavalry regiments stationed in Ireland rode to Kingstown near Dublin to join transports in Liverpool and London. Hodge was completely in the dark about transporting horses over long distances abroad and had had to buy a recently published book on the subject, but shipboard routine was soon in full swing, with a constant stamping of hooves and the eternal noise of blocks and ropes. But the ship was cleaned, horses were shifted and tubs of manure hoisted from below.

The 4th Light Dragoons were the last to leave. Lord George Paget had received his orders with mixed feelings. He had just married and his father, the Marquess of Anglesey—Wellington's cavalry leader at Waterloo, Lord Uxbridge—had just died. More, he had only recently sent in his papers, intending to retire from the army in which he had remained only to please his father, and had felt obliged to withdraw them on the outbreak of war. A man of sensibility, during his colonelcy the regiment had become known as Paget's Irregular Horse, from the loose drill it had used in Afghanistan under his predecessor.

Everyone was eager for action and no one had any doubt about the outcome of any engagement involving them. Only in the 5th Dragoon Guards was there concern. They had lost their beloved colonel, Scarlett, on his promotion to brigadier, and in his place a very different type of man had arrived from the 7th Dragoon Guards, where he had been on half-pay. Forty-three-year-old Thomas le Marchant was the fourth son of that Le Marchant who had set the seed of the military college at Sandhurst and had been killed leading the charge of the Heavies at Salamanca. But the son was a man of much the same metal as Cardigan and, taking over only the day before the regiment was due to leave Cork, his first action had been to call a parade at which he had told them that he considered they had had things far too easy under Scarlett and that he proposed to treat them differently.

His last words—'impressive but not very elegant'—'so, look out!' had seemed ominous and hardly the spirit with which to lead men to war.

6 We expect to be in it red hot

As the troops began to gather in the Middle East, fierce fighting was taking place to the north where the Russians were besieging the Turks in Silistria on the Danube, and, eager to get into action, Corporal Arthur Warner, of the 44th Foot, wrote home to his father. 'They are hard at it about 80 miles from where we lies at present,' he said, 'but we expect to be in it red hot in another month.' Unfortunately, they were not. Although the government had been warned that the army would find no transport in Bulgaria, none had been provided and, just when it was urgently needed, the British army was condemned to inaction simply because it had not the means to move itself.

The cavalry leader, Lord Lucan, however, had wasted no time. It had been the wish of Lord Raglan that divisional and brigade commanders should not accompany their troops to the war and, like many others, Lucan went via Dover, Paris and Marseilles and arrived at Scutari early in May. His staff was young and intelligent and his aides-de-camp included Lord Bingham, his son and heir. For an interpreter he had a 22-year-old member of the Consular Service, John Elijah Blunt, who, born in Turkey and with service behind him in that country, knew like his chief not only the land they were expected to fight over but also their Turkish allies. In addition, attached to the cavalry as deputy assistant quarter-master-general there was a young man who was an acknowledged expert on modern cavalry tactics. Captain William Morris was 34 years old, had taken part in three campaigns, and had charged with cavalry on four occasions, including the Battle of Aliwal in 1846 with the 16th. Lancers.[1] He had since changed to the 17th Lancers and, returning to England, had passed with distinction through the Senior Department of the Royal Military College at Sandhurst, one of the very few officers who had. A believer in physical fitness, he was short, stocky and powerful, a popular man whose nickname was 'The pocket Hercules'. He was a great friend of Captain Nolan, whom he had met in India, and with whom he shared a great enthusiasm for cavalry and mounted warfare, and he was already at Varna in Bulgaria on the shores of the Black Sea, which had been chosen as the base for operations against the Russians to the north.

According to one of them,[2] Lucan got on well with his staff and in return they took care of those details of his life to which he was largely indifferent. He was a remarkably bad dresser and was not therefore always recognised when he could be persuaded to put on uniform, and his indifference to ceremony startled the Turkish pashas. Though he was careful not to neglect such details as the insuring of his horses and those of his staff—a thing for which they were to bless him before very long—he was often unpunctual and, however good a plan he made overnight, he always overrated his capacity for work and was usually 'well out of time'. His staff were in the habit of sending him off to dine at the British Embassy with the fare for his caïque across the Bosphorus folded in a paper marked 'Boat' in one pocket and the money for the hire of a horse up the hill in another marked 'Pony'.

The 17th Lancers and the 8th Hussars were the first of his men to arrive, Captain Winter the first cavalryman ashore as he raced Cornet Cleveland through the shallows at Gallipoli for the honour. Anthony Sterling, brigade major to the Highlanders, didn't rate the chances of Lucan's small force very highly against the 27,000 cavalrymen the Russians were reported to possess, especially since their numbers were reduced even further by the state of the horses. The voyage out had been dreadful and many had been lost through fright and seasickness. Horses are bad sailors and, suffering from the appalling confinement below decks, 26 of the 17th Lancers' mounts had died. In the Bay of Biscay conditions had become 'horrible beyond words', and the men had had to stand constantly at the animals' heads although some were so sick they could scarcely keep their own feet. As the vessels rolled, the horses were pitched against their mangers, losing their balance so that they became frantic with fear, and the stamping of their hooves in the stuffy, stinking, ill-lit holds, their screams and the shouts of the men trying above the din to pacify them, created a special kind of hell. Horse after horse went down and was no sooner got on its feet again—with great danger to the men from the kicking, plunging animals about them—when another crashed to the deck.

Only a few of the officers' chargers could lie down but they were on their feet 'like a shot' the minute the ship began to roll; and in the dark battened-down holds amid the smell of the oil lamps and the stink of ammonia and the vinegar which was scattered on the deck or used to bathe the nostrils of distressed animals, the horses hung in their canvas slings, heads down, their shoulders and bellies galled, some of them already beyond help and swinging limply, until the weather abated and they could be thrown overboard. In the Mediterranean a number went mad and had to be shot.

Kicking, biting and mad with joy at their freedom, the horses disembarked through the sparkling shallows where dogs fought over the carcass of a dead pack animal. They were clearly not fit for service and not likely to be for some time, but Captain Nolan was still busy trying to acquire remounts. By the beginning of May he was at Pera, where he bumped into one of Raglan's aides, Somerset Calthorpe, who, if he admired Nolan's books, considered some of his ideas 'rather extravagant'. Since his arrival, he had managed to round up only 30 to 40 horses, because he was finding it difficult to get them large enough, though there were baggage horses by the hundred and he could have bought 1,000 of them with ease but had no authority to do so, despite the fact that the commissariat was desperately in need of them.

If the horses were unhappy, the men were equally so, billeted as they were in the dilapidated Turkish barracks which was later to gain such notoriety as the Scutari hospital. Fleas plagued them, and even the staff complained of the immense rats in their rooms which 'gambolled about all night like cats'. They had just begun to recover a little when Lord Cardigan arrived, 'looking as usual highly important'. He was not in the best of health. There had been no improvement in his bronchitis and the dust was no help, and though his bombast was tremendous, Beauchamp Walker, one of Lucan's aides, immediately noticed that he looked very old and ill and felt they would have been better off with 'young men ... with more bodily activity'.

He, too, had travelled via Paris where he had given a dinner party at the Café de Paris and been entertained by Napoleon III and his Empress at the Tuileries. Scarlett was on the same train to Marseilles, which he left, again chased by Scarlett, on 16 May He spent two days sightseeing in Athens and arrived off Scutari on 24 May. Two days later he called on Lord Lucan, and the army held its breath.

The dislike between the two men was well known. The only things they had in common were their tempers and their aristocratic arrogance, and everyone expected trouble. William Howard Russell, who had been sent by The Times to the seat of war as the first war correspondent in history, considered the government had made a 'monstrous choice' in picking Cardigan to serve under Lucan and Calthorpe commented 'Both have violent and imperious tempers so if they don't clash, 'tis passing strange.'

Nevertheless, Lucan was anxious to avoid trouble and Cardigan was happy in the assurance he had received in London about his independence, and the meeting passed off well and even ended with an invitation to dine. Lord Lucan believed in living the same sparse life as his men, however, his indifference to hardship coming as a shock even to some of his staff,[3] and his attitude to food was the same. But though he was not noted for the lavishness of his table, they got through yet another meeting, even if Lucan's aides thought Cardigan 'a great swaggerer' whom they could not admire.

Though there were no difficulties at these meetings, however, there were plenty in the making. Cardigan was soon complaining that Lucan was asking him to send brigade returns to him and not direct to headquarters, which, since he believed he had an independent command, was what he had expected. In addition, though he hadn't informed Lucan, he had already written to Lord Raglan over his head requesting permission to move to Varna with the first detachments of the 8th Hussars, the 17th Lancers and the horse artillery. And that very day, also without informing Lucan, Lord Raglan had agreed. It was to be the beginning of a great deal of trouble.

It was one of the facets of Lord Raglan's complex character that those senior officers he favoured got away with a tremendous amount, while those he disliked—and Lucan was to become one—were virtually ostracised. What happened to Lucan was to happen also to the naval commander, Admiral Sir James Dundas; the man who was to take over in the event of Raglan's death, Sir George Cathcart; and Sir Colin Campbell and Sir George de Lacy Evans, who might well have put their vast experience of war at the commander-in-chief's disposal. Some of it can be put down to Raglan's wish to avoid trouble with strong-minded subordinates, but while he was avoiding trouble with one he was causing it with another and he must have known that Lucan was a diligent soldier very concerned with the proper channels of command and not at all the type to be ignored. Without Raglan, there would have been no trouble from Cardigan and none of the things that resulted from it.

While Cardigan was happily making arrangements for the embarkation of himself and his staff, Lord Lucan received his first intimation of what was going on in the form of a note from Lord de Ros, Raglan's quartermaster-general, informing him that Cardigan was about to go to Varna and requesting him, 'as his lordship wished to leave next day', to see that arrangements were made 'forthwith'.

Lucan was concerned with things as diverse as officers who grew mustachios in defiance of standing orders—'a clean-shaved face', one old soldier felt, 'was as necessary as a clean shirt'—and the fact that due to the inefficiency of the commissariat the horses were already having to eat chopped straw and barley instead of oats and hay. He had already been snubbed once by the commander-in-chief over Mrs. Duberly, or 'Jubilee' as she was known to the troops, who had arrived with the 8th Hussars. Though she claimed to have travelled with the permission of the Horse Guards and had had accommodation provided by the Admiralty, Lucan had guessed correctly that she had in fact no right to be on an army transport and had very properly sent an aide to inform her that unless she could produce an official permit she was to disembark. While she prepared plans to overcome his objections, however, she had been saved the trouble of putting them into operation because Lord Raglan had told her that he 'had no intention of interfering with her' and she passed beyond Lucan's reach to Varna.

To the gentlest of divisional commanders the second snub over Cardigan would have been enough to annoy. Lucan was a great believer in the chain of responsibility, that passing of information through the correct channels of rank without which any commander could find himself lacking vital information at a crucial moment,[4] but he held his notorious temper in check. Instead of an official complaint to the commander-in-chief, on 2 June he wrote a letter to 'My dear Cardigan' which, even from a mild-mannered man, would have been utterly reasonable. From a man of Lucan's temper it was a masterpiece of restraint.

'It is obvious,' he said, 'that the service cannot be carried on as it should be, and as I hope my division will be, if a subordinate officer is allowed to pass over his immediate responsible superior and communicate direct with the General Commanding-in-Chief of the Forces . . . or with any of his departmental officers . . . I write privately, as I wish this . . . to be of the most friendly nature. I hope that the arrangements I made for your embarkation were, as I intended them to be, as agreeable and convenient as they could be.' Considering the gross breach of etiquette, it was as mild a rebuke as could be uttered. Not only had he barely raised an objection, he had also held out a hand of friendship. No one could have asked for more and even the stupidest officer would have accepted it for what it was. But Cardigan was Cardigan and he did not apologise or offer any sign of friendship and by 7 June he had joined his regiments at Varna.

Unable to reach him, Lucan, in his energetic way, threw himself into the organisation of his command. He never failed to rise early, lived his usual spartan life and kept his division, or what he had of it, on its toes; and while the rankers do not seem to have complained, his energy clearly didn't suit some of the officers who had been used to a much easier way of life in England. He was expecting Colonel William Ferguson Beatson, who was being sent out by the Foreign Office. He had made a name for himself for his management of irregular cavalry, and had a tremendous record of service both in Spain and India, where he had risen to the rank of general in the Nizam of Hyderabad's army. He was hoping to persuade the Turkish government to give him command of the Bashi-Bazouks, splendid-looking men of Caucasian, Negro or Arab descent, of hungry aspect and covered with weapons. Even if not much used to discipline, such men would have been a useful addition to the small force under Lucan's command, but the letters Nolan had written during his search for remounts had indicated that their horses were too small and too weak. In fact they were very hardy animals which Captain Thompson, his assistant, thought had good build and great power for their height, but Nolan's letters were sufficient to put Raglan off. His rigid Horse Guards attitude had little use for irregular soldiers, or 'Indian' officers either, and no one, not even Omar Pasha, the Turkish commander-in-chief, had much love for the Bashi-Bazouks. In the end Raglan offered no help at all.

The rest of the cavalry, including the Heavy Brigade, were beginning to arrive now. Their journey out had been no easier than that of the first units. Hodge with his men had embarked on the Deva, a sailing ship, and inevitably he was immediately seasick. By 6 June they were 112 miles south-west of Finisterre, and at Malta they had picked up the regimental sergeant-major and eleven men of the Inniskilling Dragoon Guards, whose transport, the *Europa*, had caught fire 123 miles off the Scillies. Two mates and three sailors had immediately deserted her and, though the soldiers had behaved well, in the holocaust of flame and smoke and falling rigging they had lost 57 horses, their veterinary surgeon, 12 men and two women, and every scrap of equipment they possessed. By this time the horse holds and men's quarters on the *Deva* had become like ovens, and the temperature, even in Hodge's cabin, which was the captain's and the best on the ship, had stood at 82 degrees.

The 5th Dragoon Guards had also had a difficult voyage out but for a very different reason. Scarlett's successor, Le Marchant, in a matter of weeks had transformed a happy regiment into one which was muttering with discontent. At Gibraltar, he had given the senior NCOs permission to go ashore but had told them that if any of them returned drunk or brought drink aboard he would 'break' them. They were careful to remain sober, but about midnight, one of them, Troop Sergeant-Major Franks, was informed that a keg of whisky belonging to the veterinary surgeon had been stolen, and that the colonel had ordered all berths to be searched. The keg was not found but a small bottle of brandy was found in another sergeant-major's berth, whose label showed it had been bought ashore. The sergeant-major was ordered by Le Marchant to be tried by court martial and the court assembled in the saloon. The man who shared the accused's cabin said he had carried the bottle on board for the prisoner and had helped to drink some of it, and the court, clearly seeking not to bear down too hard, acquitted the prisoner on the grounds that he did not bring the liquor on board and that the purchasing of the drink and asking a comrade to carry it aboard did not constitute a crime. Le Marchant was furious. The regiment was paraded on the quarterdeck to hear the proceedings read and he told the officers of the court that they did not know their duty and that they were unfit for the position they held. 'He seemed', Franks thought, 'to have lost all control of himself.'

The regiment had very soon been made aware of the change in their circumstances and matters were very strained, the men standing in groups discussing the court martial in subdued tones. The officers were all popular and only the advice of the older soldiers stopped the men showing their resentment openly, but when Scarlett came on board to pay a visit to his old regiment at Scutari he was greeted with particularly loud handclapping and cheers. Oddly enough, this same dislike had once faced Le Marchant's father when he had been second-in-command of the 7th Light Dragoons and the same inordinate cheers had greeted Lord George Paget's father when he had come to take over from him.[5]

To the loss of horses en route Cardigan now began to contribute a few of his own. The arrangements for landing horses at Varna had been hurriedly made and had proved quite inadequate and, on top of those which had suffered severely from the voyage, more were injured in being put ashore. Major Cresswell, of the 11th Hussars, felt that 'anything more mismanaged' could hardly be conceived, and the staring coats of the troopers grew worse as forage and water became dangerously short in the parched Middle East.

Cardigan was established by this time well ahead of the army at Devna. It was a beautiful spot alongside a lake but in the bright days and blue velvet nights no one had noticed that it was known to the Turks as the Valley of Death. Neither Raglan nor the staff had paid any heed to their helpful advice, and 'at night', Russell wrote, 'fat unctuous vapours rose fold after fold from the valleys', and they were the forerunners of disease.

As yet, however, the worst problem was still Cardigan. He was complaining about the absence of pack horses and holding field days as though he were in Phoenix Park, Dublin. 'Such a bore he is,' wrote Cresswell, '. . . going round stables as if he were a colonel instead of a major-general . . .' No one had any clear idea what they had to do and '. . . as to fighting, it is the last thing we think of'. The Turks, although allies, were treated appallingly. Most of the Europeans regarded them as an inferior race and bullied and beat them. Cardigan set the example in the cavalry, having them on his field days but giving them no orders and then 'swearing at them for not being in the proper place'.

To make life easier for himself, he had acquired a house built over a stream and shaded by a tree, and was busy sending out patrols to the north—usually Turkish cavalry accompanied by British officers, but occasionally British horsemen, to whom he made it clear that he would be disappointed if they found no Cossacks.[6] He refused to allow them to carry cloaks, considering them effeminate, and mostly they brought back little but nosegays for Mrs. Duberly.

The first had left the day after their arrival. The heat was terrific and Cardigan was careful to stay indoors. Command did not include desk work and not a single copy of his orders had been forwarded to his divisional general, and, as plans were already being made for the rest of the army to follow the cavalry to Varna, it was Cardigan who was in command of the division. Lucan had been left behind with duties that seemed to consist chiefly of watching his men pass him by. Even the Heavy Brigade did not come under his command and went straight on to Varna.

It would have been too much for a milder-mannered man than Lucan, who had always doubted Cardigan's ability, anyway, and on 11 June he wrote to Cardigan, insisting on returns and reports, and composed a long letter to Raglan, who, he claimed, was taking the field with the main body of his army and the larger part of the Cavalry Division while he, Lucan, was being left behind. 'The whole of the horse artillery,' he said, 'and the whole of the cavalry present, full half of what is expected . . . will be in the field with the headquarters of the army, under . . . Lord Cardigan. I am to be left behind without troops and, for all I can see, without duties.'

When the letter arrived Raglan had a lot on his mind. Reports of sickness were beginning to come in and the bearded figure of Russell of The Times had turned up asking for tents and rations, as arranged at home. He had found he was looked on by the staff as an interloper who had no right to be there and Raglan's military secretary had told him quite flatly that his wish could not be granted. With Lucan's letter before him, however, and aware that newspapermen with their ears to the ground could be dangerous, Raglan was inclined to be more cautious. He sent for Lord de Ros who, despite his lack of experience, quickly saw the dangers and advised the commander-in-chief to order Lucan to Varna, after all. Then, hurrying himself to the cavalry commander, De Ros managed not only to persuade him he was under a complete misapprehension—Lord Raglan had not the slightest wish to leave him behind, while Lord Cardigan had been made completely aware of his position—but also even to withdraw the letter of protest.

*

Lucan finally arrived at Varna on 15 June. As usual he had been a little 'out of time' and had missed the boat.

Backed by the blue distant hills over which the shadows of ever-present thunderclouds moved, Varna abounded in wildlife. Storks flew overhead while eagles, kites and vultures sought out the carcasses of dead pack animals. The woods were ablaze with brilliant birds and at night the countryside was loud with the sound of frogs. Unfortunately, however, Varna had been allowed to fall into a dreadful state. The main street, Henry Clifford, of the Rifles, wrote, was 'like a large drain into which is emptied all sorts of filth . . . In trying to get out of the way of a dead dog . . . I found my foot on a dead rat . . . The stench beats everything I have ever smelt.' The infantry were camping among the graves of Russians who had died of disease in the war of 1828 and the water from the wells was tainted and came up green, while the rats—grey ones which made Calthorpe shudder—were even larger than at Scutari.

The only cavalry in sight seemed to be Spahis, white-robed French native horsemen who carried their swords under their thighs to prevent the jingling sound that always surrounded the British cavalry, and when Lucan called at headquarters, Sir George Brown, leader of the Light Division, who was in command until the arrival of Lord Raglan, had to admit there were no orders for him. However, he was soon 'buying stores at speed' to send on to his men, but there was little forage and what the locals brought in was 'little else than old bed stuffing, and full of fleas'.[7] By this time, he had received Cardigan's reply to his letter. It had been written on 15 June and it was sheer insubordination.

He considered, he said, that his command was a separate and detached one, and he added that he did not feel bound to anybody except Raglan, to whom it was his intention of submitting an appeal.

Lucan decided coldly that there should be no trouble and that the only way to avoid it was that he should never if possible give an order personally to Cardigan but would always send it through an aide. When Raglan arrived for a short visit, he passed the letter on to him, and if Raglan had been anything like a commander-in-chief, he ought at this point to have realised it was ridiculous to expect the two brothers-in-law to work together. In view of Cardigan's behaviour he ought to have squashed him completely or even, as Russell felt, removed him from command. Having accepted Lucan as commander of his cavalry, he ought to have backed him up, but the brisk, imperious Lucan and the gentle, diplomatic Raglan were like oil and water. They could not mix and Raglan once again avoided the issue and a brisk exchange of letters ensued.

General Estcourt, the adjutant-general, replying on Raglan's behalf to Lucan on 20 June, insisted that Lord Cardigan's misapprehensions about his command had already been put right in a letter he, Estcourt, had written at Raglan's request and that he would now understand that Lucan could call for whatever returns he felt necessary and take what steps he wished to look into the efficiency of his command. Once again, however, great care was taken not to let the matter become official and Estcourt ended with the note that his letter to Cardigan had not been an official letter because his misapprehension had already been corrected.

Lucan was by no means mollified and, indignant at the way the chain of command by which he set such store was being constantly ignored, he pointed out that Cardigan had written a very insubordinate letter and had gone over the head of his commanding officer. Raglan still preferred not to curb Cardigan, however, and did nothing to correct him. Estcourt's reply to Lucan was that all had been done that was considered necessary and that in future Cardigan would not be permitted to depart from the regular and usual channels of communication. 'Therefore,' Estcourt ended, 'the point you urged ought to be noticed as an irregularity of Lord Cardigan's will be the subject of a letter to him, but it will be a private communication, as indeed all the correspondence on this occasion has been.'

It was an infuriating situation and, to make things more difficult, on 20 June Cardigan, together with many others in an enormous bulletin, had been gazetted major-general, Lucan's equal in rank. It went to his head at once and when the 13th Light Dragoons arrived he changed the whole cavalry camp round, taking a 'wearisome time arranging it', but leaving everyone more than a mile from water when he had finished whereas before they had been alongside the river bank.

Lord Raglan finally arrived in Varna to stay on the 24th, and Lucan was quick to ask to be allowed to join his command. Since his men were all at Devna, he said, there was little for him to do at Varna. His request was turned down. Lord Raglan thought, Lord de Ros wrote, that as detachments of cavalry were still due to arrive at Varna, he should remain there to inspect them carefully before they disembarked.

There was little wonder Raglan had demurred. Despite his promises, he had again given Cardigan his head and he was at that very moment preparing to disappear once more into the blue.

7 He neither feels for man nor horse

ODDLY enough, Omar Pasha, the commander of the Turks, whom the British and French were there to rescue, was the most experienced of all the allied commanders. Small, pale and clever-looking, and given neither to the showy panache of St. Arnaud nor to the old-womanish shyness of Raglan, he was quite unimpressed by the Russians—with very good reason. Turkish troops had defeated them on more than one occasion, and had now defeated them again.

On 23 June, the news had come in that, after 40 days of fighting whose ferociousness had made up for its lack of science, the siege of Silistria had been raised. With the assistance of Captain James Armar Butler and Lieutenant Nasmyth, two young British 'Indian' officers who had invited themselves to the fight, and General Cannon, also formerly of the Indian Army, who had got into the place with more troops—the Turks had driven the Russians off without any assistance from the allied armies. Ravaged by cholera and worried by threatening moves by Austria, they were already retreating, and Omar Pasha was anxious to discover where they were, and on the very day that Raglan had been instructing De Ros to reply to Lucan's complaint, he had issued orders sending Cardigan off to make a reconnaissance along the banks of the Danube. Time was undoubtedly short but Lucan was at hand in Varna and it would have been courteous in the very least to have informed him—especially since he had once fought across the country to be reconnoitred—but though Raglan managed to give Cardigan written orders, Lucan was not informed at all. Still trying to keep the peace, he had even breakfasted with Cardigan that very morning and was ready packed to leave himself. But not a word was said to him and the following day Cardigan disappeared into the Dobrudja with 121 men of the 8th Hussars and 75 of the 13th Light Dragoons.

He vanished over the horizon in great glee, reinforced by this demonstration by Raglan that he still had an independent command, and with only the minimum of food and forage and no tents and intending a brilliant cavalry feat such as he had dreamed about for years, he forced the pace as much as possible.[1] Yet nobody was less fitted for an independent command than Cardigan, not only because of his love of flamboyance, his arrogance, ill-health and age, but also because of his lack of skill as a horsemaster. Not only were the horses still unfit after their long journey out and now wearing saddles which no longer fitted because of their leanness but they were also absurdly overloaded with extra blankets and rations.

No one was sorry to see him go, however, and he reached the banks of the Danube in four days, only to find the Russians already on the other side. The job he had been sent to do was done but he could not resist trying to do more and followed the hot dusty roads along the banks of the river, returning by Silistria and the old fortess of Shumla. He was away so long, in fact, a second patrol was sent out to look for him but had to report to the worried commander-in-chief that it had seen no sign of him. All that was known was the news brought back by one of his officers, Lieutenant Bowen—whose horse dropped with exhaustion as it arrived and had to be revived with brandy— that the fatigue was excessive, with incessant marching for which neither horses nor men were fit.

Meanwhile, in Varna, the sickness which had broken out among the troops was declining a little, despite the heat and the wind that filled everything with dust. The Heavy Brigade were a couple of miles outside the town and the horse artillery were still at Devna, and Lucan was finding some of the regimental officers very lax in many ways. Many of them had omitted from their equipment what he considered three main essentials for active service—a spy-glass, a compass and a watch—and he issued an order that they were to obtain them forthwith and were never to appear on duty without them. He also noticed that in an effort to produce uniformity, trumpeters in the Light Brigade had been given grey horses but, considering them of as much consequence as an officer in battle, he ordered them to change their mounts for others less conspicuous.

'No officer in the army was more vigilant and careful' of his command, Russell noticed—even to the point of annoying headquarters on its behalf. There was not a single matter, great or small, that he did not deal with—the care of baggage animals, the composition of the squadrons, the picketing of horses, their shoeing and marking and heel-ropes, the carriage of ammunition, the dress of officers, the packing of valises, reports and daily states, tents, the quality and dearness of boots, trumpet calls, watch-setting, marching, drills and parades, even washer-women.[2]

Unlike most of the allied soldiers, he got on well with the Turks, and he had ordered a field day and review for Omar Pasha. But it was seventeen years since he had handled a regiment, and in the interval cavalry drill had changed. To a layman like Russell the field day seemed an unqualified success. There were one and a half squadrons of the 17th Lancers, a troop of the 8th Hussars and a troop of the 11th and, as they came up at full trot, they 'riveted the attention of the Pasha'. Nobody had understood Lucan's old-fashioned words of command but like good soldiers they had used their intelligence and put on a show. Beatson's Bashi-Bazouks, however, were proving difficult. Their horses, almost all of them stallions, spent their time kicking and fighting and, as Beatson had no money to pay them, they began to desert and indulge in their old habits of violence and plunder. Faced with Omar Pasha's profound contempt for them and an absolute lack of support from Raglan, Beatson gave up in despair and found a place instead on the staff of Scarlett who, 'blind as a bat' and entirely without experience, willingly added him to Lieutenant Elliot as an adviser.

Scarlett was beginning to clamour for his Heavies now and the 5th Dragoon Guards had arrived by this time—'very green', Sir George Brown thought, 'and in no state to move'—and another more elaborate review was put on for Omar Pasha on 6 July. Despite Lucan's wrong words of command and the white covers they wore over their brass helmets, they made a splendid sight as they went past at a gallop with two troops of Royal Horse Artillery, whose six- and nine-pounder guns bounded behind them; while a charge in line which shook the earth and sent up clouds of dust so delighted the Pasha he said 'With one such regiment . . . I could ride over . . . four Russian regiments at least.' He was so pleased he requested that they should be given an extra ration of rum, but since he didn't provide the money to pay for it the quartermaster could not draw it from the commissariat, and if he had heard the remarks of the men 'he would have found them quite the reverse of those expressed' when his request had been made known.

Colonel Hodge arrived on 8 July. With the thermometer at 90 and the land shimmering in the heat, he found an arid shore by a gentian-blue sea covered with horses and soldiers. There were twelve men to a tent, but the organisation of the army was so pathetic saddles had to be kept in the open air, no transport had been provided by the commissariat and only a regulation number of pack animals was allowed, so that the worried Hodge began at once to reduce the voluminous kit he had gathered about him. Water was two miles away and every drop had to be fetched, and though the countryside was pretty enough it was fast disappearing under the axes of the troops. The horses were suffering considerably. They were tethered in the boiling sun all day and had to endure not only a freezing dew at night but a plague of insects that drove them mad. Although protected with bandages and coverings of rags or mats, already many of them had bad eyes from the glare and were coughing from the dust, and the stink around the camp was dreadful because of the Turkish habit of leaving dead animals where they dropped. Hodge was finding active service in the East quite as bad as he had expected and even dinner with Lord Lucan did not cheer him up. 'A moderate feed, very,' he commented tartly.

On 11 July, a wet and gloomy day, Cardigan's patrol returned. According to Mrs. Duberly, who saw it arrive, it was a pitiful sight—men plodding in on foot, carrying their saddles and driving and goading 'the wretched wretched horses, three or four of which could hardly stir'. As always it was the condition of the horses not the men which drew her sympathy. 'I hope,' she wrote to her sister, 'that Cardigan, whom all abhor, will get his head in such a jolly bag he will never get it out again.'

According to Russell, Cardigan's ambitious patrol had 'effected very little service'. Despite firm instructions that if he found water and foraging difficult he was to use only a small portion of his force,[3] Cardigan had done no such thing, and his skill was so lacking he brought back no information of military usefulness whatsoever. He had more than once been lost and on one occasion had allowed his exhausted men to bivouac in full view of a Russian battery across the river. Fortunately the Russians did not fire, probably because General Lüders, the Russian commander, could not understand what they were doing as they galloped about.

Despite Lüders' forbearance, however, the patrol had taken a dreadful toll. The pace Cardigan had forced had resulted in five of his horses dropping dead while 75 more were dying, and of the remainder most of them would never be fit again for anything but light work, through a foot disease they had picked up from too much fast trotting on hard roads. Heat, violent rainstorms, want of forage and water had resulted in quite unnecessary exhaustion. At Bazarjik the cavalrymen had been quartered in buildings infested by starving cats against which they had had to draw their swords, and at Karasi several horses were lost when they were stampeded by loose pack animals. They had become desperately hungry, but when the officers shot a number of pigs they had found, Cardigan was angry at what he considered their unsoldierlike behaviour—though he was pleased to dine off the pork that evening. At one village, a dozen men, left behind under Lieutenant Percy Smith, of the 13th

Light Dragoons—a man who had injured his hand in a shooting accident and could not hold a sword without a special iron guard which he slipped over his wrist—were surrounded by a band of Turks who imagined them to be Russians because Smith wore a shako similar to those worn by the Russian cavalry seen at Silistria, and there was the ominous sound of swords being drawn before the matter was settled.[4]

Despite such experiences, however, and the problem of their failing horses, when they had run across a party of French officers Cardigan had been so eager to present his patrol in the full panoply of his glory he had insisted on them mounting, although they were already walking their horses and carrying the saddles because of the animals' sore backs. According to Captain Lockwood, of Cardigan's staff, he had the greatest difficulty in inducing the men to put the saddles on at all,[5] and when told by the doctor of the condition of his men he had answered haughtily 'I am a major-general . . . and yet, sir, I can feel for the men', which, said Mrs. Duberly, was 'an infernal lie, as he neither feels for man nor horse'.

Turkish carts, known as arabas, brought in the men who had collapsed. They had not taken their clothes off for seventeen days, and the net result of the patrol, 'the Soreback Reconnaissance to the Dobrudja' as it became known, was that the Light Brigade had lost another hundred of their precious mounts, while those that had been brought back would never be fit again. Though the patrol had left Cardigan in no state for work for some days to come, he felt he had borne it well and noted with pride in his diary that he had slept in a small tent six feet square, just big enough to cover a spring sofa bed. He did not mention how the bed was carried.

Despite his failure, Lord Raglan wrote to him 'You have ascertained for me that the Russians have withdrawn . . . and that the country . . . is wholly deserted by the inhabitants. These are important facts . . .' and ended with the old-womanly hope that fatigue would not prove injurious to his health. The truth was that he was beginning to have second thoughts on Cardigan. He had covered an ambitious 336 miles in 18 days, disappearing entirely from the ken of the army, and had the Russians been active he could have lost every horse and man. It was an unnerving thought—especially with Nolan's mission unsuccessful. He had acquired 300 Arab horses but they had not proved very satisfactory. When they had arrived, they had seemed to Sergeant Albert Mitchell, of the 13th Light Dragoons, to be wild, untamable and small, and the worst he had ever handled, as they fought together and constantly broke loose.

It was from this moment that Raglan's support of Cardigan was noticeably withdrawn. Unfortunately it was already too late and much damage had been done not only to the horses but also to the relationship with Lord Lucan who was shocked at what had happened. On the day of Cardigan's return he issued an order that no horses were to be destroyed except in the case of a broken leg, or glanders or farcy, highly contagious diseases which had been introduced to the division by the Royal Dragoons who had picked them up during their long journey from England, and he began to seek out a route up-country[6] for them to change their camp in the hope of reducing the number of fatalities.

His efforts were wasted. Lord Raglan had already decided they should go to Yeni-Bazaar, 28 miles from Devna, and, again forgetting to inform Lucan, had instructed Cardigan accordingly. It was a difficult march through waterless countryside in intolerable heat and blinding sun, and when a well was found for an evening halt there was such a rush for it Captain Lockwood's horse almost fell in. There was enough water to have supplied every regiment but Cardigan slapped a sentry on it so that everyone had to walk more than a mile and climb a steep hill on the way back. It was done, in fact, from a fear that the water was tainted with the germs of cholera which had begun to appear in Varna, but Cardigan's unpopularity was such that everyone was prepared to believe it was solely for the selfish reason that he wanted it himself. It wasn't an unreasonable assumption, because when Mrs. Duberly had selected a spot in the shade of a clump of trees to pitch her tent, Cardigan had insisted on her moving it so that he could place his own there instead, and Lieutenant Inglis, one of her admirers, had exploded. 'I wish a great damned wind would come,' he said, 'and blow down those damned trees on his damned old head!' To everyone's joy the spring overflowed during the night and flooded his tent.

The following day they moved on to Yasi-Tepe along a road littered with the stinking carcasses of horses, bullocks, sheep and dogs. After the tents had been pitched, Cardigan insisted on them being struck and repitched and when they were up once more said they were not straight, so that they had to be repitched yet again.

He was not unaware of the grumbling he was causing. He was stubborn and arrogant but he wasn't so stupid that he didn't realise his staff had to toady to him[7] to keep him in a good temper. But his was a split personality and his moods changed with his health, and a few days later when he met Mrs. Duberly he greeted her cheerfully as though nothing had happened. When he wished, he could be charming, and Mrs. Duberly was soon surprised to find herself taking rides with him—'not often', she said cautiously, in a letter to her sister Selina, 'as I detest him'.

Though Mrs. Duberly found her fears calmed, the rest of the cavalry did not. It was now midsummer and the heat in the tents had reached 110 degrees and fodder was growing desperately short. Although the men received a daily ration of one and a half pounds of black bread and a pound of thin mutton, which Lucan ate like his troops, the horses were already on a starvation diet. And by now it was growing difficult to forage because everyone who was fit was suddenly overworked for an entirely different reason. When even the Prince Consort could die of typhoid from the water at Windsor it was unlikely that anyone should be very concerned with the water at Varna, and almost overnight, it seemed, an epidemic of cholera had assumed the proportions of a plague.

8 In a state of mutiny

THERE had been a great deal of sickness in the allied camps for some time. Without doubt the heavy uniforms had not helped, while the brass helmets some of the cavalry wore became too hot to touch in the Middle East sun, and with officers wearing French kepis, fezzes and sun helmets with gauze veils, Raglan, the most conservative of Wellington's admirers, had had to allow the stock to fall into disuse in the dusty heat. He had been quick, however, to pounce on anything approaching unconventionality and complained of open jackets, coloured shirts, the absence of collars, unshaven chins and turbans.

Rations remained unreliable also and when they came they were as often as not salt pork, guaranteed to produce a thirst at any time but in the Middle East heat almost a frenzy. Nevertheless Sir George Brown stopped the porter of the men of the Light Division because, he said, 'it was a luxury and encouraged drunkenness'.[1] Instead, they went for raki, the local spirit, which was infinitely worse for their health. Every officer had his own method of dealing with the problem. Higginson, of the Guards, forced one of the vendors who appeared in his camp to drink half a pint of his own poisonous spirit so that he passed out cold, but there were also many prisoners in the guard rooms, and a sergeant-major of the Royals thought 'a little flogging would do a few men a lot of good'.

Hodge wrote to Lucan on the subject but, concerned with the results of Cardigan's patrol, the divisional commander did not manage to answer. 'He is a man of violent temper,' Hodge complained fretfully, 'and an unreasonable man to deal with.' Yet, when Hodge saw a boat come ashore to sell rum and seized it and its cargo, itching to burn them and flog the men, Lucan, doubtless aware of being in a country which, despite its official alliance, was demonstrably—even at times murderously—

hostile to the hordes of foreigners who had descended on its soil, contented himself with spilling the spirits and letting the crew go.

Suddenly, however, drink was not the only threat. To quench their thirst, everyone had been in the habit of buying local-grown water-melons whose juices, touched by tainted water, brought on diarrhoea and dysentery which the heat and the flies spread, and cholera, when it appeared, found the army in no condition to withstand it.

Cholera had been prevalent in Europe since 1847 and in 1854 had been noted in places as far apart as Dublin and St. Petersburg. In England it had been expected in the gin shops and the two-penny brothels of the poor as early as 4 March. There was little sign of it in the British troops up to the middle of July, however, though it had appeared among the French troops[2] and, less concerned with the discovery of information than with a wish to remove his troops from their stricken camps, St. Arnaud had decided to send a small expeditionary force to the north. It was a disaster. The cholera struck with such fury that in one night 600 men died. By the time they returned to Varna the force had lost more than 7,000 men. The Bashi-Bazouks began to desert en masse and the disease spread like lightning.

Flies had become a curse by this time and Hodge was busy complaining that coffee was issued unroasted though there was not only no coffee mill in the whole British army but also no fuel to roast it and nothing to roast it on, when he suddenly woke up to the fact that the disease was all about him. By 30 July his regiment was affected and the Inniskillings, who had already been so hard hit on their passage out, had 46 men in hospital.

Soldiers alert and cheerful at noon were dead—and buried—by evening, sometimes in a matter of only three or four hours, while those who recovered became mere skeletons. Trumpeter Farquharson, of the 4th Light Dragoons, lost two stone in a matter of three days, and Captain Morris, the DAQMG, was so ill he was not expected to live. The hospitals, hot and smelling of disease, were full, yet the ambulance corps was hopeless and there were no directions from headquarters. Regimental officers were left to use their own initiative, and Higginson of the Guards kept his cholera cases alive by giving them bottled Bass.

The French losses were becoming frightful by this time and at night, near the Turkish barracks which they were using as a hospital, Russell counted 35 carts containing sick, who were waiting for men to die before they could be admitted. Observing empty arabas nearby he asked the NCO in charge what they were for and got the short reply 'Pour les morts'. By 19 August it was possible to find wisps of straw sticking from the sand everywhere, and beneath them a dead face; to find corpses under the stones that were being lifted from the sea to make a jetty; and bodies floating bolt upright in the water, their feet shotted, one French corpse of enormous stature defying all efforts to sink it.

In the cavalry the onset of disease had a double effect, not only killing off the men but helping to kill off the horses as the surviving soldiers found themselves unable to groom and water the neglected mounts of the sick and the dead. Those horses which survived began to fall off terribly as forage grew even shorter. Though no less than 110,000 pounds of corn, and chopped straw were available daily, the commissariat arrangements were so bad Hodge's horses could get only 12 pounds of barley.

Whatever else he had learned from that master of logistics, Wellington, Raglan had never learned that an army that was well fed and clothed was capable of anything. He was, in fact, probably never informed of the situation, because it was always the staff's policy never to bother him unnecessarily. Captain John Adye, on taking up a staff appointment, was told 'Never trouble Lord Raglan more than is absolutely necessary with details, listen carefully to his remarks, try to anticipate his wishes and at all time make as light as possible of difficulties!' It was a policy for the care of an elderly man and was certainly not one to produce much in the way of results.

Rations remained poor and it was impossible because of the

tangle of regulations even to get coal for the farriers' forges and the artillery lost ten per cent of their shoes every time they left camp. Everybody blamed everybody else, the young officers their commanding officers, commanding officers their brigadiers and divisional generals. The fault, of course, lay with the government, and even with previous governments, and without doubt with the supineness at headquarters.

Overnight, the army began to look shabby and listless. There was no pipeclay and belts and equipment became patchy and dark, and the red jackets of the infantry turned purple with exposure to the weather. Everyone was 'growing beards and looking very wild and ragged',[3] and, despite Raglan's disapproval, casual shirts of all colours continued to be worn. Indeed, the flannel shirt and red trousers of Raglan's own quartermaster-general was one of the strangest garbs of the lot. The occupant of the post had recently changed. Lord de Ros, who had been ill for some days, had now been obliged to give up his post and return home—'He won't be missed,' Captain Robert Portal of the 4th Light Dragoons commented—and the position was given to Major-General Airey. Though he had never seen active service, Airey, who was 51 years old, had had a distinguished career, entering the army at 18 and rising by purchase to lieutenant-colonel at the age of 35, when he had been attached to the Horse Guards staff. Following the normal custom of the day he had been away from the army for some time in Canada on the estates of his cousin where he had built his own log cabin and lived cut off from civilisation, but he had returned to England and become military secretary to Lord Hardinge in 1852 and had worked with Lord Raglan, who had all along wished him to be his quarter-master-general. He had been given instead a brigade of the Light Division. He was not a popular man—Hodge thought him a 'conceited coxcomb'—but at least he had energy and a pur-posefulness that was in direct contrast to Raglan's lack of drive.

With him as aide he took the man who had been appointed to

his staff for the purpose of buying remounts, Captain Louis Nolan. Surrounded as he was by men of influence, Nolan was without influence himself and the move was an opportunity to show what he could do. It was the only sure step to the top a man in his position could take and he was eager to bring himself to the notice of the commander-in-chief. A complex character, regarded by his fellow-officers as somewhat officious and pedantic, he had already let it be known that, although he thought the men of the cavalry second to none in bravery and skill, he had not much time for their style of riding or their equipment. Compared with those of the native troops in India, their swords were too blunt, he felt, while those adornments which had become part of cavalry furniture—the shabraque and the sheepskin—were totally unnecessary.

He had been 'full of invective' against Cardigan for the Dobrudja patrol and now he did not hestitate also to let his disapproval be known of Lord Lucan. Since they had barely met and Lucan was never really aware of Nolan, the feeling can only be put down in the beginning to Lucan's dislike of the horses he had bought. He had been forthright about them and had made it very clear that he thought them of poor quality. Nolan took it very much to heart.[4] His knowledge of horses was considered to be beyond question, and it infuriated him to have this middle-aged general questioning his selection. It was the far-from-unfamiliar attitude of a young man resenting an older man's ideas and it was from this time that his diary began to fill with embittered comments on the cavalry in general and Lord Lucan in particular.

*

When the 4th Light Dragoons had arrived under Lord George Paget, compared with the rest of the cavalry they had looked well. They had marched into Plymouth to embark through triumphal arches, massed flowers and clusters of flags.

One of Paget's first jobs, however, was to face Lucan. He was now the senior colonel in Varna and immediately he had had thrown into his lap a problem which had been worrying his colleagues for some time. While Lucan's field days had provided magnificent spectacles, they had also provoked a crop of sly comments from Hodge's second-in-command, the same witty Major William Charles Forrest who had tangled with Cardigan and who had exchanged to the 4th Dragoon Guards to escape him. How much Forrest's letters home were meant to be taken seriously is difficult to assess but, since he was regularly wildly wrong, it is possible to assume they were intended chiefly to amuse. He wrote good ones full of gay scandalous news, and the disputed cavalry command was a ready-made subject for a man with a flair for words. He considered Lucan 'rum' and, though 'a very sharp sort of chap', rusty at his drill. 'All his staff,' he said not very truthfully, 'wish themselves off it' and he gaily suggested that something had happened between Lucan and Scarlett because Scarlett, finding 'he was nobody here', had disappeared. As the days passed, his tone became more critical. 'We have not much confidence in our cavalry general, Lord Lucan,' he wrote, 'and only hope he will allow his several brigadiers to move their own brigades . . . for he and Cardigan will be sure to have a row directly.' The quarrel was general knowledge by now and every slight disagreement was being greatly magnified, and the field days were excellent subjects for Forrest's witty pen.

'Lord Lucan', he wrote, 'has been so long on the shelf . . . he has no idea of moving cavalry, does not even know the words of command and is very self-willed about it . . . Officers who have drilled under him are puzzled to know what he means.' Forrest had good reason to dislike Cardigan and was not likely to admire his brother-in-law. 'He has not a very good cavalry style,' he said, and went on to criticise Lucan's staff one by one. Lord William Paulet, Lucan's assistant adjutant-general, he said, had been all his life in the infantry; MacMahon, his assistant quartermaster-general, had always been on the staff; Walker had a lot to learn;

and Lord Bingham, a second lieutenant in the Guards, like the others was not efficient for his post.

It all sounds like a good gossip made better for the benefit of adoring relatives but there is no doubt there was already a surprising tendency to run the cavalry down and Walker found one of the staff unceasingly singing only the praises of the Spahis. It didn't take long for the habit to spread and Forrest continued to enlarge on Lucan and the field days. 'If he is shown by the drill book that he is wrong,' he said, 'he says "Ah, I'd like to know who wrote that book, some Farrier, I suppose." ' This was Forrest at his wittiest, but Paget found the truth was very different. When Lucan called his colonels to his tent to explain his puzzling orders, Paget was deputised as senior colonel to present to him the colonels' problem. He did not relish the idea of facing his terrifying senior officer with what was in effect a criticism of his methods, and, like everyone else in Society, he had heard of the dispute between the two brothers-in-law and didn't fancy being caught in the middle of it.

He remembered two quarrelsome noblemen he knew, of whom it had been said 'They are like a pair of scissors which go snip and snip and snip, without ever doing each other any harm, but God help the poor devil who gets between them', and thought his position might well turn out to be similar. To his surprise, however, Lucan proved considerate and forebearing and the matter was soon sorted out to everyone's satisfaction. To the end of the campaign, in fact, Paget never had an angry word with his divisional commander, and though he occasionally caught the rough edge of his tongue, he had the wits to notice that Lucan was as hard on himself as he was on everybody else.

Nevertheless, Forrest's warning that things were not well was not far from the truth. 'I write all this to you,' he had said, 'in order that if any mishap should occur to the cavalry you may be able to form a correct idea how it happened.' He was showing a remarkable prescience, but the tragedy when it did happen sprang from something much more complicated than Lucan's old-fashioned orders, and the elements that could compound that tragedy had already come together.

Cardigan was being difficult with the petulance of an elderly, sick and spoiled man—though, like Lucan, he was always careful to keep his quarrel dignified and his communications were always in writing or through an aide—and Nolan was wasting no time in making his views felt at headquarters. By this time Lucan was on the same icily formal terms with Raglan that he employed with Cardigan, and now, following Cardigan's indifference to the chain of command, something he held sacred, he received indirect reports that the colonel of one of his regiments was also going over his head and, what was worse, that the regiment he commanded was in a state of mutiny.

*

Food was always difficult and the rations which the 5th Dragoon Guards, Le Marchant's unhappy regiment, had been receiving turned out to be very poor and on occasion failed to appear at all. Without doubt this was due to Le Marchant's indifference. In other regiments, such difficulties had been overcome by a little effort on the part of the commanding officers and a little goodwill on the part of the men, but Le Marchant had kept out of sight and the 5th Dragoon Guards were already resentful and angry at their treatment by their new commander.

In their ranks was a hardcase Irishman named John Martin who, although a good soldier, had a liking for drink. After a visit to a nearby French canteen he had been returning to his quarters, not very sober and singing loudly, when the colonel shot out of his tent and told him to stop. 'No, I won't,' Martin had said with the aggressiveness of drink, 'I will sing as much as I like.'

Le Marchant had promptly threatened him with a flogging and when Martin had just as promptly retaliated by saying he would do better to get the troops their rations instead of sneaking in his tent, Le Marchant had had him handcuffed and tied. Most of the officers had been inclined to treat the incident as a drunken misdemeanour. But when the Duke of Cambridge, whose headquarters were nearby, had passed through the camp, Sergeant-Major Franks and a few others had heard Le Marchant—though the Duke had nothing whatsoever to do with the cavalry—tell him that the regiment was 'in a state of mutiny and that he could not be answerable for their conduct'. A popular commander with a great regard for the men in the ranks, the Duke had found it hard to believe of Scarlett's regiment, but a parade had been called and at the end he had turned to Le Marchant. 'I don't see any signs of mutiny here,' he had said in bewilderment. 'I think there must be some mistake.'

The following day the regiment had left for Devna, and on arrival Le Marchant had ordered Martin's court martial. There was no doubt of his guilt but the court, trying to be lenient, had sentenced him only to the minimum of 25 lashes. Le Marchant had been livid. The regiment had again been paraded to hear the verdict and again the colonel had lost control and upbraided the officers in front of the men. He was so disgusted with the paltry sentence, he said, it wasn't worth tying Martin up for it, and he had told him to go to his duty. Martin had vanished as quickly as possible, and Le Marchant, in a wild speech, had threatened to tell his friend, Sir George Brown—again a man with nothing whatsoever to do with the cavalry.

Rations still remained sparse and the beef that was issued—killed by Turkish butchers who were doubtless keeping the best for themselves—was very poor and badly cut up, but the worst disappointment was the coffee. Knowing Turkey was noted for it, the men had been looking forward to it, but when Sergeant-Major Franks went to collect the rations for his troop, he was met by a languid young gentleman of the commissary staff who handed over green beans. The men did their best with them, roasting them on a spade and grinding them with stones, but there was a lot of grumbling and some horseplay, in the course of which a camp kettle containing boiling water was flung and Franks's horse was scalded. He was ordered to find the culprit but no one was talking and when the matter was laid before Le Marchant he was furious. He was still only being seen on parade and then only to find fault and threaten privates with floggings and NCOs that he would 'break' them.

Shortly afterwards, Scarlett visited the camp and at a parade, at which Le Marchant was not present, he told the men it was their duty to support their new colonel. What he said to Le Marchant is not recorded, but the rations improved a little. A divisional staff officer had inspected the Turkish butchers and as a result the names were asked of men who had been butchers before enlisting, the idea being to bring the cattle to the regiments on the hoof. The men were furnished with canvas clothing and the meat began to improve.[5]

Though the troubles had blown over, they soon began in another quarter. When the Light Brigade had been moved to Yeni-Bazaar, 28 miles from Devna, it had been hoped they would get rid of the cholera, but in fact they took it with them. The weather was terrifically hot and, with the flies and the sickness increasing, Cardigan was again ill and ignoring all Lucan's requests for information. Once again for several days his diary shows that entire absence of interest in things which indicated he was having to take life easy. No one was very happy. 'I would rather do anything than continue here,' Lieutenant Seager, of the 8th Hussars, wrote, while Captain Portal noticed that his men were growing daily more dispirited and disgusted with their fate. 'They do nothing but bury their comrades,' he said. On a day when Russell was writing home that the Guards had become so weak that they had to make two marches to get from Aladyn to Varna, a mere 10 miles, Hodge buried 23 of his men and it was becoming difficult to find a spot for a grave which had not been dug over already.

To add to the miseries, an enormous fire broke out on 10 August which destroyed more than a quarter of Varna and vast quantities of provisions.[6] Sailors and French and British soldiers worked for 10 hours to fight it but the brisk wind fanned the flames and sparks along the wooden streets. In his efforts to superintend the work, St. Arnaud only served to aggravate the angina from which he was already suffering, and there was a lot of plundering so that Hodge was turned out by Lucan in the glare to patrol the town with 200 cavalrymen. The fire left a sooty dust everywhere so that everyone was filthy and, with the shortage of water, unable to wash; and it was no longer possible to buy the tea, sugar, brandy and rice with which they had supplemented their monotonous rations.

Soon afterwards the 5th Dragoon Guards, hitherto free from cholera, began to have sickness. As the first casualty was buried—with all his belongings because it was believed they might carry the infection—they suddenly discovered they were camped on the site of the crumbling burial ground of Turkish troops who had died of the disease and they hastily moved to Kotlubie, hoping to leave the sickness behind. But though the new site was better, their tents were so old they would not keep out the dew, let alone the regular thunderstorms, there was no water handy, and instead of escaping the cholera they took it with them. By 11 August there were 70 sick, 15 of whom died within hours.

The difficulties of forage had occupied Lucan for some time and, discovering that the commissariat department were not bringing in their correct rations of barley, he had sent Walker out to scour the countryside. Since there was no grass, fields of standing wheat, oats and barley were bought and twenty sickles were issued to each troop. For those who had grown up in rural areas the job was not hard, but the townsmen cut themselves as often as they cut the crops, and the experts found themselves doing all the work. With so many sick this was tremendously hard on the few fit men of the 5th and their spirits fell again. The officers did all they could to help, but then it was discovered that a medicine chest containing the drugs needed for cholera had been left at Varna and the rumour started that it was entirely the fault of Le Marchant.

It was probably quite wrong but there was a great deal of muttering, the men gathering in angry groups, determined to blame the unpopular colonel for all their troubles. They were obviously planning something and it didn't take long to discover what it was. Three men had been selected to see Le Marchant and ask him point blank if he had been responsible for leaving the chest behind. What they hoped to do then is hard to say but it was indicative of the desperate state of the regiment, low in spirits with sickness and the stupidity of its colonel. Fortunately the regimental surgeon heard what was afoot and warned Le Marchant, and when the three men arrived he was not in his tent. That night he vanished and it was learned later that he had gone for good. His servant produced the extraordinary story that he had hidden himself under a pile of grass in one of the carts leaving the camp and had been driven to Varna where he had gone on board ship. It was an astonishing disappearance and, with the command falling on Captain Adolphus Burton, who was very young and inexperienced, the regiment was in a poor state of morale. There had been about 90 deaths and many men were still in hospital, where the officers, 'some ill themselves, some simply disgusted',[7] were taking their turns sitting by suffering privates.

By this time, all the cavalry, which had been harder hit by the disease than the infantry, was in poor shape. So many had died, in fact, they were borrowing each other's trumpeters to sound the last post and Colonel Douglas did away with funeral music altogether in the 11th Hussars. With the 5th Dragoon Guards useless as a regiment, Lucan decided it would be wiser to move them back to Varna, in the hope that the sea air would help their health, but the sick had to be transported by waggon and there were only seven officers and so few mounted men each one had several riderless horses to look after. The road was dusty and the horses were sweating, so that when they paraded alongside the

4th Dragoon Guards and the newly arrived 4th Light Dragoons at Varna, they cut a 'very sorry figure'.

Le Marchant had wrought havoc with the regiment and Lucan wrote to Raglan on 20 August that he had found them 'in a most unsatisfactory state'. The condition of the horses, he said, was due to 'neglect alone'.

Clearly surprised that Scarlett had not noticed 'the distressing state' of the 5th, Raglan thought the horses 'exhibited every appearance of absolute neglect' while the men were 'dirtier than I ever yet saw a British soldier'. It was Lucan's wish to get rid of the regiment, but, desperately short of horsemen, the eyes and ears of his army, and with plans afoot for further moves against Russia, Raglan seemed to suspect that the Light Brigade under Cardigan would not measure up to the tasks that might face it and he decided instead that the regiment should be attached to the 4th Dragoon Guards. Hodge was almost overcome by the honour and terrified that it might throw discredit on Scarlett. 'But,' he confided to his diary, 'Le Marchant has throwed up the command and gone home ill.'

He had indeed—much to the disgust of his officers who were firmly of the opinion that he fully intended to use the influence of his good connections to hang on to the colonelcy long enough to sell it at a profit. 'I don't believe he has the pluck to come here,' Captain Temple Godman wrote bitterly. 'The men have been saying that . . . he would not like the noise of the cannon.' In a matter of weeks, Le Marchant had almost brought about a disaster and with others was to be indirectly responsible for the bringing about of another. Lucan's observations on the 5th soon became public property and it began to be said that he was 'jealous of the regiment' and of Scarlett, and was anxious 'to have a rap at them'. For the growing number of his enemies beginning to group at headquarters round Nolan it was a delicious morsel.

Fortunately, Raglan's experiment turned out to be most successful. Franks considered Hodge 'most kindly and genial' and his example was followed by every officer and man of his regiment. Though to Franks it seemed incredible that two regiments could be commanded by the same colonel, particularly during a campaign, nevertheless the 5th began to recover their spirits a little and, with the 4th and the 5th under his command, Hodge became known as the colonel of the 9th.[8]

9 The eye-tooth of the Bear must be drawn

WITH the war apparently over after the victory at Silistria, the British army at Varna had fallen into a state of utter apathy. It was calling itself 'the army without occupation' and complaining about the inertia of its elderly commander. They had been 'too long stationary'[1] and nobody cared, it seemed, what they did.

Troops for the East had been found from Home and Mediterranean garrisons, though to find 31 battalions at war establishment it had been necessary to draft large numbers of volunteers from the battalions which were to stay at home. This meant that those who went constituted one of the finest armies ever to leave England from the point of view of stature, physique, appearance and intelligence, and these men—anything but hastily recruited levies—were the troops who the spiritless leadership of Lord Raglan had allowed to lose their sense of purpose.

Old for his age, far from robust, dreamy and forgetful, the one thing that was lacking in him that his hero, the Duke, had possessed in great measure was that streak of ruthlessness which made the Duke a great commander. Most descriptions of Raglan refer to his extreme loftiness of character and to an ability, through some strange psychological reason, to dominate almost everyone with whom he came into contact. He had great charm and his kindliness conquered everyone, so that the saintly man he undoubtedly was constantly obscured the reactionary and tender-hearted soldier who had done so little to prevent the chaos in which the British army had found itself.

Led by a commander given to ignoring details while he wrote silly letters to his favourites about trivialities and directed by a quartermaster-general whose energy was so much in excess of his commander's that at times he seemed virtually in command himself, the British army, dusty, bored and gasping in the heat, was looking bitterly at the Turks they had come to rescue, angrily aware that the Sick Man of Europe had routed the Russians without their assistance. It didn't make for amity among the allies. 'I would rather fight against them than for them,' Captain Montgomery of the 42nd said.

However, though they didn't yet know it, they were very soon to leave Turkey behind. Despite the fact that Britain had not been eager originally to go to war, when war had arrived even the gentlest of civilians had become aggressive in the extreme. John Arthur Roebuck, the Member for Sheffield, who had busily denounced Napoleon when he had become president, had changed his coat at once, and in a warlike speech 'advocating an immediate resort to the sword' had suddenly discovered qualities of great loyalty and honesty of purpose in him now he was emperor. Such men, safe as they were from the firing line, never imagined for a moment that the magnificent army sent to the East should trail home with nothing accomplished. The Times began to insist that Sebastopol, the proud new ruler of the Black Sea, should be occupied and destroyed and Lord Palmerston, whose attitude was always that of his most jingoistic countrymen, said bluntly, 'The eye-tooth of the Bear must be drawn.' A cabinet meeting in June had approved instructions to Raglan to invade the Crimea, and though the was supposed to weigh up all the pros and cons first, the instructions left him in no doubt that he was expected to go. But any attack had to be made quickly and with sureness, because it was already too late in the year to dawdle and reports had been received that the climate of the Crimea was not very reliable. In addition there were no maps and no information about Sebastopol's fortifications except that they were supposedly very strong, and there was not even any information about where a landing might be made. But the fatal decision was taken, and with Raglan suddenly optimistic and feeling Sebastopol would surrender in a matter of days, it was hoped that things might now improve.

While the younger officers, like 22-year-old Cornet Fisher, of the 4th Dragoon Guards, were eager to be away—'Hurrah for the Crimea', he wrote—older ones like Beauchamp Walker wanted to be off for a very different reason. 'I hope we shall go soon,' he wrote, 'or the army will not have stamina left to thrash even the Russians.' The decision to invade was far from secret and one officer called it 'a hare-brained undertaking' which violated all the accepted rules of war. Hodge thought it was simply the government 'crouching' to The Times, and most responsible officers were equally unhappy because, despite the fact that the army had been in the East now for six months—ample time to discover what it lacked—little effort had been made to remedy the defects. They were still even carrying water in rotten old kegs which had been in store since Waterloo and were fast breaking to pieces, and the tents were threadbare leftovers from the Peninsula, while that British clothing which had at first been so fatiguing in the heat was now considered too worn out for a winter campaign.

For this lack of preparedness Raglan must take the blame. He had been informed at the end of June in a secret despatch from the Duke of Newcastle that 'while his first duty was to prevent an advance on Constantinople, it might become essential . . . to undertake operations of an offensive nature . . . at the southern extremities of the Russian Empire',[2] but so far his letters had contained little that was alarming or urgent. Addicted to desk work so that he seemed more like a military secretary than a commander-in-chief, he wasted hours which should have been used in planning and protesting in sending what at times seem incredibly stupid letters to commanding officers about such things as sunstroke, as though he were an army welfare officer. He remained oddly old-womanish, inclined to tears, and shy before his men to the point of silliness, and all too often occupied, where the French were concerned, with honour.

It was suggested later that if Airey had been quartermaster-general from the beginning of the campaign, things might have been done differently, but by this time so much had been left undone it was too late to put it right. However, gabions and fascines, made as fast as the men could work, were being put aboard ship with sandbags, engineers' tools and stores, shot, shell and supplies, the unwanted Bashi-Bazouks were dismissed and showed their resentment by assaulting British officers whenever they got a chance, and the red dusty columns began to file down to the waterside, so 'lean, gaunt and sickly', the men of the 4th Light Dragoons had to turn out to help them carry their packs and weapons.

Nobody seemed to know what they were to take. The only thing that could be said with certainty was what was not to be taken. Transport was so short the most essential things were ordered to be left behind. One horse only was allowed to each officer in the optimistic belief that all transport would be acquired in the Crimea, and all the thousands of baggage animals that had been so laboriously collected, together with officers' ponies and favourite chargers, went into a hastily formed depot. Paget never expected to see his animals again and he was right. As neither the commissariat nor the staff took the trouble to organise it, most of the animals eventually starved to death.

When the information that they were to go to the Crimea arrived in the Light Brigade camp, to Mrs. Duberly's astonishment there were none of the cheers she had expected from men eager to get into battle. Instead the news was received with the gloomy silence of men with sickness and death uppermost in their minds. Cardigan was still unwell but somehow, doubtless without any intention of so doing, Captain Wetherall, the aide who had brought the orders for departure, led him to believe that he would be in command of the cavalry and it helped his health a great deal. The following day the troops began moving to the transports and two days later Lord Lucan received his instructions. What Cardigan believed appeared to be right! Despite being gazetted lieutenant-general with England and Cathcart on 18 August, he was to be left behind in Varna, Raglan's idea apparently being that Cardigan should be given one more chance on active service while Lucan was to be comforted by the fact that after all he did command officially. It was an extraordinary plan of sheer favouritism. Lucan was supposed to be Raglan's adviser on cavalry and how he was to advise from a distance of 300 miles with an ocean in between is difficult to understand. The fact that Raglan should have disliked Lucan and yet been a friend of Cardigan's is also hard to comprehend, and it can only be supposed that in Cardigan there was something of the weak, spoiled child that appealed to him, while Lucan, of much tougher metal, was never likely to be fobbed off. He wasn't on this occasion.

Cardigan had sent in no reports on the Dobrudja patrol, neither concerning its activities nor its return, and had still not bothered to send any returns to divisional headquarters and, very angry by this time, Lucan wrote Raglan a letter which made it quite clear that he had no intention whatsoever of being left behind. 'I find myself,' he wrote, 'as on former occasions, left without instructions . . . except, as I read them, not to accompany the Light Brigade or to interfere with their embarkation . . . I cannot conceal from myself what has not been concealed from the army . . . that during the four months I have been under your lordship's command, I have been separated as much as it was possible to do so, from my division; being left at Kulali when the force was at Varna, and at Varna when it removed to Devna.' He could hardly, he said bitterly, be considered responsible for troops beyond his reach and under the command of Lord Cardigan who had long since repudiated his authority altogether, and who had left him as ignorant of his men's positions, their duties, efficiency and discipline as he could.

There was a lot more in the same strain and, like all Lucan's letters, it was beyond all doubt tediously correct, and there was little Raglan could do about it. If Lucan were driven to throw up his command in disgust, he was by no means the man to suffer in silence, and any questions that might be asked would prove difficult to answer. He had no alternative but to give way.

As he waited for a reply, Lucan made a point of inspecting Cardigan's troops and weeded out the men he considered unfit for service in the field. He clearly didn't think much of Cardigan's management of his brigade. The yellow dust was blowing up enough in the heat to make Hodge's ink muddy and the watering problems that Cardigan had caused had had their effect. Lucan delivered a blistering broadside about them on 30 August. 'The men are not cleanly,' he wrote, 'in their appearance or in their persons . . . their clothes are unnecessarily dirty and stained, their arms are not as clean as they ought to be; their belts, leathers and appointments, both of man and horse, are rusty and dirty; it would appear as if the object were that every soldier on service should look as unsoldierlike, slovenly and dirty as possible.' He advised pipeclay and continued with another broadside on the cavalry's sense of its own importance and superiority. '. . . In the infantry no such mistaken ideas appear to prevail.'

His opinions seem to have been well justified. Forrest saw Cardigan's camp site a few days later and observed 'You never saw such a depot as the Light Brigade left.' Walker could only collect the deserted chargers and baggage animals with the help of Colonel Douglas, of the 11th Hussars.

While the cavalry was still digesting Lucan's blast, Raglan had been chewing over his letter and when Lucan went to see him, he made a final attempt to persuade him to stay in Varna. The Heavy Brigade, who were sailing later, he said, should be properly inspected. There was no reason whatsoever why Scarlett could not do this and Lucan quite rightly refused. He quoted regulations pointing out that it had been laid down during the Peninsular War that a divisional general might accompany any part of his division he wished, and since the Duke's pronouncements had always been Holy Writ to Raglan, he had to agree. It was decided that Lucan should go after all, while Cardigan was yet again to be informed that Lord Lucan, and not himself, was in command of the cavalry. Once more, however, Raglan was careful to make sure that Lucan's complaints should not become official.

Cardigan's disappointment was tremendous. Despite his continued ill-health, he had been happy with his command from the day of landing at Scutari. He had had under him not only the Light Brigade but also two or three heavy dragoon regiments and the horse artillery and the fact that Lucan was to take it from him—on some old regulation of the Duke of Wellington's, he noticed bitterly—rocked him on his heels. 'From this day,' he wrote in his diary, 'my position in the cavalry was totally changed, all pleasure ceased . . . and I had nothing to guide me but a sense of duty.'

Dangerous sides began to be taken once more. While Lucan's aides could not stand Cardigan, Fitzhardinge Maxse, of the 13th Light Dragoons, Cardigan's aide, wrote 'Lord Cardigan is . . . rather disgusted at having the command of his brigade taken away from him. It is rather hard . . .' Like Cardigan, he had got hold of the wrong end of the stick. No one was taking Cardigan's brigade away from him. They were merely preventing him behaving like the divisional commander he was not.

The embarkation started on 1 September, the first of the 80 staff horses being embarked on the *Ganges*. With the sea very rough, it took time to put slings on them, but the sailors were equal to the task, hauling them about in a way no groom or batman would have dreamed of doing. One skittish animal would not allow the slings to be put under it and kept lashing out with its hind foot and delaying the embarkation until one of the sailors coolly grabbed hold of the flashing leg and hung on to it. To everyone's astonishment, the animal stood still, snorting nervously, and a second later it was swinging in the air.

Mrs. Duberly, who had become surprisingly friendly with Cardigan while he was at Yeni-Bazaar, was also busy. She was hoping to go on with the army to the Crimea, but Lord Lucan had said she was not to go an inch further, and she had appealed to Cardigan who had hurried on her behalf to Raglan. But Raglan was listening to the divisional commander at last and he turned down the appeal. When Cardigan brought his answer she burst into tears and Cardigan, always an easy prey to a pretty defenceless woman, said 'Should you think it proper to disregard

94

the prohibition, I will not offer any opposition to your doing so.'
It was as good as an invitation.

The cavalry moved to the coast on 5 September, Colonel
Shewell, of the 8th Hussars, so ill he was almost falling off his
horse. At Kotlubie they were assailed by the stench of death and
the barking of dogs scratching up the bodies, and shocked by the
sight of corpses starting from the graves where the local
inhabitants had dug them up for the sake of the blankets. By the
time they arrived at Varna, Shewell had collapsed and was being
carried in an araba. As they assembled in a stubble field they
could see the forest of masts in the harbour, but the troops were
listless and despondent and showed little excitement. Mrs.
Duberly was sick herself by this time and wrapped in shawls. Her
hired groom got drunk and her cart stuck in the sand and, still
ill, she was smuggled to Cardigan's transport, the Himalaya, a
converted steamship carrying 700 men and 390 horses. She was
sitting in a native cart disguised as a Turkish woman, while her
husband, afraid of the consequences of her daring on his career,
watched anxiously 'like a hen with young ducks'. Lord Lucan
missed her, she said, because he was looking for a 'lady'. Not
being recognised as 'quality', she received no assistance up the
ladder except from Captain Longmore.

The embarkation was a scene of noise and confusion, and
little thought was given to space or order. It had never occurred
to headquarters that things like tents which would be wanted
first should be put aboard last and when the time came to need
them these and other essentials were found to be at the bottom of
the holds under tons of baggage and shot. Into the Simoon, an old
screw man-of-war with the guns removed but in no other way
prepared for the transportation of troops, 1,300 men were
packed. Any troopship in the first hours of embarkation is a
scene of chaos but this time it was just too much. It was impossible to get all the men below and 200 of them had to be marched
off again. Others, infected by cholera, were being sent ashore as
fast as they were put aboard, and on the evening of 1 September,

as they waited to sail, Captain Longmore, who had helped Mrs. Duberly on board the Himalaya, was taken ill and lay dying in the cabin where the rest of the officers of the 8th were dining, separated only by a screen as the champagne corks flew. His body went ashore the following day in a rough coffin as Paget, on board the Simla, was watching another boat pass under the stern containing a corpse covered with a Union Jack and a man sitting in the bow with a spade.

Sanitary arrangements were disregarded entirely and men were crammed in everywhere. Lighters were made by lashing two boats together and constructing a platform on them, and slowly all the 22,000 infantry and the 1,000 cavalry were embarked. It took much longer to get the horses on board than the infantry, and their embarkation was checked for a time by an awkward wind from the north-east which set up a swell. At the last moment, the women of the regiments, who had followed their husbands to the beach to see them off, began to wail, and it was discovered that nothing had been done to provide them with accommodation, food or pay or even the means of going home, and since they could hardly be left behind to starve, they were allowed on board to swell the number of unnecessary mouths the army had to feed.

The bulk of the flotilla was still anchored at Varna, filling the hot, heavy air with the roll of drums and the sound of regimental bands, but the signal for departure came on the morning of 5 September and the bay was filled with clouds of thick smoke as the steamers stoked up and the transports began to move. The disease-hit Heavy Brigade, left behind for lack of transport, and the convalescents who had been given the duty of providing the garrison for Varna, watched them go. Hodge's thoughts were gloomy.

'Our men have no clothing for the winter,' he wrote. 'The flannels and things they brought from England are nearly worn out . . . I think a fortnight in wet weather and mud will make nice figures of us all . . . The season is too far advanced and we must depend upon a very stormy sea for feeding the army.' With a rare insight, he concluded, 'I hope this may not prove a second Walcheren affair.'*

He was to discover that he was far more right than he had imagined.

* A disastrous campaign of the Napoleonic War when the casualties were caused less by battle than by disease.

10 A pleasant march, though rather hot

THERE were no such gloomy thoughts in the minds of the troops on the transports. They were glad to turn their backs on scarred, scorched, unhealthy Varna. They anchored again opposite the minarets of Balchik, the great vessels dwarfed by the magnificence of the coast, then on 7 September guns woke the fleet and by seven in the morning the steamers were busy picking up the sailing vessels they were to tow. Within an hour they had covered half the horizon.

Above them the sky was filled with smoke but otherwise there wasn't a thing in sight, not a bird, not a fish, not a sail. In the forbidding stillness, signal flags ran up from time to time and about 3 p.m. they joined eight steamers towing 50 small brigs and schooners under the French flag, and shortly afterwards large French men-of-war steamers with transports in tow. The following day more ships joined the fleet. The weather had become raw and cold but boats went backwards and forwards between the ships as the commanding officers debated what to do. St. Arnaud was suffering from his heart complaint again and since Lord Raglan, with his one arm, was quite unable to climb the steep side of a ship to visit him, much of their planning had to be done by their deputies.

Meanwhile Cardigan was beginning to be aware of what the presence of the divisional commander meant. Recovering from his disappointment, he was in such good spirits that when the *Himalaya* gained ground it was considered to be due to 'his silly vanity',[1] but in the close confines of a troopship, it would have been almost impossible for him to avoid finding fault with someone and with 700 men on board it was equally impossible to keep out of his way. When he issued an order for a court martial, however, Lucan reacted quickly with a reminder that he had no such right and a request that he should submit embarkation returns immediately on landing. Already beginning to chafe, he replied indignantly that Raglan, previous to leaving Varna, had informed him 'in the most distinct terms' that Lucan did not intend to interfere or deprive Cardigan of the Light Brigade.

In this, of course, he was quite right and this was doubtless what he had been told by Raglan. No one, least of all Lucan, who had fought all along to avoid annoying him, was trying to deprive him of the Light Brigade—only to stop him usurping the over-all command of the cavalry—but somehow, with his great gift for getting things twisted in his narrow mind, Cardigan was assuming that Lucan's very proper divisional instructions were outright interferences with his own duties. The letter must have seemed to Lucan hardly worth replying to after Raglan's capitulation, and when Cardigan received no immediate reply he reacted by sending across to Lucan, on board the Simla, a more aggressive letter in which he said it was impossible to carry out his duties until his position in the expedition was made clear.

Lucan's staff were all aware of the difficulties he was under with Cardigan and they were not surprised when his secretary was ordered to write a flat, sensible reply which still managed to contain a barb in the tail. 'To circulate a memorandum,' it said, 'that disembarkation returns would be required on landing, a memorandum which has been circulated to all senior officers, is not an irregularity, nor is it disrespectful or any encroachment on your authority, and Lord Lucan much regrets that you should entertain what his Lordship considers a great misconception. In reference to the rest of your letter the Lieutenant-General instructs me to add that whilst he knows his own authority he equally respects yours; and that your position as a major-general commanding a brigade in the Cavalry Division, will not, so far as depends on him, differ from that held by the other brigadiers, of whom there are so many in the six divisions of this army.'

While Cardigan was still digesting it, the fleet continued on its way to the Crimea. As on the voyage out, great suffering was caused to the horses. They had endured much on the journey from England, had put up with a lack of water and forage and burning sun at Varna, and now they were crowded into the stuffy, stinking holds again, and beginning to feel the effect of short rations. Some of the troops had now been on board for 17 days and many of the ships were suffering dreadfully from cholera. Calthorpe reported that 70 dead were lost in the infantry while in the cavalry whose numbers were smaller the proportion was greater—22 deaths and 104 very sick. The French were suffering even more, because they were more crowded than the English and they lost over 1,000 men on the short voyage. They were hastily thrown overboard but they were improperly weighted and rose to the surface again, their swollen features above water to grimace at the passing vessels out of the blankets and hammocks that shrouded them. It was almost possible for the following ships to find the route by the line of floating corpses.

At dawn on 12 September, land was sighted and, as everyone rushed on deck to look at the Crimea, Mrs. Duberly noticed that while most of the officers gazed at the future battleground silently and thoughtfully, Cardigan was very excited and impatient. Throughout the day the fleet ran along the coast and at noon anchored off the pretty town of Eupatoria, situated on a spit of land where windmills and bathing boxes were visible. The governor immediately surrendered, but Cossacks had hidden all cattle, and the post coach from Sebastopol to Odessa had been seen going at speed, doubtless with the information of the Allies' arrival.

The fleet finally anchored in the ominously named Calamita Bay, opposite a low strip of beach forming a causeway between the sea and a stagnant salt-water lake to the north, and the French were first ashore. They immediately raised a flagstaff and broke out the French tricolour, and as the troops began to climb down the ships' sides into the boats, they were greeted from below by the sailors with catcalls and, to the Highlanders, shouts of

'Come on, ladies.' To the creak of oars and the slap of the sea they were rowed ashore to join the scene of confusion on the beach where officers were trying to assemble their companies and stragglers were shouting the numbers of their regiments as they trudged through the sand between the gossiping staff officers, the horses, guns and piles of equipment.

There was no sign of the enemy, except for an officer with a troop of Cossacks who appeared on the low hills about 1,000 yards away. He was seen to be wearing a dark-green uniform with silver lace and to be riding a fine bay horse, and he was making notes and sketches very calmly. As the English boats neared the shore, it was seen that the Cossacks were pointing with their lances to a point near the cliffs and it was then noticed that Sir George Brown and General Airey had landed there. Sir George Brown had failed to see the Cossacks riding stealthily forward while the energetic Airey was concerned only with the capture of a string of arabas he had spotted nearby. Suddenly the Cossacks made a dash and the commander of the Light Division was only saved from capture by a party of the Royal Welch who had been stalking the Cossacks as busily as the Cossacks had been stalking the general. The first blood split in the Crimea was that of a boy who was with the carts and was hit in the foot.

By the afternoon, Lord Raglan and his staff, 12 guns and 14,000 men of the Light, First and Second Divisions were ashore. Outposts were quickly pushed forward and Cossack vedettes were seen in the distance, but by this time the weather had changed, and it began to rain. Before long it was coming down in torrents and sloshing in streams to the beach while disconsolate generals squatted on powder barrels, huddled in their dripping rubber mackintoshes. Nearly 24,000 men had now been landed, together with 19 guns, while the French claimed to have landed 22,000 men and 53 guns. Unfortunately, as fast as they were landed, many were sent back aboard sick. The rain came down pitilessly and while the doctors searched for their medical chests, sick men lay in rows in the downpour, suffering from diarrhoea and dysentery, their only cover their greatcoats. Sir George Brown took refuge under a cart and the Duke of Cambridge under a gun carriage.

Because of the wind that had got up, the landing of the cavalry was left until the following morning. Since the boats that carried them couldn't be beached, the horses were pushed overboard and they were swum ashore and caught on the beach by sailors who sprang on their backs and galloped them up and down with all the confidence of practised riders. Their condition was dreadful. After two months' shortages, they were shaggy and desperately thin and weak[2] and it had long since been discovered that the army-issue saddles had become too heavy. The men were in as poor shape as the horses and Mrs. Duberly kept her sick husband on board when he was ordered ashore by Cardigan, who, she noticed, was eager for the fray, and she suspected that he would be doing something 'directly he . . . landed'. His opportunity came within a matter of hours.

Carts and food were necessary and he was ordered into the interior to capture arabas and cut off a regiment of Russian chasseurs that had been seen, which might be carrying information to the Russian command. It was important to be careful, however. No one knew where the Russians were or the strength of their forces and Raglan was not willing to push the cavalry too far forward to find out. Apart from a few French Spahis, they mustered no more than 1,000 sabres and, with Cardigan all eagerness, it was important to restrain him from anything foolish. Lucan's first order reminded him that defence, not pursuit, was the duty of the Light Brigade for the time being and said they were not to engage the enemy without authority. While it restrained him, it didn't stop him exhausting his command as usual. He left with 250 horsemen, 250 men of the Rifles, and two guns. He saw no enemy and brought in only a few carts, but they travelled about 30 miles, and the Rifles complained that he had not noticed that men on foot travelled slower than men on horses, even when these were ridden at a walk. The captured carts were used to carry the exhausted men back, while the horses suffered as usual from the shortage of water. They had seen hardly any wells, and even where they had, there had been no means of hauling the water up. The streams and rivers were brackish or salt and though they had passed one wide river, the horses would not touch it and remained without water for 30 hours. The French had done somewhat better, and Spahis drove in flocks of sheep and cattle and a long string of country carts and camels heavily laden with grain.

Viewing the results, Raglan seemed to think once again that Cardigan had not shown much efficiency and decided to leave the foraging to the infantry. General Airey, in his energetic way, decided to use officers of his own department and sent them in all directions to bring in supplies. Nolan was among the more successful and, though without a cavalry escort, cut in on a convoy of 80 government waggons laden with flour. It was a great boost to his morale. He was longing to see his ideas on mounted tactics put into operation—his belief in sharp swords had, to a certain extent, been justified as the cavalry were already coming to consider the lance useless—and with his feet on Russian soil, he was itching for the opportunity he felt would not now be long in coming.

It had been expected that there might be resistance to the landing but all they had met so far was blank indifference. Several unwary infantrymen had been killed by hovering Russian horsemen, however, and Cossacks had appeared in considerable strength before the patrols of the 13th Light Dragoons and set fire to villages and corn nearby. Now, after dark, with the cavalry unsaddled and the army nervous in the silence, there was a sudden flurry of firing and a picket of the 11th Hussars, deciding that the enemy had got between themselves and the main body, tore in at full gallop. Rising ground protected the men from the flying bullets but everyone sprang for their weapons, and there was a clicking of firelocks in the dark as they prepared for attack. Cardigan's guess was shrewder than most and he rode in the direction of the firing to find it came from an outlying infantry picket not sure of its bearings who had mistaken the cavalrymen for the enemy. No one was hurt apart from one of the 11th Hussars who was shot in the leg by Captain Cresswell, but what Cardigan told the infantry picket can well be imagined.

At midnight Raglan's orders came to break camp at dawn the following morning and at 3 a.m. reveille sounded. Cholera was still with them and Captain Cresswell, hardly recovered from the excitement of the night, had been unexpectedly taken ill and was now, to everyone's horror, dying in the village where he and his men were quartered. He was a great favourite with the men and, at that moment, his wife was preparing to follow him from Varna.

In a scene of utter chaos the tents were dragged down to the beach. One of the brigades of the Fourth Division and Paget's 4th Light Dragoons were to be left behind to clear the stores and embark the sick. By this time the contempt of the French for the British staff was becoming obvious. Their troops wore modern loosely fitting uniforms and were equipped for quick movement and, as Cornet George Wombwell noted with envy, they landed with tiny tents d'abri, shared by three men, each of whom carried one part. Already the alliance was becoming trying for both sides. Raglan detested the fuss and flourish that the French so much enjoyed while the French considered Raglan old-fashioned and pedantic.[3]

It had been Raglan's intention to move off at 6 a.m. before the heat became too intense, but, according to Calthorpe, 'the confusion was so great' it took three hours to get the army in motion. Nolan had drawn up the plan for the march and had made certain that the cavalry could come into action immediately if necessary. The divisions marched in great lozenges of colour, with bands playing and colours snapping, and, since they had few cavalry, the French marched on the right, the seaward side, where they were protected by the fleet which moved along with the army in magnificent order. The British, on the left or landward side, were preceded by the advance guard of the 11th Hussars and the 13th Light Dragoons, under Cardigan, while the dangerous left flank was covered by the 8th Hussars and the 17th Lancers under Lucan. The 4th Light Dragoons under Lord George Paget brought up the rear. The British were in two dense columns, on the left the Light Division and the First Division and on the right the Second and Third Divisions. The Fourth was to follow later.

It was a brilliant morning, with a blue sky and a sea as quiet as a millpond, but though they could see for miles, there was a need for wariness because it was perfect cavalry country with folds of ground that could hide a whole division of horsemen, and they knew perfectly well that the enemy had vast forces of Cossacks at hand. The turf was springy and, as they pushed through the undergrowth, the crushed wild thyme on which they trod gave off an overpowering scent, and hares and coveys of partridges started up and were chased by the soldiers.

The troops presented a splendid appearance as they swept over the ridges and folds of ground, rank after rank of them, regiment after regiment, the sun playing on the forests of glittering steel. But the day was excessively hot and those men who were recovering from dysentery or diarrhoea or were already suffering from cholera soon began to fall out from exhaustion. There was soon a dire need to find water and as throats dried the bands gradually stopped playing and the army started to labour badly. The earlier high spirits disappeared and a heavy silence fell over the marching men. Their feet made little sound as they pushed through the grass and low scrub but though the larks continued to sing, no one had any breath left to comment on the fact as they plodded doggedly on, bathed in sweat and leaving behind a litter of abandoned equipment.

Every now and then a man in the ranks began to show a blue tinge round his mouth and cry out for water, then the inevitable vomiting followed and in a moment he had collapsed with cholera. Lady Errol, riding on a mule, was carrying the rifles of several men of the 60th, who were fully occupied only with keeping upright and moving forward. They had barely marched ten miles, and there had been frequent halts. To most men it had been a nightmare, though to Trumpeter Parker Kelly, a Guernsey-man in the Royal Artillery, it was 'just a pleasant march, though rather hot'. Kelly was fit, however, and the whole rear of the army was littered by sick, dying and exhausted men so thick on the ground the following 4th Light Dragoons found it difficult to avoid riding over them.

As worrying as the disease was the absence of foraging. It had been hoped that cattle and grain would be picked up quickly but the Russians had learned the value of scorched earth forty years before and all carts, animals and inhabitants had disappeared into the interior. To the men in the ranks the emptiness of the land brought the same sense of dread that had been felt by Napoleon's men in 1812, for apart from glimpses of solitary Cossacks in the distance, there was no sign of the enemy until soon after midday when, as they breasted the brow of a hill, they caught sight of burning houses and empty, smouldering farms. The smoke rose into the cloudless sky, spreading out in the light wind, and the whole of the stumbling army knew what it meant. They were at last treading on the heels of the Russians.

*

At two o'clock, the leading riders under Cardigan reached the River Bulganak. Nearby houses, one of them the Imperial Post House, were burning, and a solitary peahen stalking near the ruins was picked off by Russell to be added to the day's rations. The sight of the glittering water in the sunlit valley was too much for the parched men and with the exception of the Highland Brigade, who were kept in hand by Sir Colin Campbell, they broke ranks and dashed into the shallows to drink alongside the horses of the cavalry.

Beyond the river the land rose in a succession of blue ridges and hollows and as they lifted their heads from the water they saw they were being watched by a line of Russian cavalry vedettes. Raglan ordered the advance guard to investigate what lay behind them and Cardigan sent two troops splashing across the river, following himself with the rest of his men. Pushing through a melon-field, they soon reached the spot where the Cossacks had been seen and from there saw a large body of cavalry on rising ground a mile away, with a valley between them. When this was reported to Raglan, he at once ordered up the Light and Second Divisions, and sent for the other two regiments of cavalry from the flank. Meanwhile Cardigan had thrown out a troop in skirmishing order and, when the Russians opposite did the same, both sides fired at each other for twenty minutes from the saddle.

By this time the 8th Hussars and the 17th Lancers had come up, the 17th picking up melons from the ground on the ends of their lances as they approached. Knowing Cardigan's eagerness to cover himself with glory, Lucan pushed forward to join him and Private Spring, a Dubliner in the 11th Hussars who was nervous with the cavalry commanders around because he was a deserter from the 17th Lancers, heard what took place.

'What are you doing?' Lucan asked as he rode up. Cardigan replied tartly that he was going to advance.

'You must not do that,' Lucan said. 'They have numbers of men behind those hills and the Brigade will be annihilated.'

Cardigan was immediately on his dignity and harping on the eternal theme of his independence: 'Then haven't I any command at all?' he demanded.

Lucan's reply was blunt and to the point. 'Yes . . .' he said, 'but not just now.'[4]

Of all those who wrote about the incident at the Bulganak, Russell was nearest the action. He was riding well up in front with Lieutenant-Colonel Collingwood Dickson, of the artillery, who had served in the Turkish Army and was on Airey's staff as chief interpreter, and he now saw the Russians come quickly over the slope in three great blocks. The British skirmishers began to look round anxiously for the horse artillery. 'Now we'll catch it,' Dickson said. 'Those fellows mean business.' Russell could see Cardigan was still eager to try his strength, but now more dark columns were seen in the folds of the hills beyond and he heard Lord Lucan order him to gather in his skirmishers.

By this time the supporting British infantry had reached the brow of the hill, but Raglan had also now seen the mass of Russians beyond the rise by the sun on their bayonets and he had no wish to bring on a general engagement. Instead of issuing a straightforward formal order, however, he preferred to rely on the diplomatic methods which were so deeply ingrained in him and, as Maude's troop of horse artillery moved up, bounding across the turf to cover the cavalry, he sent Airey forward to make his wishes clear in the form of a suggestion. Eager to feel he had been under fire after all the years he had spent in safety in India while everyone else was fighting, Nolan advanced with Airey among the flying bullets to the skirmishers. It had already been noticed that a few staff officers were in the habit of placing themselves in prominent positions where they would be noticed —when the Victoria Cross was instituted it became almost a nuisance—and, without influence, Nolan *needed* to draw attention to himself. Despite the closeness of the Russians, he dismounted and put on a show of inspecting his horse. 'Those Russians are damned bad shots,' he said gaily.[5]

The one thing Wellington had always disliked was unnecessary heroics. 'There is nothing on earth so stupid as a gallant officer', he had said, but Nolan—brave, impulsive, intelligent—was itching to see the cavalry in action and gain some kudos therefrom. Though a lot of what he had written in his books was regarded with derision by some cavalry officers, there were others who regarded it highly and the numbers of the Russians opposite meant nothing to him. He believed well-led cavalry capable of passing through guns and breaking squares—indeed he had been in India when it had happened at Aliwal—and like

Cardigan was dying to fling the four glittering squadrons forward.

Raglan had other ideas. It was his wish to keep a tight hold on his cavalry and by this time Airey had reached Lucan, who was still arguing fiercely with Cardigan in an effort to restrain him. As he added his authority to the divisional commander's Cardigan sullenly gave way and the cavalry began to retire by alternate squadrons, 'as quietly and as orderly as if at a field-day on Hounslow Heath', facing front every 50 yards. They moved at a walk, except for the 11th Hussars who were the most advanced and whose colonel, Douglas, could see no sense in exposing his men to unnecessary fire and led them off at a trot. As they retired, the enemy moved after them down the hill, uncovering a battery of guns which immediately started to fire.

Russell was covered with dust as the first round shot bounded along, passed the cavalry and rolled between the ranks of the infantry who were just coming up. The second shot hit one of the 11th Hussars, taking off his foot at the ankle, and a shell, burying itself in the body of the horse of a paymaster-sergeant of the 13th, blew it on to its head and scooped out the hollow between its ribs so cleanly its backbone could be seen. There was no alarm, however. The cavalry remained rigidly disciplined, in bright blocks of colour, and Williamson, the hussar who had been hit, rode up to Cornet Roger Palmer, his foot hanging by his overall, and quietly asked permission to fall out. 'Had they been of iron, they could not have been more solid and immovable,' Russell said. No one enjoyed it, however, and for the rest of his life Private Pennington never forgot sitting motionless while the round shot flew overhead to bounce and roll among the infantry.

The horse artillery were replying now but their six-pounders were outranged and Raglan ordered up heavier guns which opened fire with visibly greater effect, and they saw one shell burst right in the middle of the Russian cavalry. Meanwhile the French had moved round on the right and opened up with nine-pounders[6] and having by this time lost about 12 men killed and 35 wounded, with 32 horses out of action, the Russians limbered up and retired. The skirmish, according to Calthorpe, was 'the prettiest affair I ever saw . . . If one had not seen the cannon-balls . . . bounding like cricket balls, one would really have thought it only a little cavalry review.' On the English side, six horses were lost and four men were wounded. They were regarded without sympathy by the envious footsore infantry, however. 'Serve them bloody right, silly peacock bastards,' one soldier said as they rode past.

It was late in the day now and, as the army bivouacked, the cavalry were placed in advance to guard against any night attack. They picketed their horses with their heads facing inwards, their equipment in the space between, and lay down with their saddles as pillows and their cloaks as blankets. As soon as the rations of rum and meat were served out, the casks were broken up and the staves used to make cooking fires that were fed by fragant shrubs and undergrowth. It was a cold night with a heavy dew and stragglers kept wandering in calling the numbers of their regiments. Russell, that inveterate critic of the army, admitted that 'as a military spectacle, the advance of our troops, and the little affair of the artillery, as well as the management of the cavalry', had been 'one of the most picturesque and beautiful that could be imagined', but to the cavalrymen, who had not seen what Raglan had seen, the affair had been disappointing. The Russians had jeered as they had retired and they felt they were being withdrawn 'like a pack of whipped dogs to their kennels'. Cardigan was frustrated and, furious at having glory snatched from under his nose, took it out of his men with trivial complaints about dress and forage nets. He was livid with Lucan, the Light Brigade, and even with his old regiment, the 11th Hussars, for their more hasty retreat. He told the officers, Forrest later claimed, that they were 'a damned set of old women' and, when Colonel Douglas complained, he was promptly told that a colonel had no right to remonstrate with a major-general.

The comments flew round, most of them not very well informed, and Lucan was considered to have shown too much caution, but in his despatch to the army, Raglan said of the Light Brigade '. . . it was impossible for any troops to exhibit more steadiness than did this portion of Her Majesty's cavalry . . .' while in his despatch to the government, he referred to Cardigan as having 'exhibited the utmost spirit and coolness, and kept his brigade under perfect control'. Cardigan was pleased to note them both down in his diary. It wasn't really a bad start.

11 The infantry will advance

As they lay down that night in the damp grass, many of them too exhausted to eat, the cavalry outposts looked across the plateau in the direction of their next day's march, and they knew exactly what the masses of watch-fires twinkling in the dark meant. The immense extent of the ground they covered indicated that a formidable army was waiting for them.

It was obvious that the allies were facing a tremendous struggle to get across the Alma, the second of their river crossings towards Sebastopol, but little or no plan had been made, and Raglan had retired without making any special dispositions for the next day, except to warn commanding officers that their men were to be wakened without noise of trumpet or drum. The morning of 20 September dawned bright and clear and Lord George Paget, passing the ruined posthouse, saw Raglan outside with Airey and Estcourt. He was looking anxious and since the staff officers round him were all wearing the cocked hats that made them easily distinguishable in battle, he knew it meant business.

The troops had been roused at 3 a.m. but such was the quality of the staff work they were not ready to move until the sun was high, and while Raglan was waiting with his staff for the forward movement to begin, a handsome grey pony appeared, neighing and screaming so that no one could hear what was being said. It was decided its rider must be a newspaper reporter and that he ought to be moved on, but it turned out to be Alexander William Kinglake, a British barrister who had arrived in an unofficial capacity as one of the travelling gentlemen—or 'T.G.s' as they were known—who were accompanying the army at their own expense. A writer of some distinction and a military historian who had followed one of St. Arnaud's flying columns in Algeria, he was a very different kettle of fish from the working journalists like

Russell, and when the pony finally threw him Raglan even took the trouble to enquire how he was.

With the British still wheeling into line in great blocks of colour against the grey-green slopes, the two allied armies lost touch with each other for a while and it was six hours after the first move before they were at last properly aligned for the commencement of their advance. In front of them, from a ridge of high ground the land fell gently down to sea level, then it rose in a series of steep hills that stood out sharply enough to look like a precipice. Along the foot of the hills ran a patch of green where cypresses, willows, gardens and vineyards grew near a couple of small villages, and from the crest of the northern slope, where they stood, the British could see the sparkle of the River Alma in the valley between them and the dark masses of the Russians on the opposite slopes. At noon the allies halted again and a strange hush fell over the massed men, so that it was possible to hear the neigh of a horse, the chink of a bit or the clatter of a man's musket against his ration tin. Sir Colin Campbell ordered the Highlanders to get loose their cartridges and the order was taken up by the other brigades and the silence ended in a rattle of equipment.

Prince Mentschikoff, the Russian commander, uncertain which of the two possible routes to Sebastopol the allies would take, had chosen to meet them at the Alma because of the steep hills there. At one point, the Kourgané Hill, they rose to a height of 450 feet, and this he chose for the centre of his position. His only prepared fieldworks were here, a shallow breastwork about 300 yards long containing twelve heavy guns and known as the Great Redoubt, with the Lesser Redoubt, further to the east, containing nine guns. Another battery straddled the road that crossed the river but not a trench had been dug anywhere else and most of the Russian infantry was simply disposed round the Kourgané Hill while the cavalry covered the right flank.

About one o'clock, the British skirmishers were within range of their opposite numbers and shortly afterwards a single gun fired, the shot kicking up a spurt of dust in front of the Light Division. It was a windless day and the dust hung in the air, catching the sun, but, though the shot did no damage, it scattered in all directions a group of onlookers which had gathered round Raglan and his staff.

Almost immediately, more round shot started to fall, kicking up clods of earth, and the order was given to deploy the leading divisions into line. Not enough ground had been taken, however, and the right-hand regiment of the Light Division found itself behind the left-hand regiment of the Second Division. Raglan saw the trouble but left the matter to take care of itself and by the time Sir George Brown's brigadiers realised what was happening the cursing men were intermingled.

As the lines came under fire the failure to make a concerted plan began to be obvious, and Raglan decided he must wait for St. Arnaud. With round shot and splinters of shell beginning to pick out men he ordered the army to halt and lie down, and the troops had to wait on the open slope under fire for more than an hour.[1]

The cavalry, drawn up on the left—with the 13th Light Dragoons in a melon-field and the 4th Light Dragoons to the rear near the Fourth Division, to which they had been attached ever since landing—were still waiting for orders. With them were two troops of horse artillery, one under Captain Maude, the other under Captain John Brandling, another skilful officer, who was given to the wearing of exotic dress of his own choice. Their eyes on the glitter of bayonets opposite, they, too, now began to come under fire. A cannon ball took off the head of an artilleryman, and Paget's dragoons, dismounted and dozing in the sunshine, were kicked to life as more began to fall among them. Another shot narrowly missed Lucan, while yet another leapt over the hindquarters of Cardigan's horse so that he had to move his men out of range.

Despite their lack of experience, the troops stood up well to the ordeal and, as they waited, the little knots of mounted senior officers in their cocked hats and blue frock-coats made an inviting target, Raglan particularly conspicuous with his empty sleeve.[2] He was enjoying the excitement of being under fire again but remained as calm as ever, sending his aides away with the instruction, 'Go quietly, don't gallop.'

The French on the extreme right had crossed the river by a sandbar at its mouth, and the information was brought to Raglan by Nolan who, with his fluent French, was employed on liaison work between the two armies. He was in his element, and it was with difficulty that he curbed his exuberance to the pace set by Raglan.

By this time a lull had fallen on the field. The main body of the French had still to make contact with the Russians and, though the skirmishers were now exchanging a lively crackling fire with their opposite numbers, most of the British were still waiting for something to happen. It was at this moment that a French aide appeared in front of Raglan in an agitated state and said that unless something could be done the French on the extreme right would be in danger. The message made up Raglan's mind and, turning to Airey, he said, 'The infantry will advance.' It was the only real order he gave during the whole battle.

The decision was carried to the divisional generals by Nolan but as he reached the Second Division his horse was shot dead under him. As it sank down the message was snatched up by one of Evans's staff who carried it on to the Light Division, and, as the orders were given out, the British line rose to its feet, dressed ranks, and moved forward in perfect step down the slope towards the river.

Sir George Brown rode his horse through a shallow crossing but while some of the men around him had to wade only up to their ankles others found themselves breast-deep and had to hold their muskets above their heads. A few more, stepping into holes, were drowned by the weight of their equipment. The musketry from the southern hills was cutting the surface of the water to foam and more men fell, while on the opposite side they were faced with a steep cliff-like bank where the river had eroded the soil, and, above it, a slope that was entirely devoid of cover.

Sir George Brown forced his way out of the confusion by spurring his horse at a break in the bank, and sat waiting for his division to get itself aligned. General Codrington, in command on the right of the division, seeing the danger as the troops clustered together, some with bunches of grapes snatched from the vines between their teeth and laughing at their friends who had had a ducking, gave the order to fix bayonets and spurred his pony at the bank. Colonel Yea led the 95th forward, shouting 'Never mind forming! Come on anyhow!' and they advanced towards the rolling sun-touched smoke which was split here and there by the fiery tail of a rocket or a distracted flight of frightened birds. Russell, well up with the troops, noticed a formidable-looking mass of burnished helmets tipped with brass which he saw plainly were infantry, but Sir George Brown mistook them for cavalry and Russell heard him giving appropriate instructions to an aide so that one regiment on the left flank was ordered to lie down while another formed square.

As the Light Division began to push its way upwards, the Russians—only 400 yards away now and looking oddly blank and expressionless with their white faces—began to lower their sights. Men were being knocked over regularly and Russell saw an officer of the 7th with his back against a wall, surveying his ruined legs without bitterness. 'I wish they had left me one,' he said, as medical men tried to stop the bleeding.

Salvo after salvo of canister, grape and round shot were now cutting swathes through the ranks of the advancing Light Division, but, as the hanging smoke that hid the Great Redoubt began to disperse, it was seen that the Russians were limbering up their guns and hurrying to the rear. 'Stole away!' some fox-hunting enthusiast yelled and Codrington, still unscathed,

116

waved his men forward and leapt his pony into the redoubt.

*

Having got the army in motion, Raglan ought now to have been attending to the provision of support for the first line, but instead of stationing himself somewhere in the centre rear where he could see all that was going on, he and his staff had taken a path which led into the heart of the Russian position and to a spur of land where they were to have a clear view over the whole Russian army.

Although the Great Redoubt had fallen, it left 2,000 British soldiers unsupported in a very vulnerable position with a huge Russian column in place nearby and 4,000 Russian cavalry close at hand. But with Raglan beyond reach, nothing was done to support them; the only orders Lucan had received were that he was not to move until told to do so.

Lucan had a tearing energy, an impulsiveness and a capability for ruthlessness that might have made him a good cavalry leader, given the chance. He had formed a firm—and correct— impression in his days with the Russian army that there was little to fear from their cavalry and a forward movement at that moment might well have driven the Russian horsemen from the field. Paget, in fact, sent a message begging him to let them 'come on', and Cardigan expressed his annoyance loudly and forcefully. Instead they had to sit in their saddles, bursting with impatience, and watching them, Nolan was livid. He believed that charges should be carried out with the 'greatest impetuosity and speed', and it had been his hope that the cavalry would thunder at full gallop on to the Russian flank. In his absolute faith in what they could do, it was heartbreaking to watch them doing nothing.

But Lucan's orders left no room for personal initiative and Raglan was too far away to grant it to him. As he faced east on his knoll he could see the whole line of the river with the smoke-wreathed Great Redoubt and the Russian positions on the

Kourgané Hill in front of him. Almost directly below not a quarter of a mile away were Russian battalions and batteries. 'Now!' he said. 'If we had a couple of guns up here!'

In fact, the guns were already moving forward. De Lacy Evans, with the Second Division, was the only commander who seemed to realise it was wiser to assault the Russian positions with artillery instead of a wall of flesh and blood and had been collecting guns from whoever would lend them, and he now had a solid battery of 30 which was beginning to get into position. Noticing the Russians' vulnerability from the knoll where Raglan waited, two guns had been detached and were already on their way up.

Though the regiments in the redoubt were intermingled they were not lacking in discipline, but there was no sign of help and as a second Russian column, four battalions strong, appeared round a spur of the Kourgané Hill someone among the British shouted 'Don't fire! They're French!' The crackle of musketry died away and a bugler sounded the Cease Fire on the order of an unidentified officer. The call was taken up by other buglers and then, again without any good reason, someone sounded the Retire. At first it was thought there had been a mistake and it was not obeyed but, as the calls rang out again, Codrington's men finally accepted that they must be genuine and began to scramble out of the redoubt.

Even as they began to retire, the Duke of Cambridge had set the second line in motion, the rear brought up by the Third and Fourth Divisions, while the cavalry, still guarding the left flank, moved forward alongside on the order of Lord Lucan. The Guards, presenting a solid wall of black, red and blue, waded the river and proceeded to dress ranks as though on parade. The Scots Fusiliers were the first to move off but as they went up the slope ahead of the other regiments, the retiring Light Division, coming down from the redoubt in a disordered mass, sent them flying. The other two regiments, however, were nudged forward by Evans and, with the Highlanders on their left, began to advance. Tired of waiting for orders, Lucan ordered the cavalry down to the river on his own initiative.

The First Division, extending over a front of a mile and a half in a solid wall of men, topped by the bearskins of the Guards and the bonnets of the Highlanders, were advancing in perfect formation. Pursuing the fleeing Light Division, the Russians were moving forward again by this time but the left platoon of the Grenadiers stopped them dead in their tracks with a volley, and the firing was taken up by the whole line. On the extreme left, Lucan, acting closely with Sir Colin Campbell, sent the cavalry across the river at a ford, with Maude's battery in support. The men snatched bunches of grapes from the vines as they went but the horses, desperate for water, had to be spurred ahead as they tried to drink. Some crossed by the bridge, moving so close to the left of the Highlanders that the 17th Lancers were soundly berated in broad Scots by Campbell for getting in the way, and as they began to climb, they opened their ranks carefully, so that their horses would not tread on the dead and wounded. They arrived at the forefront of the battle at a very opportune moment. As they reached the tableland, they could see the Russian army retreating in the afternoon sun, covered by their cavalry. The fleeing soldiers were just being gathered together and formed into a column 10,500 strong when the guns opened fire. They did tremendous damage and Captain Tremayne, of the 13th Light Dragoons, later saw rows of men with their skulls blown off. Before long, these Russians, too, were streaming to the rear and British and French soldiers stood along the whole line of the heights cheering, waving their shakos on their muskets and watching the enemy pour away to the south. A few, like Trumpeter Parker Kelly, stood on a construction rather like a racecourse stand which had been built by Mentschikoff in his overweening confidence so that civilians from Sebastopol, who had driven out in carriages, could see him win his victory. Others lay exhausted, a few were in tears, and yet others were still carried away by the excitement of the afternoon and were on the edge of hysteria.

But now, with the Russian army streaming away in demoralised confusion, was the time for pursuit not hesitation and both Airey and Lucan were eager to move.[3] It was an ideal moment for attack. There was nowhere for the enemy to stand between the Alma and Sebastopol and the cavalry, fresh and unexhausted and wild with eagerness, itched to get at the enemy. Private Pennington was firmly of the belief that they could have scattered the Russian horse and turned the retreat into a rout, but they were just settling themselves in their saddles for the sound of trumpets, when General Estcourt arrived with instructions that under no circumstances were they to attack the fleeing enemy. No advance, Estcourt insisted, was to be made without artillery support and they were to do no more than escort guns which were at that moment being sent to take up positions in advance. No doubt was left about what was to be done. 'Mind now,' Estcourt finished, 'the cavalry are not to attack.'

Unwillingly the order was obeyed and the brigade moved ahead of the guns, taking prisoners, most of them dazed with drink and eager to surrender. One of them, a man of the Imperial Guard, was so drunk he almost put out the eye of Sergeant Bond, of the 11th Hussars, as he handed over his weapon, and in the excitement some of the Russians who resisted were roughly handled. An officer whom Private Wightman, of the 17th Lancers, tackled fired a pistol at him point blank and carried away the ring of his horse's bit. When he felled him with the butt of his lance, his colonel, Lawrenson, whom he had all along thought a 'little too dainty for the rough and ready business of warfare', called him a coward, a word he found hard to stomach. But Lawrenson was already a very sick man, so doubled up in his saddle with the cramps of cholera his men wondered that he didn't fall off his horse.

As they continued to move forward, eager to feel they had taken some part in the battle, Raglan sent a second infuriating order, instructing them to return to their duty of escorting the guns and, when they continued to take prisoners, a third order arrived peremptorily ordering their recall. John Blunt, the young consular official, was near Lucan when the message arrived and it was handed to him. As he passed it over he saw Lucan's anger, but the order left no doubt. They were to cease pursuit forthwith. In his frustrated fury Lucan turned loose all his prisoners and galloped back to the guns while the men, knowing nothing of the reasons, began to mutter bitterly as they imagined the fault lay with their divisional general.

Raglan's anxiety was not entirely without reason. A general of ability might well have taken a chance but it was true that on the cavalry depended the safety of the army, and against the thousands of horsemen the Russians could call on he had only a few hundred. The Heavies, under Scarlett, were still in Varna and he had seen Cardigan in action once already, and all those old injunctions of Wellington's were in his mind. The cavalry were 'incapable of movement', Wellington had said, 'except on Wimbledon Common . . . merely an indisciplined stampede of a rabble going as fast as their mounts could carry them', and, though the things the Duke had noticed had been learned as lessons by cavalry leaders and trainers since Waterloo, Cardigan was never a man to be trusted. Nothing he had done so far indicated that he might not irreparably damage his squadrons by over-reaching himself in some mad chase after glory. Raglan's reasons were not bad ones under the circumstances, especially since a mere 900 men 'on fagged horses', desperate for water and half-starved, would have been opposing almost 4,000 untouched Russians with well-fed mounts, but Lucan's assessment of the Russian cavalry was correct. They possessed little of the dash of the British and a determined assault on them might well have opened the way to a general rout.

The restriction led to an enormous amount of ill feeling, and from this moment there began to arise the steady hostility between the smart young staff officers at headquarters and the cavalry commander that was to so sour all relations between them. Cardigan's obsession with his independence had started it

and from Raglan's unwillingness to curb him had come the
Dobrudja patrol and Raglan's decision to keep a rigid control over
his horsemen, from which in turn sprang the growing doubt in
the army about Lucan's ability, the witty comments against the
cavalry and the fury of Captain Nolan.

12 They ought to be damned

THE battlefield was a dreadful sight, the mangled bodies of French, English and Russian soldiers everywhere. Where the fighting had been heaviest, the dead and dying were lying in heaps, the groans and cries for water mingling with the curlew-keening of the Irishwomen who found themselves widows. 'It made my heart sick for the rest of the day', one soldier of the Black Watch wrote home, while a naval surgeon, from a ship at anchor off the mouth of the river, said 'I have been literally in a sea of blood.' The musketry had dropped men in rows, while the artillery had scattered headless trunks, arms and legs among the shattered waggons and the litter of cartouche boxes, broken weapons, bugles, helmets, shakos, trampled rations, equipment, and the bodies of the dead, whose blood filled the little hollows and gathered in the river.

The casualties had been high but the troops felt they had not let anybody down. 'I think they'll say we did our duty,' one mortally wounded Guardsman said to his officer. It had been a regimental officers' battle and despite the impression that Raglan gave in his despatch that he had had a plan, no one else had noticed one, and as the men prepared their letters home their doubts emerged. Headquarters had not exactly shone and there had been several instances of staff officers—naturally never identified—turning up at crucial moments with panic-stricken cries of 'Retire.'

One senior officer complained that the only orders he had received from the time he had left the Bulganak were 'March' and 'Halt' and Russell considered that nothing more than 'a bulldog rush at the throat' was attempted and wrote of Raglan, 'he had lost, if he ever possessed, the ability to conceive and execute large military plans—and that he had lost, if he ever possessed, the faculty for handling great bodies of men, I am firmly persuaded

. . . that he was a great chief, or even a moderately able general, I have every reason to doubt.'

Captain Patullo, of the 30th, summed it up in seven succinct words '. . . there was a great want of generalship . . .' and there was a feeling among the troops as they bivouacked among the dead that they were now missing an opportunity to finish a war that was rapidly becoming detested by everyone. Cathcart told Paget that he thought the Russians had had such a dressing they would never come into the open again, and Windham, of his staff, said 'The more I think of the battle the more convinced I am that it might have ended the campaign.'

The cavalry held the same view. 'What an opportunity was lost!' one of them said, and Captain Portal complained that they were commanded by 'a pack of old women who would have been better in their drawing rooms'. Even the men in the ranks aired their anger. One man wrote home that the cavalry 'was not made use of' and that when they had shown themselves at the end of the action more than double their number of Russian cavalry 'ran away from them like sheep'. Russell, like any good newspaperman, was quick to pick up the controversies and lay them before his readers. He was writing in his tent when Nolan burst in, his face dark with anger. Obsessed with his ideas, he believed that the cavalry had not been allowed to do their duty. Despite Wellington's view that 'cavalry should always be well in hand and . . . not used up in wild and useless charges', the battle had failed to change his opinion that nothing in the world could withstand light horsemen armed with sharp swords. Their manoeuvrability and speed were part of his whole conception of cavalry tactics and he had no time for heavy men on heavy horses, and the jeers of the staff were acting like a goad to his troubled spirit. He had been thwarted by Evans's staff officer in his dramatic appearance with Raglan's message to advance and, in his impulsive intolerance and already annoyed at the disapproval of the horses he had bought, all the irritation of a young man too certain of his skill burst out in an intense hatred for the older officers.

124

'There were one thousand British cavalry,' he said bitterly, his rage at white heat, 'looking on at a beaten army retreating —guns, standards, colours and all—with a wretched horde of Cossacks and cowards who had never struck a blow, ready to turn tail at the first trumpet, within ten minutes' gallop of them. It is enough to drive one mad. It is too disgraceful, too infamous! They ought to be damned!' He did not hesitate to air his disgust even among the officers of the cavalry themselves, though he must have known it was heavily frowned on. Wellington detested junior officers spreading idle gossip and discussing the short-comings of their seniors, and constantly endeavoured to devise means of putting an end to it, in case, he said, it 'put an end to us'.

The hot-headed Nolan was not deterred and the correspondent of The Morning Post heard him using expressions 'not made for the tongue of an aide-de-camp', while his diary began to teem with impatience at the inaction to which the cavalry had been condemned. This diary, though it no longer apparently exists, was before Kinglake as he wrote his vast history, and to him it disclosed a clear belief—'based apparently . . . upon somewhat wild processes of reason—that the commander of our cavalry was the man upon whom the blame should rest'. It was already firmly in the mind of this cavalry enthusiast who had so far not been chilled by the harsh facts of war that the cavalry should have been performing miracles and he could only imagine that nothing but perverse mismanagement and an evil choice of leaders prevented them from doing their work properly.

The contempt of the infantry, already clear after the affair at the Bulganak, was easily spread, as those who had been in the fighting jeered—as soldiers do—at those who hadn't. Surrounded by the wreckage of battle, it was a humiliating thing to have to endure but the cavalry were all well aware how little they had contributed to the battle and they knew that in the vast list of casualties that went home with the despatches, under the heading 'Cavalry' would come the entry, 'One horse wounded'.

It doesn't take long for just one active tongue to start ideas working. The irascible Lucan had never been popular, and Maude wrote 'The more I see of Lord Lucan and Lord Cardigan, the more thoroughly I despise them. Such crass ignorance and such over-bearing temper.' Lucan was no fool and, no slower than anyone else to hear the complaints, he went to see General Estcourt with a message he wished to be passed on to Raglan: Lord Lucan trusted that Lord Raglan had that confidence in him, as commanding the cavalry, that he would allow him to act on his own responsibility, as occasion should offer and render advisable, for otherwise opportunities of acting would frequently be lost to the cavalry. It had no effect. Raglan had made up his mind.

The exhausted army settled down to cook its rations, breaking up casks and tearing down vines and cottages, even burning broken Russian muskets which exploded from time to time to send bullets whistling across the steppe. While a few were drunk on vodka they had found, thousands of others struggled to get water for themselves or their horses at the river in the dark and the confusion. With his usual kindliness and concern, Raglan was occupied with the sick and wounded but, while his humanity is to be admired, it was no part of his job as a commander-in-chief.

There were no bandages or splints, no chloroform or morphia, and the wounded had to lie on soiled straw from a farmyard or old doors, or sat waiting for transport on tubs or boxes. Because there were not even any candles the surgeons, their aprons drenched with blood, finally found themselves working by moonlight. Those who had pointed out the shortages at Varna had been rebuked by Airey for being 'frivolous', but now one of Raglan's tents was given up for sick and wounded officers while ruined houses were turned into field hospitals where surgeons worked surrounded by newly amputated limbs. The numbers defied their efforts. Between 400 and 500 wounded were brought in, only a third of the British injured, and there were still thousands of Russians lying about who only received any attention at all through the humanity of British regimental officers.

In addition the cholera had not ceased. General Tylden of the Engineers was dying in agony and Colonel Lawrenson of the 17th Lancers had had his horse led from the field by a dismounted man and was now being taken on board one of the ships lying at the mouth of the river. A long stream of sick and wounded went with him, together with trophies in the shape of helmets, blood-covered muskets, bayonets and swords.

While everyone else was concerned with the aftermath of the victory and the state of the wounded, however, Lord Cardigan was occupied only with his own grievances. He had somehow got his baggage and his tent and was sitting inside it composing a long shrill letter to Raglan. Though he accepted that it was an inopportune moment, he brought out all his old complaints and still could not get rid of the idea that the Light Brigade was to be independent of Lord Lucan. He reiterated the promise he claimed had been made to him that the divisional commander would not trouble him and ended with a request that the commander-in-chief should inform Lord Lucan of his rights and duties.

Lucan wearily forwarded the letter to headquarters, but in his covering note he could not resist putting his side of the question. 'I cannot . . . in justice to myself,' he wrote, 'omit to add that I have neglected nothing to show courtesy and attention to Lord Cardigan . . . To avoid any personal difference, I have studiously communicated on all matters of duty with him either by written memoranda or divisional orders; and on no one occasion have I ever allowed to drop from me one sentence of reproof, reserving my opinion when I could not approve, and only expressing it when it was likely to be agreeable to him; nor can I charge myself with having done an unfriendly act towards him since his Lordship has been under my command.'

It was late when Lord Raglan settled down to something to eat. Although he did not trust the cavalry alone, he still felt that some follow-up should be made to the army now trailing away to the south. It had always, he knew, been a maxim of the Duke of Wellington's to pursue a beaten enemy and he proposed to St. Arnaud that the untouched Fourth Division should go forward with the cavalry and an equal number of French troops. St. Arnuad, however, made the excuse that the French needed to recover their packs which they had dumped at the beginning of the battle, and nothing was done.

As Raglan sat down by lantern-light to dine, Kinglake was with him. Raglan had come across him wandering about lost after the battle and had invited him to join him. His charm captivated the writer and he made a supporter who defended his reputation to the end of his life.

The army was astir early the following morning, digging vast pits to bury the dead, while more sick and wounded were sent jolting in agony in unsprung arabas and litters to the river mouth four miles away where they were lifted into boats and hoisted painfully aboard. Their destination was Scutari, where their chances of survival proved to be very slender. The cavalry were saddled ready for a move by 5 a.m. but, sitting on his trunk waiting for orders, Paget gradually became aware that no move was contemplated. By the next night, there had still been no move and the wounded were still lying in rows along the banks of the Alma, some of them complaining that they had not yet seen a doctor.

As he made the rounds of his regiment, Paget bumped into Raglan dining in the open and, since his father was an old friend of the commander-in-chief and he had been known by him ever since childhood, he was invited to join. Raglan was very dissatisfied with the French, he found, and when their trumpets sounded while they were eating, he said 'quite petulantly', 'There they go with their confounded too-too-tooing; that's the only thing they ever do.' Broaching the sore subject of the cavalry, Paget asked if more use could not have been made of them, but Raglan shook his head stubbornly and admitted frankly that his object all day had been only to 'shut them up'—or as he put it to

ord Lucan. Mezzotint by Herbert
Davis after Sir Francis Grant.
: shows Lucan much as he must
ave looked on the day of the
harge. In the background is the
•lain of Balaclava, with the
arbour and the Genoese fort
uarding its entrance.

Lord Raglan (wearing civilian hat).
Photographed by Roger Fenton
in the spring of 1855 when
Pelissier—on Raglan's left—had
become C. in C. of the French.
This picture probably more
than any other indicates Raglan's
character. At the extreme left
is Lord Burghersh, one of Raglan's
five nephews who were on his
staff.

MAJOR GEN. THE EARL OF CARDIGAN

Top left: One of the rare pictures of Louis Edward Nolan. It appears to have been taken from the portrait in the officers' mess of the 15th/19th The King's Royal Hussars; he is dressed in the uniform of the 15th Hussars.

Top right: Lord Cardigan. Engraving by T. W. Knight. This portrait of the leader of the Light Brigade shows him as he was at the time of the charge, and does not attempt to romanticise him.

Right: General Airey's order to Lucan which initiated the charge. The almost illegible scrawl suggests the haste with which Airey must have written the order. (See pages 196–7)

Top: This *Punch* cartoon indicates the British attitude to their Turkish allies. Though the Turks had actually defeated the Russians before the allies had even gone to the Crimea, they were never given any credit as fighting men. The cartoon is headed 'How Jack makes the Turk Useful at Balaclava'; the sailor 'jockey' is saying '. . . Riding's a deal pleasanter than walking about here, and when this chap's tired—I mounts t'other Cove.'

Above left: William Howard Russell, by Roger Fenton. Russell is dressed as he must often have been seen by the men in the Crimea, in civilian clothes but wearing odds and ends of uniform.

Above right: Paymaster Henry Duberly, of the 8th Hussars, with his wife, Fanny, known to the troops as 'Jubilee'. Photographed by Roger Fenton in the spring of 1855.

'English Cavalry surprised by Cossacks while foraging near the Tchernaya.'
Engraving by H. Linton after E. Morin. It gives an idea of the kind of terrain
where the cavalry had to operate, with narrow gullies from which the enemy
could emerge unexpectedly.

Top: Balaclava Harbour, photographed by James Robertson, a contemporary of Fenton. This appears to be the end of the inlet, and shows why the arrival of Cardigan's personal yacht must have created quite unnecessary difficulties for the harbour authorities.

Bottom: The Tractir Bridge in the valley of the Tchernaya. Photograph by Robertson. It gives an idea of the terrain where the charge actually took place. The left of the picture shows roughly the point reached by Major Low, of the 4th Light Dragoons.

Top: Lord George Paget, by Fenton. Although this photograph was taken after the winter, on Paget's return to the Crimea, it gives some idea of the shaggy ungroomed state of the horses at the time of the charge.

Below: Sir James Yorke Scarlett. Mezzotint by F. Bromley after Sir Francis Grant. The picture of the commander of the Heavy Brigade launching his men into their charge shows him as he must have been on the day of Balaclava, wearing a helmet instead of a cocked hat, so that the Russians mistook his aide for the leader.

Top left: John Penn, of the 17th Lancers. Engraving by G. Stodart from a photograph by J. E. Mayall. It appears to have been made after the Crimea, when cavalry tunics were increased in length.

Top right: W. H. Pennington, of the 11th Hussars, taken in later life. Pennington was fond of putting on his old uniform for photographs and remained as proud of having ridden in the charge as he did of his fame as an actor.

Left: A Fenton photograph of an infantry private in full marching order.

Top: 'Before the Charge of the Light Brigade at Balaclava.' Watercolour by Orlando Norie. This shows the 13th Light Dragoons taking their place at the right of the first line. They came out of the action with only two officers and eight mounted men.

Bottom: 'The Charge of the Light Brigade.' Anonymous contemporary watercolour. Cardigan can be seen leading the first line, consisting of the 13th Light Dragoons and the 17th Lancers. Behind them the 11th Hussars are falling back, so that the 4th Light Dragoons are almost catching them up on their right to form the second line. The 8th Hussars, held in check, alone form the third line. The Heavy Brigade is seen falling far behind on the right.

Top: 'The Charge of the Light Cavalry at Balaclava.' This illustration from *British Battles* by James Grant, published c. 1885, is one of the few drawings which show the Lancers and the 13th Light Dragoons in the proper position in the first line. Although it is not quite correct in showing hussars arriving at the same time, it does depict the British cavalry without plumes and the Russian gunners in the flat 'muffin' caps.

Bottom: Contemporary print showing how Sergeant Berryman of the 17th Lancers, unhorsed during the charge, won the VC by rescuing Captain Webb, of the same regiment.

Top: Cornet (sometimes referred to as Lieutenant) Yates, of the 11th Hussars, a newly commissioned ranker, who was with Cardigan during his interviews with the artillerymen on the Causeway Heights after the charge. Photographed by Fenton.

Bottom: 'The Roll Call—Balaclava', by R. Caton Woodville, a popular painter of battle scenes. It shows survivors of the 17th Lancers with one of the 13th Light Dragoons just behind, and hussars on their left. Judging by the white stockings on the horse's hind- and forelegs, the figure in the right foreground is intended to be Cardigan.

Our Cavalry Dec.ʳ 1854

Top: Huts and clothing for the army. Drawn by W. Simpson, a war artist. During the winter the cavalry were ordered to give up their horses to carry supplies. They had reached such a condition by this time that 80 pounds was considered the maximum they could carry. Very few of the huts seen in the background were erected until reinforcements arrived.

Bottom: 'Our Cavalry, December 1854.' Contemporary sketch by Captain H. J. Wilkinson. Chargers starved to death after trying to gnaw at gunwheels and each others' tails and manes. Those which survived looked 'more like costermongers' donkeys'.

Top: Party of French and English at the camp of the 4th Dragoon Guards. Photograph by Fenton in 1855. Before huts arrived, a few officers managed to erect shacks for themselves. The woman is one of the army wives allowed to accompany the army, who supported themselves by cooking or doing the laundry for officers. The officer on horseback might well be English despite his French headgear; kepis became very fashionable with British officers.

Bottom: 'The last survivors of the Light Brigade at the coronation of George V, 1911.' Watercolour by A. S. Martrick. The short man fifth from the left is Private Spring, the deserter from the Lancers who was discovered in the 11th Hussars after the charge had reduced the Brigade's numbers. The tall man next to him is Wightman's friend, Private Mustard.

another officer, to 'keep them in a bandbox'—because of the enemy cavalry's superiority in numbers. It was the obsessive attitude of a slow, stubborn old man and, because the victory at the Alma was not followed up, it was a wasted victory.

Although the fleeing Russians had been told to halt and re-form at the River Katcha to the south, it was impossible to stop them and the fords and drifts became jammed with panic-stricken men. The Katcha was only a matter of ten miles away and there was a good post road along which a few batteries could have bounded to send their projectiles among the terrified soldiers, but when Raglan urged this on St. Arnaud the French marshal refused, saying his men were tired. He was, in fact, desperately ill and was behaving with the stubbornness of a sick man.

The following day, however, it was Raglan who was being difficult. When the French proclaimed themselves ready at last he claimed it was necessary to complete the burial of the dead and the embarkation of the wounded. Yet there were men in both French and British armies who had not been involved at the Alma and the cavalry, despite their half-starved horses, were more than willing to provide flank and vanguards. There were also 10,000 Turks who had not been involved at all but they were not even considered, any more than they were ever considered to be in need of food, water or camping facilities.[1]

It was three days later when the allies moved on to the Katcha where the cavalry were joined by the Scots Greys who had landed at the mouth of the river and were eager to make up for their absence at the Alma. Compared with the rest of the cavalry, whose uniforms were shabby and covered with mud, they looked as though they had just come off parade in Hyde Park, and Paget was disgusted when they did not take over from him the onerous duties of rearguard which always meant being saddled in the early morning with the rest but getting in after dark when everything eatable had been found and cooked. Since they had not been at the Alma, however, Raglan was anxious to show them with their conspicuous horses to the Russians to indicate that his cavalry was more numerous that it seemed. In fact, the Russians thought simply that he had mounted the Guards.

Despite the fact that he had once been a cavalryman himself, Raglan never seemed quite to understand them and he had sent Lucan ahead without giving him time to water horses, ordering him to take possession of a village called Duvankoi, shown on the maps to be within easy march of Sebastopol and situated on a river bank two miles away. The maps at headquarters were inaccurate, however, and the cavalry had to approach the village down a tremendous hill by a dangerously narrow defile. They were watched all the way by Cossacks and to Lucan it seemed pointless merely to leave a patrol there because there were 2,000 Russian horsemen hanging on his flanks. He placed three guns at each entrance to the village but, cooped up there, he was powerless if attacked by infantry and artillery, and after a few hours the order was given to quit the place and they returned up the dangerous defile in the dark, along a road so narrow several of the baggage carts were upset. Even before they left the village the Cossacks were hovering in their rear again. There had been little time to water the parched horses and many of them had had none at all for 24 hours, and the patrol had achieved little except to exhaust the already exhausted horses even more and give Cardigan the opportunity for malice. 'Lord Lucan was in command,' he said to Paget. He seemed to feel it was the whole reason for the difficulties.

The moment had now been reached when the allied commanders had to make up their minds whether they were going to attack at once the north side of Sebastopol which contained strong fortifications poorly manned or march across the peninsula to the south. The defences on that side were not yet developed and apart from one or two batteries there was neither ditch nor gun. Raglan took the idea to St. Arnaud for his views but he was sitting rigidly in his chair, his hands gripping the arm rests, and he was able to do no more than nod his head. A few hours later he was in the agonies of cholera.

The information coming in suggested the allies should hurry. Though no attempts were being made by the Russians to defend rivers or destroy bridges and even wells still had their buckets, already a line of battleships had been sunk across the entrance to Sebastopol harbour and a position was being prepared at the mouth of the River Belbek, just outside Sebastopol. Cardigan was sent off to reconnoitre it with a squadron of the 11th Hussars and one of the 13th Light Dragoons but he returned to report that he had been faced with a marsh, crossed by a causeway which was held by a battery of heavy guns and a strong force of infantry and cavalry.

No one wanted another set-piece battle so soon after the Alma, and with the French advising a march round the city for an attack from the south, the allies turned their backs on the sea to head inland. The Russians were in no state to do much harm and there were signs of retreat all round them in discarded weapons and ammunition, but the route was still one of incredible danger because not only would they be cut off from their ammunition and the heavy guns of the fleet, but they were also entering country where an enterprising enemy could have landed them in desperate trouble.

They were moving now through a thickly wooded area intersected by lanes, towards Khuton Mackenzie, or Mackenzie's Farm, which had once been the home of a Scottish settler. It was intended to make a halt there and orders had been issued for the cavalry and artillery to reconnoitre the place while the infantry made its way through the woods by compass. Lord Lucan was supported by a battalion of Rifles and guided by Captain Wetherall from headquarters who was considered to be so able it was felt he could not possibly lead them wrong.[2]

The route was not a good one and it soon became overpoweringly hot. The infuriated infantry had to carry their rifles above their heads, while the branches constantly snagged on their equipment and the briars tore at their flesh, and in the confusion the regiments and brigades became inextricably mixed. Having

131

watched them depart, Raglan, who, to the surprise of a Prussian observer with the army, always persisted in riding at the very head of his army, cantered off alone with his staff to look at Sebastopol and, diverting from the track to the shoulder of a hill, was confronted with a glittering panorama of the city. There appeared to be a large number of stately buildings, barracks and forts and many fine private houses, and, since everything was built of white stone, they were dazzling in the sunshine, while on the vivid blue water of the wide harbour those ships of the Russian Fleet which had not been sunk were quietly at anchor.

Cantering back to the track, Raglan happily imagined himself to be following the leading units of his army, but instead of being behind, he was now in front. Wetherall had arrived at a fork which was not marked on his map and had led the way up the unmarked road only to find it was leading north-east. As he was riding back on his tracks, Raglan, whose map must have been better, had not mistaken the fork and as the trees began to thin, he and his staff moved forward.

Maude's troop of artillery, having also kept to the correct route, had found themselves in a position where they were 'devoid of all proper protection and support', while Brandling's troop, fighting its way from the wood, came across Raglan and his staff examining hoofmarks in the white dust. As much in the dark about Mentschikoff's movements as Mentschikoff was of theirs, Raglan and his staff were trying to decide whether the marks were made by friendly or enemy horsemen. One of Brandling's farriers was called on for an opinion and, though it is hard to decide how he came to the conclusion, he gave it as Russian. 'This appeared to be conclusive' and the staff continued with greater caution.[3]

By this time the worried Wetherall, hearing Maude's troop of artillery somewhere near him on the correct route, had galloped off to find them and learned that Raglan had passed them and was now leading the army. The staff had just moved ahead of the battery in single file, fully expecting the cavalry to be in front, when Wetherall burst from the trees and bumped into them—at just the same moment as they bumped into the rearguard of Mentschikoff's army.

Kinglake gives a highly adulatory version of this incident to show Raglan sitting on his horse, a noble figure holding the Russians in awe simply by the calmness of his demeanour. It takes a lot of swallowing and Calthorpe's version is more likely. According to him, Raglan was still wondering why he had not yet seen the cavalry, and two officers had just been sent into the wood to try to find them when two of his escort of the 8th Hussars and an officer of the staff who were riding ahead came hurrying back to report Russian troops on the road in front. Airey rode forward to investigate and almost immediately reined in and, without speaking, held up his hand. In front of him, not far away, was a Russian waggon-train and a body of Russian foot-cossacks, the rearguard of Mentschikoff's army, and they were halted and resting.

Raglan who had been hurriedly packed off to the rear,[4] was growing irritated by this time and again sent some of his staff to look for the cavalry and hurry on the Rifles who were nearby in the wood with the Light Division in their rear, while the artillery were moved up in readiness, and Raglan's Hussar escort, under Captain Chetwode, was thrown out in skirmishing order. They were all found in these positions by the worried Wetherall who now galloped off at full speed to inform Lucan.

One group of Russians fired at Chetwode's men but no one was hit and, by now informed of what had happened, Lucan was bringing his cavalry up at full speed. They were not sorry to be out of the wood. They had been obliged at times to move in single file, a formation that could easily have brought disaster if the enemy had thought to place a few sharpshooters in the undergrowth, and they were relieved to break clear, even though they were emerging in penny numbers.[5] Led by Lucan they galloped towards the Russians and as they passed Raglan the commander-in-chief called out sharply, 'Lord Lucan, you are late!'

A detachment of Greys, eager to make up for missing the Alma, crashed after the Russians as they fled into the thickets and, as the cavalry continued to emerge, Maude unlimbered his guns and brought them to bear on the waggon-train, stopping its retreat, while Cardigan, cheerfully offering five pounds to anyone who could shoot a Russian who was sniping at them from across a patch of marshland, was sent ahead after a column of the enemy seen in the distance over the next rise.

He set off with the 17th Lancers down the hill, as usual in his eagerness pressing too far ahead—so far, in fact, he was warned by his aides that he was in danger himself. He paid no attention to the warning but when he called up the 8th in support, Lucan decided the starved horses were becoming so weak they might not get back up the hill again and recalled him and sent another regiment, until it became obviously useless to pursue, and the brigade major, George Mayow, was sent instead to discover what he could.

A few Russians had been killed and a few taken prisoner—one of them an officer who was drunk—in return for a British sergeant who had been sent too far ahead by Cardigan and captured. The troops soon broke open the carts and immense quantities of boots, shirts, coats, dressing cases and jewellery were found as well as a military chest. There were rich hussar jackets of fine light blue cloth and winter cloaks lined with furs, to say nothing of champagne and pornographic novels in French. Nolan's friend, George Evelyn, who was riding with the Greys, noticed a quantity of ball cartridge in some of the carts and tried to set fire to the hay around it with his cigar. Colonel Darby Griffiths, of the Greys, offered him a lucifer but the hay was too damp, and the carts were eventually blown up by the artillery.

13 Wait till I get a chance

THE allies were now in the extraordinary position of being ten miles inland, with the port they had come to besiege between them and their own fleet. To the disappointment of the hard-pressed cavalry, few horses had been taken at the skirmish, but at Mackenzie's Farm they were at last able to quench their thirst and fill their water bottles, and cook their rations on the smashed fragments of expensive furniture. The halt lasted for about two hours then the march was continued, with a bivouac for the night by the Tractir Bridge. The headquarters staff were as badly off as anyone else for rations, but Captain Thomas, of the Horse Artillery, had found a side of wild boar in the captured Russian waggons and sent Lord Raglan a leg, and he and his staff sat cross-legged on the ground, using their fingers instead of knives and forks, the chief subject of gossip the ridiculous incident in the wood.

Raglan's shouted criticism had not been lost on Lucan. He had not asked for a guide, but he had been publicly and—as he rightly thought—quite unfairly rebuked in front of everyone. As for Raglan, the incident only served to remind him of the Duke of Wellington's strictures and when Cardigan appeared he caught the full force of the commander-in-chief's anger. The letter he had written after the Alma demanding that his position should be clarified was still rankling with Raglan and he was sharply accused of having the cavalry in the wrong place. Smug in his self-righteousness, however, Cardigan merely reminded the commander-in-chief that he was no longer in command of the cavalry, and went off cheerfully to wrap himself in his cloak and go to sleep by a fire of the 13th Light Dragoons, oblivious to the chatter of Fitz Maxse, his aide, who was exchanging greetings with his brother, Fred, a lieutenant on the *Agamemnon*, who had ridden through unknown and unoccupied territory with despatches and information from Admiral Sir Edmund Lyons and was about to retrace his steps with a request to the navy to make for Balaclava, a small port on the southernmost tip of the peninsula.

As Fortescue described it, the incident in the wood was a 'trifling and ludicrous' affair which had sprung chiefly from Wetherall's indifferent map and Raglan's casual attitudes, but it did untold and unrealised damage. It was seized on with glee by the gossips at headquarters and the jeers at the cavalry increased. Nolan did not hesitate to say his piece. Blunt noticed that when he visited the cavalry, as he did regularly, he was not slow to 'speak disparagingly of the divisional commander', and he astonished Russell by the angry way he spoke both of Lucan and Cardigan. Raglan's decision to keep a tight hold on the cavalry had driven him to a white-hot rage. 'Did anyone ever hear of cavalry in a bandbox doing *anything*?' he fumed, and went on in a fury about the patrol to Duvankoi where, he said—declaiming about something everybody who had been there had well noted—a battalion of infantry could have disposed of every man-jack in twenty minutes. The heat never cooled down, and he maintained that the cavalry's work had been deplorable and that they had been exposed to utter destruction.[1]

Somehow it had got around that he had rendered great service at the Alma with his superior proficiency in cavalry tactics and that it was entirely due to his judicious suggestions that the small force of horsemen had kept at bay the vast mass of Russian cavalry;[2] certainly he had been brave and he had been conspicuous and even the cavalry began to believe the stories that were being bandied around.

'It is common gossip', Lieutenant Seager, of the 8th Hussars, wrote, 'that Lord Raglan thought the cavalry was being wretchedly handled.'

On the 26th, after a chilly night, the army moved on towards Balaclava. It was clear now that the Column they had seen at Mackenzie's Farm belonged to Mentschikoff who had marched it out of Sebastopol to pose a threat to the flank, yet Lucan, whose job it was to frustrate the design, had his hands completely tied by Raglan's orders. The only officer, according to Russell, in the whole army with any knowledge of Russian methods, he had told the newspaperman that the regular Russian cavalry were 'as bad as could be', though the Cossacks 'could be damnably trouble-some . . .' and certainly they always worried the British horsemen. Small in number, the British never knew whether to attack and chance being caught by a larger force hiding behind the next rising ground or whether to stay near the main body and prevent Russian attacks, a method which made it impossible for them to function as scouts.

The dew soon cleared and it became very hot once more and the army left its trail of dead and dying behind as it marched. The village of Kadikoi to the east of Sebastopol was deserted and, with infantry heading for the heights overlooking the south side of the city, Raglan and his staff rode into Balaclava. At first it appeared to be deserted but a shell was fired from the old Genoese fort that dominated the entrance, and burst near them in a puff of smoke. It was only a token resistance, however, and, when the *Agamemnon* replied, a white flag was hurriedly raised, and they were warmly received with flowers and trays of bread and salt, the old Russian tributes of friendship.

Balaclava was an attractive fishing village and summer resort for the people of Sebastopol, and its green-tiled cottages were covered with honeysuckle and clematis and fronted with vegetable gardens. But it had an oddly ominous look because it lay in the constant shadow of steep cliffs which rose from either side of a long and twisting inlet. The waters were deep enough for big ships to moor right alongside the wharves but it was clearly not big enough for both allied armies, and though the British, holding the left of the line, would—when the armies turned to face north towards Sebastopol—normally have taken over the wider but shallower harbours of Kamiesch and Kazatch on the west coast of the peninsula, on the advice of Admiral Lyons it was decided to allow the French the use of these two harbours. They would thus be well protected by the British, who, except for the few Spahis, still had the only cavalry.

The decision immediately threw on the British all the responsibility for defending the dangerous right flank against Mentschikoff's army hovering to the east and north. But few people worried as it was assumed that the Russians were in such disarray after the Alma that the assault on Sebastopol would begin at once and give the armies the benefit of that vast deep-water harbour. There was no reason why not. The cavalry had even discovered an Englishman named Upton whose father had built the dockyards. He was married to a Russian woman and, though he objected to using his knowledge against the country which had sheltered him, his wife had no such scruples and told them they could walk into Sebastopol any time they wished.

The same view was held by Cathcart, whose Fourth Division was looking straight down on to the defences. He was, he said, 'in the strongest and most perfect position . . . 20,000 Russians could not disturb me . . . They are working at two or three redoubts, but the place is only enclosed by a thing like a low park wall, not in good repair . . . I am sure I could walk into it with scarcely the loss of a man at night or an hour before daybreak.'

Unfortunately, the French were dragging their feet again. St. Arnaud was failing fast and, though he was recovering from cholera, his heart was affected and his place had been taken by General Canrobert, a man of too great a sensitivity to be a commander-in-chief. He baulked at the responsibility and Raglan gave way, and Airey and Nolan rode to the bleak heights round Sebastopol to place the infantry divisions in camp. Cathcart was furious when he heard that siege trains were to be landed. 'But my dear Lord Raglan,' he said, 'what the devil is there to knock down?'

Raglan's coolness towards Cathcart was already marked and he took no notice, but it was dangerous to delay because the siege was not yet—and never was—properly a siege, in that it was still possible to move in and out, and by 1 October 14 battalions of Russian infantry had entered the city. Within another few days, a further 28,000 had moved in and what had been a ripe plum ready to fall into the hands of a determined attacker had become a fortified city ready to withstand an assault.

*

Long before this, Balaclava had lost its attraction. The streets were jammed with men and beasts and vehicles, as supplies, guns and ammunition were dragged from the ships up to the heights overlooking Sebastopol, and it had become a shambles where the chaos was equalled only by the squalor. Gardens had been trampled flat and, as little had been done to provide the troops with firewood to cook their rations or roast their green coffee beans, like all troops they took matters into their own hands. Doors, huts, fences and roofs were torn down to make fires, and bushes were ripped up and the clematis and honeysuckle disappeared. When the cavalry had first ridden down, it had been possible for the men to reach out and help themselves to grapes without leaving their tents and they had even fed their hungry horses on them,[3] but within days Blunt found there was not a scrap of fruit within reach as the vines and trees were demolished to feed the camp fires of British, French and Turkish soldiers.

Admiral Boxer, in charge of the port, was a stubborn old man who, according to Raglan, had no system whatsoever, and the waters were soon jammed with ships and the quays so crowded with stores and equipment everything was lost track of and left to rot in the worsening weather. The end of the harbour was used as a butchery and all the offal was thrown into the water or even allowed to lay where it had fallen to send up its stench and gather flies. Within a fortnight the place was in a revolting state.

The retention of the port undoubtedly presented grave problems for the British. The long inlet ended in rising ground where the road wound out of town. To the left was the village of

Kadikoi, backed by a small hill which was joined by other rising ground to the Chersonese Hills, a high plateau which circled Sebastopol. On the other side of the road was another hill, while to the east of Balaclava was a further small range behind the British base. To the north was a wide bowl divided by the road to Prince Woronoff's estates at Yalta. This road ran along a range of broken heights, and small hillocks, known as the Causeway, to join other heights to the east, which circled the north side of the valley and finally joined another range known as the Fedioukhine Hills which almost joined the Chersonese in the north at the Sapouné Ridge. Thus, above Balaclava on the south side of the Causeway was a plain—known as the South Valley—open in the east at a dangerous gap in the hills near the village of Kamara; and, on the north side, another narrower plain—known as the North Valley—also open to the east along the banks of the River Tchernaya.[4] The river was the safe limit of British-occupied territory, though it was always dangerous to linger there as the Russians could always push hidden troops through the gaps in the hills.

To visit Balaclava for supplies from the camps round Sebastopol it was necessary to traverse the uplands, descend the slopes and then cross the plain to the bay, a distance by road—and a poor road at that!—of about seven miles. Though Balaclava was the only port of supply, through which every item of equipment, every morsel of food, every bullet and bag of powder had to come, it continued to remain isolated from the main armies with a separate defensive system. The defence was given to the 93rd Highlanders and about 800 Marines who served the ships' heavy guns which had been landed and posted on the heights behind and to the east of the port overlooking the plain.

In support were Turkish battalions—'scarcely 4,000 men', according to Blunt—who were commanded by Rustum Pasha, an able, intelligent man, and the cavalry division under Lord Lucan. No one in particular was put in command, however, and Lucan alone was responsible, sending detachments of his cavalry along the Tchernaya and past Kamara along the highway to Baidar to the east from which direction an attack might come. His camp was at Kadikoi, two miles above Balaclava at the western end of the South Valley near the slopes where French guns on the Sapouné Ridge under the command of General Bosquet could give him support. Though placing the cavalry in a position to take any attack on Balaclava in flank, it also, however, left them in the very front of the defences.

The Light Brigade had been joined by this time by the 4th Light Dragoons, who had made a nervous passage through the woods to the north of Sebastopol, Paget worried sick all the time at the possibility of ambush. He had found the litter of the wrecked convoy and blown up the rest of the waggon train and discovered an abandoned pack horse with, twisted underneath it, baggage which to his delight he found was his own. His charger by this time was so weak with lack of food it stumbled at every other step, while five others died of exhaustion. He made strenuous efforts to load up his surviving horses with hay found at a deserted farmhouse, deciding bitterly that the staff thought they rode a peculiar breed of animal that did not need food, but he had to leave it all behind when an urgent message called him to detach his regiment from Cathcart and join the Third Division.

With the days still hot but the nights growing surprisingly cold, the Light Brigade had also been joined by this time by the Heavy Brigade. With their horses 'done up', and so short of officers they were on duty nearly every day, the Light Brigade were glad to see them, but they had been sadly reduced in numbers. On the *War Cloud*, embarkation officers had packed 100 horses into a space designed for 56 and when the ship ran into one of the gales common in the Black Sea 75 of them either died or were so injured that they had to be destroyed. More died in the *Pride of the Ocean*, but the worst disaster occurred in the *Wilson Kennedy* carrying part of the Royals. They already had horses down in dozens when a deck collapsed, throwing the officers' chargers on to the troop horses below in the hold. Horses which had cost

hundreds of pounds were lying with broken backs and legs, and
. . . animals and saddles, carbines and swords, were mixed up
together 'like as they had been shook up in a bag'. They were now
reduced to a single squadron, and according to their C.O.,
Lieutenant-Colonel John Yorke, had lost 150 horses during the
night of the gale—more than at Waterloo.

Altogether, the Heavies had lost 226 horses in their passage
to the Crimea and Lucan found the remainder in such a condition
he could scarcely recognise them.[5] They set up their camp to the
right of the Light Brigade but the cavalry were so overworked
they were roused at daybreak the following day and sent on
patrol. The Russians were not aggressive but they could not be
ignored.

Lord Cardigan was up at the front, however, indefatigable as
ever and itching to get at the enemy. Lord Raglan watched him
warily. The commander-in-chief had set up his headquarters in a
low one-storeyed farmhouse, with a deep roof of red tiles. From
each side of it ran a series of cottages and sheds joined by a low
stone wall to form a square. The staff lived in tents with two
companies of infantry and the hussar escort.

Cholera was still rampant and regimental bands had been
broken up so that the men could be used for ambulance work,
and Russell found the British camps gloomy compared with the
bustle and noise of the French. There was no bugle call or music
of any kind, and to The Times correspondent it seemed an error to
deprive men of the only bit of cheer they could find in the
chillier days of autumn.

Russell had long since noticed a lot wrong with the army and
had written home to say so. He had a great capacity for anger and
a greater capacity for putting it into stinging words. Henry
Clifford, of the Rifles, thought 'he had a gift . . .' and said that
'more than one "nob" had thought it best to give him a shake of
the hand rather than a cold shoulder'. He advised his relations to
read his articles on the staff and thought his description of
conditions 'not exaggerated . . . in any way'. Russell was disliked

intensely by Lord Raglan and his staff, however, not only because he was a 'tradesman' but also because it was felt, probably rightly, that the information he was sending home was going straight back to the Russians via friendly embassies. By this time, though, since Russell showed no sign of disappearing, Lord Raglan was treating him as he treated all unpleasant problems and was ignoring him. 'Lord Raglan', Russell wrote, 'never spoke to me in his life . . . I was regarded as a mere camp follower.'

His opinions made little difference anyway, and for the cavalry none at all. Though they were busy posting vedettes along the Causeway and other high ground overlooking the roads and passes and guarding the wells in Kamara from being poisoned, Raglan's distrust of them had long since communicated itself via the staff to the rest of the army, and Russell heard that they had never been properly handled since arriving in the Crimea, and had lost golden opportunities from the excessive caution of their leaders. Russell had little time for the gentlemanly Raglan and put the blame in its proper place, considering Raglan a man 'of strong prejudices and weak resolution', but Russell's was a newspaperman's shrewd assessment and most people, caught by Raglan's undoubted charm, laid the blame for the indecision at the door of a far less friendly character, Lucan.

Lucan was well aware of the feeling against him but there was little he could do about it. Raglan was a complex character, and they were barely on speaking terms. Yet Lucan's unpopularity was not total. The bluff and experienced Colin Campbell—no man to endure fools and always persona non grata at headquarters—got on well with him, while his brigade major, Anthony Sterling, who does not seem particularly to have liked Lucan, considered him a man of 'considerable ability'. Paget even *enjoyed* being in his command, feeling keenly that Lucan was much wronged, though at times he, too, felt the lash of his tongue, while Colonel Mayow, Cardigan's brigade major, had long since noticed the indefatigable way he worked for the division.

The self-satisfied young officers of the staff were less discerning, however, and Nolan's tongue was active. Judging by the number of men who noted in their letters or diaries that they heard his comments, he must have done a great deal of irresponsible talking. Almost everyone who knew him mentioned it, and he was often in the cavalry camp spreading stories which were far from justified. The Russians were continually roaming about to the east and the cavalry were working under difficulties, and though it was true that over the years of peace the desire for splendour had made them a show force of too-big men on too-big horses, that was not their fault and it was growing so cold at night now and the horses were in such a miserable state the regimental colonels were praying that French cavalry would arrive soon and take a little of the load off them.[6]

And what the staff in the comfort of Raglan's headquarters never took into consideration was that everyone down in the plain—the Turks and the Highlanders as well—were constantly under arms. It didn't stop the dangerous tale-carrying, however; Walker noticed that Nolan was 'dangerously hostile' to Lucan, and what he passed round as opinion was seized on as fact. The officers of the infantry, already beginning to feel the nip of approaching winter on the heights and dodging the stray Russian shots that passed through their camps to fall so often among the troops moving to the trenches through the Woronzoff Ravine behind it became known as the Valley of Death, were sufficiently in envy of the cavalry in the plain not to hesitate in following them up.

The cheerful gossipy Forrest was soon busy writing home again—'We have no faith in the generalship of my Lord Lucan. We are all agreed that two greater muffs than Lucan and Cardigan could not be. We call Lucan the cautious ass and Cardigan the dangerous ass. Between the two they got us into two or three very awkward positions at Alma and also on the previous day.' Forrest, of course, had not been there but had still been in Varna waiting to embark for the Crimea, and perhaps he was following the instructions of a satirical book of advice to officers—published some years before—'When at any time there is blundering and confusion . . . lay about you right and left. This will convince people it is not your fault'—because his own commanding officer, Colonel Hodge, was grumbling about the way he was doing his duty. 'He seemed,' Hodge said, 'to think he is to do nothing.'

Nevertheless, not just Forrest but other officers, too, were complaining—that the Light Brigade were useless in one of their most important duties, the collection of supplies for the army, and that they were always 'above their business, and too fine gentlemen for their work'. Everyone followed the view, even Punch with its satire at the heavy plungers of the cavalry itching —with a little infantry support—to take Sebastopol. It was claimed they should have followed the flying enemy after the Alma, and above all should have been more aggressive at the affair near Mackenzie's Farm. But the young men of the staff who slept in their beds at night were not aware of the whole picture. The cavalry were near enough to the enemy for shells to fall regularly in their lines and they were working night and day, stamping out their fires and mounting at five every morning to remain under arms until daylight. The horses, wretched, 'starved to death' and lacking shelter, with many already lame, had 'coats like sheep' and were never groomed because there was never time.[7]

Water had been laid on by cutting an aqueduct which carried supplies to Sebastopol but food was always difficult and Paget found himself carefully hoarding a few onions, half a loaf of bread and a ration of salt pork in his trunk. Despite his dislike of rearguard duty, he had enjoyed serving with Cathcart because he was not a fussy general—'So different from . . . our cavalry', he added, thinking of Cardigan. 'I suppose service improves people,' he wrote home, a little puzzled, '. . . especially the "tyrant" Lucan, as one has heard of him.' Despite the divisional commander's reputation, he found he could always adjust differences with him in a friendly and workmanlike way.

Cardigan was not very happy, however. He had received a considerable blow to his self-esteem in the letter Raglan had written in reply to his demands at the Alma. It had reached him as the cavalry had set up its camps and it had jolted him badly. As a commander, Raglan had finally had enough of him.

'I have perused this correspondence with the deepest regret,' he wrote, 'and I am bound to express my conviction that the Earl of Cardigan would have done better if he had refrained from making the assertions which he has thought fit to submit for my decision.' A general of division, he said, might interfere as much as he pleased with the duties of a general of brigade; his judgements might be right or wrong, but he was always the senior officer, and all his orders and suggestions claimed obedience and attention.

It was enough to put any man firmly in his place but, unfortunately, Raglan continued a little further, and while the beginning of the letter made it quite clear that Cardigan was wrong, the end seemed to suggest Lucan was wrong also.

'The Earl of Lucan and the Earl of Cardigan', it continued, 'are nearly connected. They are both gentlemen of high honour and elevated position in the country independently of their military rank. They must permit me, as the Head of the Forces, and I may say the friend of both, earnestly to recommend them frankly to associate with each other, and to come to such an understanding as that there should be no impression of the assumption of authority on the one side, and no apprehension of undue interference on the other.'

While it was the end of Cardigan's hopes of independent command, to his narrow stubborn mind the suggestion that Lucan was also wrong was enough to allow him to continue his criticism of his senior officer.

Fortunately for the cavalry his health precluded him from being too difficult. At the beginning of October he was sick with diarrhoea and was ordered by the divisional medical officer on board the *Star of the South* in the choked harbour of Balaclava to recover. It was not too arduous a convalescence, because Mrs. Duberly was on board also.[8] She was already being accused of having 'followers' and certainly Captain Lockwood, Cardigan's aide-de-camp, had been very attentive, and now the appearance of Cardigan himself led to rumours that she was his mistress. Certainly, though her published journal was careful to leave out the details, her letters to her sister showed a sudden marked difference in her attitude to him. He was kind to her, lent her horses—even his favourite charger, Ronald—and went into details about his troubles with Lucan. It was probably merely Cardigan unable to resist a woman in distress but there was a guardedness about her letters home that suggested that it might be more, and certainly Cardigan enjoyed advantages not known to her husband.

However Mrs. Duberly found him, his disappearance had been hailed with joy by the Light Brigade. He was still itching to cover himself with glory but Raglan's precise instructions that the cavalry must hold themselves in check were irksome in the extreme and an alert in the afternoon of 30 September when it was reported that 30,000 Russians were on their way, had set him by the ears. But nothing was seen or heard and he had returned to camp very disappointed.

By this time the effects of bad staff work were beginning to be felt by everyone. Lucan's aide, Walker, was so reduced he bought an old pair of trousers at the sale of a dead man's belongings to mend his own with, and his coat was ready to fall to pieces, while Strange Jocelyn, of the Guards, wore holed shoes and a shirt that was in rags, and was eating salt pork without complaint. What was of greater concern, however, was the state of the horses on which fell the responsibility of guarding the eastern approaches to Balaclava. Walker noticed that they were actually starving now and were 'almost done for', and Lord George Paget, in desperation, was planning a foray down to the dangerous area of the Tchernaya where he had heard there was hay for the taking. Unfortunately, there was never time to allow them to recover their strength and condition because it was already clear there was a Russian move in the wind: A long train of carts carrying civilians had been seen leaving Sebastopol and it was known that the Russian field army was drawing nearer and beginning to gather menacingly in the folds of the hills.

By this time the more energetic officers were beginning to consider that Sebastopol ought already to have been captured—indeed an immediate attack was the only justification for the risky flank march round the city—but in the dawn of 7 October an outlying picket of the 4th Dragoon Guards under Cornet Fisher, their noses wind-nipped in the cold, was surprised by a formidable force of Russians of all arms. Three of the patrol were wounded and taken prisoner but the rest thundered away, heads down from the flying bullets, to raise the alarm, and to the jingle of bits and the clink of equipment the cavalry division led by Lord Lucan moved across the plain towards the east with the horse artillery and halted on the high ground overlooking the Tchernaya. There they were joined by Nolan and Captain John Hackett, one of Airey's DAQMGs.

The Russians halted and manoeuvred backwards and forwards about the plain as if at a field day, and the British cavalry settled themselves in their saddles, firmly convinced the Russians were inviting an engagement. In this they were quite correct because they were trying hard to tempt the British beyond support. The ground was perfect for cavalry. The countryside was clear and without woods, narrow lanes or rocky eminences to hinder them, and the whole of the division was present. It was all a cavalryman could wish, and none was more enthusiastic than Nolan.

Keen to show himself, he had moved forward with the 17th Lancers as they had escorted the guns towards the ridge overlooking the Tchernaya and he now waited eagerly for the action to begin. He loathed any system that frittered cavalry away with constant marching and had a firm belief that Englishmen, with their love of fox-hunting, were natural horsemen. While regimental colonels, more careful of the lives of their soldiers, heartily disliked the young men of the staff who did not hesitate to rush to the front and urge them on in the hope of gaining a little glory for themselves, the impulsive Nolan was not concerned with caution. Despite the growing belief that musketry was already spelling their end and notwithstanding the proofs of Waterloo, he was firmly of the belief that nothing, neither infantry in square nor artillery, could resist them if they attacked with determination. It was the key to his whole character. Just as he marred the good sense in his books with untried theories, so in his own mental make-up obvious intelligence was unbalanced by headlong enthusiasm.

Lucan, however, had little time for Nolan's excitement. He was bound rigidly by his orders and, whether he liked them or not, he was sufficiently a believer in the chain of command not to fail in them. The trumpets did not sound the charge. Well aware of his defensive role and firmly warned by Raglan's orders, he refused to be drawn. When the gunners asked permission to open fire, he seemed to Maude 'all hesitation' and only willing to watch the way the Russians were moving and, while the division sat waiting, and without knowledge of Raglan's orders, Nolan offered his advice unasked and had it sharply rejected.

Lucan finally gave Maude permission to fire, and after the first round the Russians retired, their horsemen moving off at a gallop to leave behind two wounded men and a few discarded weapons. Beauchamp Walker was sent after them and crept forward to count 16 squadrons of cavalry and 1,000 to 1,800 infantry lying in wait for any advance. It more than justified Lucan's caution but Nolan, the expert, made no secret of the opinion that he had neglected his 'bounden duty' and thrown away an opportunity. With his outspoken comments he aggravated what was becoming an impossible situation.

Raglan was said to be very annoyed. In fact, like Bosquet, he praised Lucan for his work and, if the gossips had stopped to consider, it would have been obvious at once that he was by no means anxious to get himself involved in fights in the plains to the east. The most important thing in his mind at this time was the siege of Sebastopol and his instructions to Lucan were that nothing was to be done which would in any way draw troops from that object. Even Lucan's request for an additional troop of artillery and a few more infantry was turned down. It was hard on the cavalry and when Paget thought they were being 'miserably handled' his criticism was not directed at Lucan.

It was as a result of the affair of 7 October that Lucan got his nickname—Lord Look-on. Who first used it is not known but it was inevitable. It was clever and funny and it stuck and spread round the army. It might well have been Nolan who thought of it. He had a pretty turn of phrase and a fine contempt, and he was telling his friends that he had told Lucan 'to his face' that he had failed in his duty. It was all highly dangerous and self-important and a habit the army had always frowned on. When the colonel of the 10th Hussars had been accused by his officers of slowness at the battle of Toulouse, the Duke of York, then commander-in-chief, had said 'When the officers of a corps prefer accusations against . . . their commanding officer, nothing but the most conclusive proof . . . can justify a proceeding which must otherwise be so pregnant with mischief.'

It *was* a situation pregnant with mischief and Calthorpe was one of those who 'heard great blame given to Lord Lucan for not ordering the Light Cavalry to advance and charge the Cossacks . . .' while Captain Shakespear, of Maude's battery, decided that 'the finest opportunity for thrashing the Russian cavalry had been thrown away'.

The constant alarms were irritating everybody, of course, and as they were dragged from the comparative warmth of their camp regimental officers were complaining that there could not possibly be any need to turn out the whole of the cavalry every time. Paget, as annoyed as anyone that the name 'Look-ons' was being used against the cavalry as a whole, took a different view. He thought it was better to have 500 alarms than one surprise, and he had learned from those whose opinions were worth anything that the allegations of missed opportunities were entirely unjust. Oddly enough, for once it was even Cardigan's opinion.[9]

The cavalry were annoyed and hurt at the jeers that followed them around. Hodge thought it 'must be Lucan's fault', while Forrest, in his cheerful irresponsible way, helped the picture along with an account of the skirmish that was colourful but not very accurate. On 10 October there was another skirmish when Cossacks surprised a French working party and the Royals under Yorke chased them. On their starved horses they never had a chance of catching them, and as the stories continued to spread they were being diligently written into his diary by George Evelyn, Nolan's friend—'Our cavalry is the most inefficient in Europe. They certainly have not done as much as was expected of them.' They even reached Mrs. Duberly in Balaclava, and were seized on joyously by the staff at headquarters, who had never liked Lucan's habit of criticising them. Known as 'that nest of noodles', they were held in contempt by the fighting troops. 'The greatest set of muffs possible', they were called, and 'a parcel of lazy, idle, drinking and swearing fellows'. All these sound very much like the complaints of all fighting men for the staff and doubtless all of them were not justified but, judging by their performance, they had only themselves to blame, and Raglan, chained to his desk instead of getting among his troops, seemed quite unaware of their inefficiency.

Nolan did not consider such descriptions fitted himself. As the staff appeared before the ragged army, magnificent in snowy linen and gaudy lace, 'gallant-looking, handsome cavaliers', Nolan was always among them, 'impetuous, vehement, restless', always raging on about Lucan.[10] So far, deriding the Establishment and on edge at the prospect of action, he had behaved more like an excited boy than a responsible staff officer, and his small successes had gone to his head a little.

'Isn't this fun?' he had shouted to an old friend. 'I think it's the most glorious life a man can lead.' The only drawback was that he could find no one to put into practice those theories he had written so ardently about in his book and he blamed it all on Lucan. His precepts, his suggestions, were being ignored and there was little wonder he disliked the cavalry commander. His faith in cavalry, said Edward Hamley, of the artillery, was 'carried to the extreme' and he considered that what laurels were being won were being captured by the infantry, while the cavalry were being molly-coddled like a lot of invalids. As he set down his views in his diary, his quick temper didn't permit him to ask why or to question whether the caution might not have originated with Raglan or Airey.

'Wait till I get a chance,' he told his friends, 'and you'll see what they can do.' It had an ominous ring.

Disliked by the staff—'Lord Lucan fearfully mismanages the cavalry', wrote Fred Maxse, now at Raglan's headquarters—distrusted by those middle-class officers who felt that high command should have gone to a man of less exalted birth, distrusted by his junior officers and loathed by Nolan, Lucan's position was growing daily more difficult. He was hard-working and concerned for his men but he always remained unpopular and reviled, and it was even being considered that he did not ride forward enough with his troops.[11] He did, of course, and short of issuing an order to his division laying the facts before them he could only hope that the situation would change.

Again and again, Lucan has been portrayed as a haughty brainless aristocrat with a violent temper and an irascible disposition. Ruthless he certainly was, not allowing opposition when his mind was made up, irritable, harsh, and often irritating, but Cathcart and Pennefather were both bullying men and Sir George Brown was said even to have 'persecuted' his troops without incurring the dislike Lucan suffered. Unfortunately he was all too often linked with Cardigan, and Raglan's rigid orders were causing him to be swept along in the contempt everyone had good reason to feel for his brother-in-law. But his job remained, and the pickets seemed to be occupied almost nightly in weather that grew steadily colder. He knew, and those in command knew, that he was not to engage in a pitched battle but was there merely to keep the Russians away, and this the cavalry was doing very effectively.

He was coping not only with Cardigan and Raglan—and through him with Wellington!—but also with Nolan, who was in danger of becoming a troublemaker. But there seems to have been little complaint from the overworked men in the ranks as they huddled fireless in their cloaks in the dark along the Tchernaya. Harassed, exhausted, trying to sleep without shelter, they seemed to feel, unlike so many of their officers, that it was all part of the job. Their chief concern was with obtaining food and drink for themselves and their horses and with the fact that the gorgeous uniforms that proud colonels in the past had devised for them were singularly ill-suited for campaigning in the growing cold. Their overalls were useless in the mud and the smart jackets which hardly came to their waists, while excellent on the parade ground, didn't give much protection to a man's back at night and were so tight it was impossible to wear anything warm underneath them. But they rarely met Captain Nolan and were concerned chiefly with keeping alert for the crackle of shots and the thud of hooves in the shadows.

14 The poorest fun I know of

By this time, foraging down by the Tchernaya was growing extremely hazardous with prowling Cossacks in every valley, and the nights were sharp enough now to kill off the weaker horses. Douglas, of the 11th Hussars, was wearing a fur coat he had captured from Prince Mentschikoff's baggage train and Paget was so cold he could hardly hold a pen to write to his wife.

The night of 12 October was bitter as the wind changed to the north and began to howl down from the wide Russian steppes. Captain Stocks, of the Royals, had never felt so miserable in his life. Two days later he was on picket for 21 hours at a stretch '... the poorest fun I know of', he said. He saw plenty of Cossacks but as the British approached the Cossacks retired, and when the British retired the Cossacks advanced. 'They remind you of rabbits,' Stocks wrote, 'only not quite so harmless.' Nevertheless, the British never allowed the Cossacks peace, following them up so closely at times they even stole the Russians' picket posts while the Russians were looking elsewhere for the British.

They were never allowed to forget the myths which had started about their inefficiency, however, and Lucan was becoming convinced—and rightly, too!—that there was a clique against him at headquarters. Unaware of Nolan, not hearing what he was saying, he wrongly laid the blame on Raglan, but he continued faithfully to follow orders and Paget found little fault in him. Even Hodge, who had no love for belted earls and was full of resentment for the rewards they received from the sheer accident of birth, had found to his surprise that he was beginning to get on with him.

Cardigan was still trying him hard, however. He had been off duty sick during the affair of 7 October and when he had turned out for an alarm on the 8th, he had to go back to his quarters grey-faced and ill. When he had returned to duty on 12

October, he was in a bad temper and, according to Paget, 'the two of them were at it at once'. With a brigadier as co-operative as Scarlett, Lucan might have done well—indeed, there seems to have been no disputes between these two—but Cardigan was unbalanced, brainless and ill and it was impossible that they could work in harmony.

By this time Cardigan had acquired a nickname too—The Noble Yachtsman. Because of his health, Raglan had given him permission to sleep aboard his yacht, the *Dryad*, which had arrived in Balaclava harbour. It was an arrangement that involved sending an officer or an orderly down with a message every time he had to be informed of anything, and it was a duty that grew increasingly onerous and time-consuming as the road grew worse. It also meant that the commander of the Light Brigade had little idea how his men were having to live and did not even permit him to be on the spot in the event of an alarm. Not only that, but his yacht occupied space in the narrow harbour at a time when it was becoming almost impossible to berth ships with badly needed supplies and when Cardigan's men—even his divisional commander for that matter!—were enduring short rations and a life under canvas in the increasingly wintry conditions.

Cardigan was accompanied everywhere by his friend, Hubert de Burgh—a civilian known to the army as The Squire—who kept him supplied when on duty with hot soup and brandy, and he slept whenever he could in a feather bed and dined off champagne and food prepared by a French chef. Any commander-in-chief worth his salt would have put a stop to the self-indulgence at once but Raglan still failed to curb him. He was so difficult he was even given a separate camp for the Light Brigade but all this achieved was to make Cardigan convinced once more that his was a separate command. 'All this . . .' Paget said, 'to part these two spoilt children.'

Cardigan was looking very ill now and Paget thought the campaign would finish him. He had little cause to like his senior officer who had been involved in a scandal with his brother's wife but, deciding he was going to have no trouble, he gritted his teeth and called him 'my lord' as often as he could. It didn't prevent explosions but the treatment worked so well it brought the congratulations of John Douglas, who had suffered under Cardigan for a long time.

Lucan's position became worse on 14 October, by which time the Russians had occupied in strength the village of Tchorgoun just across the Tchernaya. After nearly three weeks, when no one in particular had been responsible for Balaclava, Sir Colin Campbell was at last sent down to take command. By now, even the fact that Lucan preferred the spartan way of living his men endured was giving rise to accusations of meanness—it was believed that he would not even feed his own son, Lord Bingham —and his reactions to the 'mutiny' in the 5th Dragoon Guards had become responsible for a suggestion that he was feuding with Scarlett.[1] As it happened, Campbell's appointment made little difference. Campbell had always assumed that he would be under Lucan since he was junior in rank and, as they were on excellent terms of mutual trust and consulted regularly, Lucan more than willing to defer to the advice of the experienced Scot, the matter was largely academic.

It was Cardigan who was indignant. Why should Campbell, he demanded, have a separate command when he had not? The fact that Campbell had experience of battle covering forty years never entered his head.

It didn't take the army long to notice that the defence had been given not to Lucan, who was a lieutenant-general, but to Campbell, who was only a major-general, and it soon became the gossip that Raglan didn't trust him. It is hard not to suspect Nolan in all this. Fred Maxse, on Raglan's staff, heard him waxing indignant at the little the cavalry had done and talking bitterly against the cavalry commander, and his diary was filled up to 12 October with his strong feelings against the inactivity of the mounted arm and Lucan's unfitness for command. The day after Campbell's appointment he was with Mrs. Duberly in Balaclava, by now carrying the plumed hat of a staff officer. Evelyn was still being kept well informed—'Our men had to gallop for their lives', he wrote gleefully and 'The commander of our cavalry has given much dissatisfaction at headquarters—no wonder'—and now Nolan's sense of security was lacking again when he advised Mrs. Duberly to be at the front because the bombardment was due to start. He stayed to lunch and lent her his horse, while he borrowed a pony, and they rode up to camp to see her husband. His position on the staff seemed to be going to his head a little because, despite his professed dislike for shabraques and sheepskins as 'useless encumbrances', he was now cutting a dash with a tiger skin over his saddle holsters.

The defences of the British base remained worrying and, knowing how isolated they were and the weakness of their force, 'neither Lucan nor Campbell were at their ease'. Campbell, an old soldier with more experience than the troublemakers, was sympathetic of Lucan's position. On the sore subject of the 7 October affair he was very irate against 'those young officers of cavalry who would fall out from their regiment, and go to the front and give their opinion on matters they knew nothing about'. 'These young gentlemen,' he told Paget in his broad Scots accent, 'talk a great deal of nonsense and though he [Campbell] might be criticised, he was indifferent because he was not there to fight a battle or gain a victory. He was there to defend Balaclava and he was not going to be tempted out of his strong position by jeers.' He was, of course, right. The country people, who were Tartars and had no love for the Russians, said troops were already marching from Simpheropol and Baktchiserai towards the Tchernaya, and Rustum Pasha's Tartar spies brought the same information.

When the reports were forwarded to headquarters, Lord Raglan ordered a series of redoubts to be made on the Causeway Heights near the Woronzoff Road. These works—'wretched molehills', Russell thought—were to guard against an attack on

Balaclava up the hidden North Valley, and were hastily constructed by Turkish troops under the direction of British engineers. According to Hamley, they were 'mere sketches with the spade, and a donkey might have ridden into some of them', while Blunt noticed that only three of them were armed. The one on Canrobert's Hill, furthest east and part of the Russian-held hills to the east, had three guns, and the two succeeding ones, Numbers Two and Three, two each, all iron 12-pounders from H.M.S. Diamond. According to Rustum Pasha, some of the ammunition supplied to them did not even fit the bores, and a Prussian engineer with the army insisted there should be a second line and a brigade or two of infantry behind them because they were too far away from anyone to be of any value.[2]

These three works, together with Number Four, were garrisoned by about 1,400 Turks, most of whom, so their officers informed Blunt, had never been under fire before or seen any active service. Despite their excellent showing along the Danube, the Turks were still regarded with contempt by the British. They were often kicked and called 'curs', and a sarcastic cartoon in Punch showed a British sailor riding one like a horse and leading a second by a rope as a spare for when the one he was riding fell exhausted. Only Lord Lucan and Sir Colin Campbell who worked closely with them and got on well with Rustum Pasha had any regard for them at all. Some 600 of these men garrisoned Number One Redoubt on Canrobert's Hill and the remainder were divided between Two, Three and Four Redoubts. Numbers Five and Six were not armed or manned, nor was Number Six even completed.[3] It was a fragile and dangerous defence and the distance of Canrobert's Hill from any real support made any defence of it 'problematical' so that the onus for protecting the army still rested on the shoulders of the overworked cavalry.

It was becoming obvious now that the army was going to have to winter in the Crimea, yet, with a British ambassador almost within sight across the Black Sea, the army was already in difficulties and no preparations were being made for the bad

158

weather ahead. Charles Cattley, on Raglan's staff as an interpreter, had been a consul at Kertsch and warned of the bleak winds, snow and bitter cold; Upton, the Englishman, was also able to warn of the terrifying difference between the hot summers and the freezing winters. Still nothing was done, but by this time, of course, with everyone looking forward to the bombardment of Sebastopol, there was a tendency once more to feel it would all be over by Christmas.

They had firmly expected that a quick 48-hour bombardment would reduce Sebastopol to ruins which would then be occupied by the allies, but the digging of trenches, parallels and gunpits had been more difficult than they had expected, and all the time the Russians, men, women and children, had been visible through glasses, working like bees to strengthen defences which when they had first arrived had been almost non-existent. There had also been constant friction between the fleet and the shore commands, because Raglan still did not get on with Admiral Dundas, but arrangements had been made for that most dangerous of all naval operations, bombardment by ships of shore batteries, to take place as the siege guns opened fire.

When the guns started on the morning of 17 October, however, it was noticed that the sea bombardment had failed to materialise. Due to a disagreement with the French Fleet, this had been put back until the afternoon, when it proved a disaster. Despite the navy's failure, however, the land bombardment was not without success. Shells, shot and rockets smashed down on the Russian defences in a torrent of smoke, flame and flying debris and Russian troops were drawn up to receive the expected assault. Unfortunately, no assault took place. The British were ready but Raglan, not prepared to damage the alliance, was unwilling to act without the French and during the morning a Russian shell destroyed a French magazine, while a few moments later another blew up an ammunition dump. The firing of the unnerved French died down and the British assault battalions were never sent in, and the bombardment died at nightfall, to allow the Russians to effect repairs. The next day was the same and on the third day the same again. It went on for a week until everyone was sick of the noise and smoke, and by the end of it the allies were growing short of ammunition and they had achieved absolutely nothing because a bombardment without an assault was pointless. Even Lord Cardigan, who was watching with his friend, De Burgh, had the wits to realise that. 'I have never in all my life seen a siege conducted on such principles,' he said, and for once he was right.

All this time it was growing steadily colder, with rain and bitter wind as a foretaste of winter, and the Russians were still far from subdued. The whole invasion of the Crimea, in fact, was beginning to look like a ghastly mistake. Life was becoming irksome in the extreme with everlasting duties in the trenches, digging, the fatigues of fetching food all the way from distant Balaclava, the mud, the growing cold and the absence of rest. Alarms were frequent and there were unexpected raids on unsuspecting outposts, and a few hasty withdrawals by nervous officers. Tempers grew thin and friendships strained, and everyone blamed each other.

With the petulance of a sick man, Cardigan was carrying on his silly feuds with greater energy than ever. It wasn't simply that he disagreed with his divisional commander. He disagreed with everyone. His quarrel with Lucan now was because Lucan objected to the number of orderlies he had to send to Cardigan's yacht. Cardigan's luxurious living infuriated him but he was careful even now not to make it a personal issue. Instead, he produced a divisional order which stated that when an officer was prevented by sickness from attending a brigade turn-out, he was to report the circumstances immediately. To Cardigan it seemed a personal insult; and there was another tremendous flare-up from him when Lucan refused to allow anyone, not even officers—not even Cardigan!—to have forage until the men guarding the outer perimeter were supplied, a stand Paget admired enormously.

Cardigan was becoming impossible by this time and he

quarrelled with Paget because, detached to one of the infantry divisions, he had not brought his regiment on parade; Paget gritted his teeth, determined not be drawn, and went on 'my lord'-ing him as much as he could.

The indefatigable Lucan continued to ride round the outposts, checking on his men, putting under arrest commissariat officers who failed to provide what his troops needed, requesting his regiments when they were called out and expected to be attacked always to hold themselves well in hand. His solicitude for his division had intensified if anything and he was always insistent on the need to spare the horses as much as possible. He was plagued, however, by officers who were unskilled in campaigning, some of them ignorant of the most elementary duties. On 2 October he found a picket without their belts on and 'as unprepared for action as if they were in Hounslow Barracks', and expressed his displeasure at the 'unsoldierlike manner' in which some regiments were discharging their duties. Again and again he stressed the management of foraging and the need to water horses before going on picket duty, and pounced on an officer who, because he was interested to see what was going on in Sebastopol, relinquished his position and brought his picket into camp without reporting what he had done.[4]

It didn't stop the jeers, however. Sterling had long since noticed that Raglan's favouritism towards Cardigan put him in an impossible position, and even Forrest, no lover of the divisional commander, was aware that he had 'enemies at headquarters'. Blunt knew who they were. Fred Maxse had often heard Nolan sounding off in his bitterness against Lucan, and now Blunt heard him, on one of his visits to the cavalry camp, remark to Major MacMahon, the AQMG, that had he, Nolan, commanded the Light Brigade at the Alma, 'he would have pursued the retreating Russians to the very gates of Sebastopol'. Paget was already anticipating a catastrophe and the chorus had grown by now to such a pitch that the envious infantry, by no means discouraged by the staff, regarded the cavalry as 'more ornamental than useful', and Sir Colin Campbell, like Paget, was foretelling that they would be involved in a disaster 'from the way he heard them taunted by young gentlemen who were called staff officers'.

The situation remained an unhappy one and both men and horses were weary. The position they held, while it was sound from the point of view of the defence of Balaclava, was still a difficult one. As Paget was well aware, when mounted their place was outside the army, but their camp should have been inside because, dismounted, they were helpless. Yet the cavalry camp was virtually in the front line, and they were constantly at work, probing to the east, their patrols from time to time having to gallop for their lives. Several neat little rearguard actions were fought as they bolted for safety but there were a few casualties, some through carelessness, and when Captain Oldham, of the 13th Light Dragoons, lost a sergeant by sending him across the river against instructions Lucan was angry enough to put him under arrest.

The Russians were clearly trying to draw them and it wasn't difficult to exhaust them. Whenever there was an alarm, they all had to turn out, even though the threatening forces might be small in number, because in the dark there was never any telling when they might be the advance guard of an army. Certainly the information that came in indicated that they could expect an attack at any time. Lucan's horses were gaunt and rough-coated by now, and he was bitter at the lack of confidence with which his officers regarded him. When Lord Raglan instituted a patrol along the side of one of the hills, with a precipice on one side and woods on the other, Forrest, as inaccurate as ever, busily told his relations at home how he expected it to be wiped out at any moment and how Lord Raglan, ordering them to be discontinued, had found great fault in Lord Lucan for sending them out at the same hour for the same distance every day. Only a few, like Robert Portal, knew the truth. He was one of those concerned and had protested, only to be told by Lucan that he considered the patrol '. . . a most dangerous one . . . quite unfit for cavalry at all unless accompanied by infantry, but that it was by Lord Raglan's order, not his'. His protest resulted in Portal, when next sent on the patrol, being joined by a party of French cavalry and rifles, under the command of a major-general. Lucan himself had now got beyond complaint. There seemed to be only one answer, and that was to carry out every order exactly as Raglan requested. There must never be any suggestion that he had refused a duty. Like other soldiers before and since, his attitude was 'Obey the order first and complain afterwards', and he was careful to retain copies of all his correspondence so that when the war was over he would be able to exonerate himself as the truth came out.

Nobody was 'crowing much' about the siege now and the cavalry, indignant at the suspicion of cowardice or slothfulness that hung about them, were in a combative mood when, during the morning of 18 October, a large force of Russians was seen marching along a ridge about five miles from Balaclava. A vedette was seen circling energetically on the hills to indicate the approach of infantry, and the horse artillery assembled with the cavalry, while the 93rd Highlanders got under arms. The batteries on the heights were manned, and the Turks began to fire from the redoubts. A dense white fog covered the whole of the plain and it was a perfect morning for an attack, but only a few shots were fired. Then once more the Russians halted and it was possible to see their watch-fires through the mist till dawn.

The cavalry shivered. They had been under arms for sixteen hours. 'If you keep a cabman out all night,' one officer said, 'he charges you double, whereas a Heavy gets nothing extra but a cold,' and as usual when the sun drove away the mist the following morning, it was found the Russians had vanished too.

It was expected that the next night might be a quiet one. But by no means. A vedette was this time seen signalling the approach of cavalry and once more they had to be turned out, everyone on edge at the hurry and bustle, the shouting, the trumpet calls, the cries of 'Lights out!' and the banging of cannon and the clatter of musketry in the distance. 'They worry us a good deal', Forrest wrote, 'by constantly making believe that they mean to attack us.'

Paget regarded the alarms philosophically, even putting some of them down to nervousness on the part of half-frozen pickets because there was a dead cow lying not far in front of the defences. Nevertheless, each turn-out meant that everything had to be packed ready for an instant move and, since the alarms all too often came at mealtimes, rations were wasted or lost—a matter of great importance, because there was no fuel for cooking anywhere and even the roots were being grubbed up now, while the hay for the baggage animals was cut to nothing. There was not a blade of grass to be had[5] and the hay ration for a charger was restricted to six pounds daily. Men went hungry too and, short in numbers and overworked, they were ready to drop in their tracks. Cornet Roger Palmer, of the 11th Hussars, going round his sentries, found Private Jowett asleep at his post. The orderly sergeant-major wanted to put him under close arrest but Palmer, knowing him to be one of his best men, let the matter go with a reprimand. He didn't know it, but it was to save his life.

Not the least affected by the weariness was Cardigan's health and he got leave, on the night of the 19th, though no one else quitted their posts, to go to his tent nearby. He was loud in his view that the constant turning out was unnecessary because he had heard it said—doubtless by some young sprig who knew nothing about it—that it was without precedent for the enemy to attack in the dark. His ill-health was as hard on everyone else as it was on Cardigan, and the following day, when he was late turning out, Paget, as senior colonel, was asked by the brigade major, Mayow, to form up the men for the divisional parade. Five minutes later Cardigan appeared and flew into a temper to know why. When Paget explained, he flew at Mayow.

Nerves were growing ragged by now, of course, and in the hope of bringing the matter to a head Lenox Prendergast, of the

Greys, was sent to headquarters with a plea that the cavalry should be allowed to attack when opportunity offered. But headquarters were obsessed enough with the siege to overlook the danger on the plain and Prendergast was informed that there was on no account to be a major offensive down at Balaclava.

On the evening of 21 October a report came in that 20,000 Russian infantry and 5,000 cavalry were marching on Balaclava from the east, and a message went up as usual to Raglan. Cathcart's Fourth Division were marched down from the Chersonese to support Campbell, and Lucan turned out the cavalry, considering an attack so imminent that he urged on them the need for desperate courage. But after a few bangs from the artillery the Russians retreated as usual and the Fourth Division, like the Grand Old Duke of York's men, were marched back up to the top of the hill. Cathcart was livid with headquarters but the only men to be involved with the enemy were a party of twelve men from the 4th Light Dragoons, who noticed a patrol of Cossacks trying to ambush them as they watered their horses at the river. As they withdrew, a group of 200 appeared in chase.

Once more, nothing had been achieved except an increased sick list among the cavalry, who had stood to their horses throughout the whole of the bitter night, and the death of the commanding officer of the 17th Lancers. When Major Willett died of exposure the irrepressible Forrest reached for his pen again. 'They say it killed poor Willett', he wrote. 'Some say it was Lord Lucan's fault.' Yet once again Forrest was wrong, and the Lancers knew better. While the other regiments were properly cloaked, Major Willett—'a tyrant', who had succeeded to the command on the disappearance of Colonel Lawrenson after the Alma—would allow neither officer nor man of his regiment to cloak, and he was his own first victim and died of cholera brought on by exposure. 'He was a corpse before sundown of the following day,' Private Wightman commented.

The Russians were using the alarms as feints to hide the fact that they were reinforcing Mentschikoff's force and the only victims were the overworked cavalry. There was another alarm in the afternoon of the 22nd when the Russians were reported in force to the east, and the cavalry were turned out yet again in the evening and stood to their horses all night before managing to get an indifferent breakfast of broken biscuits and coffee. With no real effort being made by Raglan to drive them away, by 24 October the Russians had a second army threatening the British from the flank. It was a horrifying situation. Their force consisted of 25 battalions of infantry, 35 squadrons of cavalry, and 38 guns, 25,000 men in all, under the command of one of the Russians' best leaders, General Liprandi. The weakness of the Balaclava position had not escaped the notice of the Russian outposts in the hills, and this time they were intending to swoop down on them and cut the British army off from its base.

15 Those Turks are doing well

THE evening of 24 October was wet and cold and, as the pouring rain lashed at the flapping tents and soaked the huddled sentries, everyone was low in spirits. They all knew the Russians were coming soon.[1] The belief was confirmed when a Turkish spy employed by Rustum Pasha appeared through the mist with the news that the attack was imminent and was to come from the direction of Baidar to the east. He was sent at once to Campbell, who examined him with Lord Lucan. With the help of Blunt they decided that the information was sound and they regarded it as serious enough for Lucan to write a letter immediately and send it to Lord Raglan by his son, Lord Bingham.

Lord Raglan did not like spies. Though the Russians had no such scruples,[2] his obsession with honour gave him a detestation about anything he considered underhand, and he was very conscious of Cathcart's anger after the last false alarm. He gave no other acknowledgement of the message Bingham had brought than a terse 'Very well', but when he met Bingham later he said that if there was anything new it was to be reported to him. Why he did nothing else can only be put down to the belief that seemed to obsess him that everything that happened near Balaclava was a mere feint to hide an attack from Sebastopol. It was clear to everyone in the plain that the attack they had been expecting for so long was now hanging over them and suspicions were confirmed when engineers in the forward trenches heard Russian bands playing loudly in the villages by the river.

Russell was in the cavalry camp that evening and very conscious of the uneasiness there. He was informed that the Ruskies were very strong, and 'all over the place', but, as he left, Nolan overtook him on his way to headquarters, loud in his contempt for Campbell's anxiety and very critical of the information that had been sent to headquarters.[3] All the way back he 'let out' at the cavalry generals. 'We are in a very bad way, I can tell you,' he said. But he had been complaining so long now no one took any notice of him and when Russell told the other occupants of his tent what he had been saying there were immediate cries of derision. 'He's an inveterate croaker,' one of them said. 'I wish he was away in Jericho with his cavalry.'

There were no alerts during the night, but Lucan, as usual, was up and about with his men before dawn on 25 October. In the thick mist the troops were waiting stoically for the order which would allow them to return to their lines to water horses and cook breakfast. In the ranks of the 13th Light Dragoons Lieutenant Percy Smith had turned out virtually unarmed. He had been unable in the dark to find the iron guard he normally wore to enable him to hold his sabre with his maimed hand and, fearing to miss the parade, had decided to parade without it. So sure, however, was Douglas that the day would bring the expected attack he made a point of telling the 11th Hussars they were not to cut but to use the points of their swords.

It was still an hour before daylight and still very dark when Lucan, accompanied by his staff and his field trumpeter, Trumpet-Major Joy, of the 17th Lancers, jogged off on his inspection. Cardigan was still asleep on his yacht seven miles away and, as was so often the case, Lord George Paget was in command of the Light Brigade. As Lucan passed, he joined the little cavalcade—which shortly afterwards bumped into Campbell —accompanied by Captain Fellowes, his DAQMG.

A flagstaff had been erected on Canrobert's Hill and, as they approached in the first light of dawn, Lord George noticed that it stood out against the sky. Then he realised he was staring not at one flag in the half-light but at two, and at that moment, Lord William Paulet, Lucan's assistant adjutant-general, spoke. 'Hello,' he said, 'there are two flags flying. What does that mean?'

MacMahon, his AQMG, was staring with narrowed eyes. 'That, surely,' he said, 'is the signal that the enemy is approaching.'

'Are you quite sure?' Paget asked, and at that very moment his question was answered as one of the guns in the redoubt opened fire and a picket of the 4th Light Dragoons, surprised near Kamara, came thundering up the valley. They had had a narrow escape. Exhausted by the constant turn-outs, only Major Low's timely arrival had roused them out of their drowsiness as the enemy began to pour through the defiles of the mountain ranges which bounded the horizon to north and east, and an army corps, strong in infantry, artillery and cavalry, began to swing into the valleys from Tchorgoun. The Russian spies knew the positions of the Balaclava defences exactly by this time and they had learned by experience that it took all of three hours to bring down any support from the infantry camps on the Chersonese.

Paget went galloping back to camp to bring up the cavalry and horse artillery, while Lucan and Campbell sent a messenger at full speed to inform Lord Raglan. Learning of the alarm, Paymaster Duberly, at headquarters on escort duty, sent a messenger down to his wife. He was in no doubt about what was happening. 'The Battle of Balaclava', he wrote, 'has begun, and promises to be a hot one. I send you the horse. Lose no time . . . do not wait for breakfast.'

Meanwhile, Lucan and Campbell, followed by Fellowes and Blunt, rode to the foot of Canrobert's Hill where they immediately saw a body of Russian infantry some 4,000 strong climbing the slopes to attack the redoubt against which a fierce cannon-ading had been started from Russian positions at Kamara. In the cavalry lines, the order had just been given to proceed to breakfast when the guns started. Paget arrived at a gallop a moment later and the order was changed at once and the cavalry was mounted and brought forward across the plain to halt just out of range of the Russian fire.

Douglas was leading the 11th Hussars and Paget the 4th Light Dragoons. Shewell was on the sick list, and the 13th Light Dragoons, their colonel sick, were commanded by Captain Oldham. The Lancers, since Willett's death, were led by Captain Morris. Still weak from cholera and hardly in a fit state for active duty, he had only recently rejoined and had been faced the night before with the dilemma of whether to remain where he was on the staff or, as senior captain, claim the right to command his regiment. Still wearing a blue frock-coat and gold-peaked forage cap, he was not even known among his men.

'Who is he?' they asked, and someone who had served in India told them. 'That's Slacks,' they said, giving Morris the more prosaic nickname by which he had been known in the 16th Lancers. Well aware of the hazardous nature of the cavalry operations in the valley, Morris had written a letter to his wife which he had given to Nolan, to be sent to her in the event of his death, and in return he had received one from Nolan which was to be sent to Nolan's mother in the event of the aide's death.

The Russian infantry had now pushed up a narrow bowl that separated the Causeway from a small spur projecting into the North Valley and the Turks' fire was being returned from their supporting guns. Round shot like huge cricket balls were sailing over the hill to bound down on the cavalry. One caught a horse of the 4th Light Dragoons and went into its belly with a 'slosh', while Cornet Goad, of the 13th, was injured as his mount was knocked flying. A shouted warning to Paget caused him to kick his horse forward but it only served to bring him in line with a shot that scuttled through the animal's legs. There were shouts of congratulation and Parkes, his orderly, laughed. 'It went right through your horse's legs,' he said. Paget didn't think it quite so funny and when a splinter of shell struck his stirrup he asked sharply, 'What was that?'

'A piece of shell, my lord,' Parkes said with the same grim humour. 'Pretty nigh taking your foot off.' As he dismounted to pick up the splinter, another round shot sailed over the hill, bounced through the ranks and killed a horse alongside him.

On Lucan's order, they moved forward again and Maude's battery of two howitzers and four six-pounders, with the Greys in support, raced up on to the Causeway to unlimber between the first and second redoubts. The mist in front was still thick and the gunners, with the low sun in their eyes, couldn't see the enemy but they could see flashes in the mist which indicated a long line of guns at the end of the North Valley. They opened fire on them but were immediately fired on in return. Five horses were killed before they could be withdrawn to the near slope, but though the gun carriages were scored by shell splinters the men escaped. Coming up behind on the north of the Causeway was Barker's battery, which had been sent forward by Campbell, and now, as it grew lighter, the cavalry vedettes could be seen circling right and left to indicate an attack by all arms.

The Turks were still resisting stubbornly. Despite the warning Rustum Pasha had sent, they could see no troops coming to their assistance except the small force of cavalry in the plain, and the Russians outnumbered them by as many as twenty to one, with ten times as much artillery. Paget saw splinters of broken guns, horses' legs and men flying through the air, and the cavalrymen around him could hear the Russians' cries of triumph. Although the Turks were later jeered at by the British, the men on the spot could tell how stoutly they were fighting, and both Campbell and Lucan showed their approval.

'Blunt,' Lucan said, 'those Turks are doing well.'

But by this time they had lost half their number and when the Russian infantry charged with the bayonet they at last fell back, leaving 170 dead behind. They had given the allies an hour and a half's respite to bring up reinforcements. The time was 7.30 a.m.

The cry 'They've taken Canrobert's Hill' went up as the Turks retired, leaving a few wounded prisoners in the enemy's hands. The guns, not very efficiently spiked by the British gunners who were serving them, were abandoned. Despite their stand, little had been done to help the Turks beyond the moves made by Lucan and Campbell, and it was now perilously late, and the Russians were establishing batteries on the Causeway and along the spur sticking out into the North Valley. True, Canrobert, the French commander, had sent forward two brigades of infantry and two regiments of Chasseurs d'Afrique, who had recently arrived, and Raglan had ordered the First and Fourth Divisions down to the plain, but it had taken the Duke of Cambridge and his men half an hour to begin their march while Cathcart was even slower. When Raglan's staff officer, Ewart, brought the commander-in-chief's message he was just sitting down to breakfast.

'Lord Raglan,' Ewart panted, 'requests you, Sir George, to move your division immediately to the assistance of the Turks.'

Long since disgusted with Raglan's command, Cathcart replied that it was quite impossible. Ewart tried again. 'My orders were very positive,' he said. 'And the Russians are advancing on Balaclava.'

Cathcart was at his most obdurate. 'I can't help that,' he snapped. 'It is impossible for my division to move; the greater portion of my men have only just come from the trenches. The best thing you can do, sir, is to sit down and have some breakfast.'

Ewart politely refused and reiterated the request to move to the plain, pointing out that Campbell had only the 93rd Highlanders and that he had seen the Turks in full flight.

A plea to help the Turks was never likely to produce much in the way of a result and Cathcart was unmoved. 'If you will not sit down and have breakfast,' he said, 'you may as well go back to Lord Raglan and tell him that I cannot move my division.'

Defeated, Ewart mounted his horse and began to ride away, but, after a few yards, he decided that Cathcart's behaviour was just not permissible. He turned round and tried again. He had received an order for the Fourth Division, he said, and he was not going to leave until he saw it being carried out.

Cathcart gave way at last. 'Very well,' he said. 'I . . . will see if anything can be done,' and at last bugles began to sound through the camp and the 4th Division began a leisurely march towards Balaclava.

The delays had been too long, however, and already the situation in the plain was becoming very difficult. The Turks were out of the redoubt now and their flag had been hauled down and a Russian flag hoisted in its place. Those who paused in their flight to raise their arms in surrender had them cut off with scythe-like swings of Cossack sabres, and, seeing them streaming down the hill, Lucan sent the Heavies to try to protect them and directed Blunt to tell the survivors to form up behind the Highlanders just to the north of Balaclava, near Kadikoi.

Blunt set off at full speed. The Turks were angry, parched with thirst and exhausted. They had fought off the Cossacks but they had lost many of their men, and one of them, bleeding from a wound in the chest, asked 'why no troops were sent to their support'. Another pointed out that the guns in the redoubt were too small and could not be properly served, while a third complained that during the last two days they had had nothing but biscuits to eat and very little water to drink.

As they were being pushed into some sort of order Blunt rode back to Lucan. Seeing no support coming from the Chersonese, he was trying to move his division in a way that would pose the greatest threat to the Russians without putting his own men in danger. With no guns under his command beyond the horse artillery's six-pounders he was faced by five battalions near Kamara and a detachment of riflemen on Canrobert's Hill, both of which bodies had with them guns heavier than his own, and they were now well within range. Cardigan had still not appeared.

The cavalry moved about the plain, making threatening moves without seriously compromising themselves, but by this time the Turks in Number Two Redoubt, seeing large bodies of Russian cavalry rapidly advancing towards them and by now beginning to expect no support at all, made only a token resistance and fled towards Balaclava. As they trudged along with their kits on their shoulders, their arms full of bedding, kettles and plunder, they blocked the road Mrs. Duberly was taking to the Chersonese and she was advised by a commissariat officer to get among her own people as soon as possible. 'For God's sake,' he said, 'ride fast or you may not reach the camp alive.'

The situation was certainly serious. Two of the six redoubts had been occupied by the Russians by this time and Campbell, who had never been very happy at the placing of the redoubts so far from the base, began to be alarmed for Balaclava itself and ordered Barker's battery to fall back towards Kadikoi. Maude's battery was also out of action. It had all along been outranged and a shell had struck Maude's horse as he was drawing attention to Russian skirmishers advancing through the brushwood. He was fearfully wounded by the explosion and was carried to the rear in a limber blanket, literally covered with his own blood and that of his horse.

Lieutenant Dashwood, who took over the battery, had two horses killed under him almost immediately and, with them still heavily under fire, Lord Lucan rode up. The waggons under Captain Shakespear, which had been in Balaclava to transport shot to the trenches, had not come up and the battery was growing short of ammunition, and he ordered it to retire before the heavier Russian guns. They had lost twelve horses killed, several men wounded and a gun disabled. The Greys had also had casualties, but it was typical of Cardigan, who had arrived at last, that he should stop them as they left the field and demand to know why.

Seeing themselves apparently left to the Russians, the Turks in the third redoubt now also fled, followed shortly afterwards by those in the fourth. A troop of the Light Brigade was sent to drive away the Cossacks pursuing them and Blunt was sent once more by Lucan to order these Turks also to go to Kadikoi. Raglan, who by this time had reached the Sapouné Ridge on the edge of the Chersonese 500 feet above the plain, had taken in the manoeuvrings in full view below on the plain. Russian infantry and artillery were now pushing in ever-increasing numbers along the Causeway Heights and several squadrons of their cavalry were also trotting unopposed up the North Valley. The redoubts had been occupied and the Russians had firmly established themselves with artillery on the Fedioukhine Hills.

Lucan, still anxiously manoeuvring his men, found they were now within range even of the Russian riflemen in the captured redoubts and also in the line of fire of Campbell's guns and, on Campbell's advice, he withdrew them up the South Valley. Mrs. Duberly arrived on the ridge just in time to see them take up a position on the south slopes of the causeway, just beyond the fourth redoubt, carrying out the movement by alternate regiments in precise and careful formations, protected by Maude's battery, now under Shakespear who had finally come up with more ammunition. To Paget it was humiliating that the Turks had been allowed to be overrun. 'Our retreat across that plain . . .' he wrote, 'was one of the most painful ordeals it is possible to conceive, seeing all our defences successively abandoned as they were, and straining our eyes all round the hills in our rear for indications of support.'

By this time the mist had gone and the day had changed into one of brilliance so that the watchers round Raglan had an extraordinary view over the plain and could even see a patch of blue sea at Balaclava. Heavy grey clouds still hung on the top of the mountains but they made the hills stand out more sharply and the sun sparkled like diamonds on the points of thousands of bayonets advancing from the east. It was clear enough to see the Highlanders in their kilts and feather bonnets drawn up to the north of Balaclava and in the silence it was possible not only to hear the clink of bits and the rattle of sabres but also the yells of the Turks and the shout of orders below. As the cavalry moved towards the top of the South Valley it was even possible to identify individual officers. 'There's Lord George Paget,' someone said, and 'That's Low!' Douglas, Jenyns, and Morris were all also identified.

Raglan was still studying the scene. He had worried that the advance in the plain was a feint to draw troops away from Sebastopol but it was now becoming clear that the main attack was towards Balaclava, and all that stood between it was Campbell's Highlanders, together with 100 invalids, the few Turks who had been rallied by Blunt and formed up alongside the Highlanders, and the Cavalry Division, who with their light guns were in no position to oppose the vast mass swarming along the heights with their heavy artillery.

Lucan's new position was a sound one, however. He was clear of the cavalry camps yet protecting them, and he could attack in flank any attempt swinging down to Balaclava and at the same time provide excellent support for the Highlanders. But Raglan still had Wellington's dogma about his cavalry in his mind, and, taking advantage of the lull that had fallen over the battlefield, he sent Captain Wetherall down to Lucan with his first order of the day. It demanded that he withdraw his division from his position south of the fourth redoubt to a new position under the guns of Bosquet on the escarpment. From there it was quite impossible to support the Highlanders and it was too far away to be a threat to the Russian flank and abandoned the cavalry camp to the Cossacks now swarming across the South Valley.

Lucan was furious but there was no mistaking the order's intent. 'Cavalry to take ground to left of second line of redoubts occupied by Turks', it ran. It was a humiliating order, because it implied not only that the cavalry could not be trusted but could not even look after themselves. Lucan was so unwilling to move, in fact, he insisted on Wetherall waiting until the order had been carried out so that afterwards it might not be said that he had misunderstood it. Followed as closely as they dare by the Cossacks, the cavalry carried out the order sullenly but with precision, moving once more by alternate regiments in careful formation, and Cardigan formed up the Light Brigade in two bodies, one under himself facing the redoubts, from which came sporadic fire, the other under Paget facing the Woronzoff Road at a gap in the Causeway Heights leading from the South Valley to the North Valley. From the ridge the French artillery kept up a steady fire over their heads. In the abandoned cavalry camp the tents had been dropped so that the Cossacks chasing the Turks wouldn't see it, but they had not been deluded and were now hacking and stabbing at the sick and spare horses.

Neither Cathcart nor the Duke of Cambridge had yet appeared, and with the cavalry, the only support Campbell had, now in a position where it could pose no threat to any advance on Balaclava, the Russians were not slow to grasp their opportunity. The situation could hardly be more serious, and the threat was increasing by the minute. Already the first line of defence had gone and the Russians were still moving forward in over-whelming strength.

Apart from the Russians established in the redoubts along the Causeway, however, there was nothing at that moment happening to alarm the defenders of Balaclava, but to the people on the Sapouné Ridge, who could see what they could not see, move-ments were taking place which were rapidly to change the picture. A vast mass of Russian cavalry, accompanied by artillery and infantry, was slowly moving up the North Valley round the projecting spur and it was obvious that they were intending to turn to the south and throw their weight against the fragile defences of the British base. They posed an immense threat and, watching them, Nolan's agitation in his wish to see the light cavalry in action was noticed by several people.[4] With little experience of war and none of command, all he could see were mounted units below waiting aimlessly in the plain instead of crashing into the attack as he believed they should. The advancing Russians were worrying Raglan, too, now, and he sent a second order to Lucan.

Kinglake's version of what happened next is somewhat suspect, and doesn't always tally with the positions the troops occupied or what was said by those taking part, and it becomes safer to rely on the accounts of eye-witnesses, who do not agree with him. At last realising that the Russian objective was Balaclava, Raglan changed his mind about the cavalry. He could see the Cossacks wreaking havoc in the cavalry camp—inside the British lines, in fact!—and he could see now that their original position had been a good one and wished them to return to it. The order was for eight squadrons of the Heavies to support Campbell and the Turks and, according to the officer who carried it, Captain Hardinge, it instructed them to guard Kadikoi and the position of the cavalry camp.[5] Raglan was almost too late because the Russians on the Causeway were already starting a probing attack against the batteries that were bothering them with four squadrons of hussars and dragoons.

Receiving the order, Lucan turned to Cardigan, not trusting his excitable brother-in-law. 'I'm going to leave you,' he told him. 'You'll remember you are placed here by Lord Raglan himself for the defence of this position. My instructions to you are to attack anything and everything that shall come within reach of you,' and he made his instructions clearer still so that there should be no impetuous charging '. . . but you will be careful of columns or squares of infantry'. Satisfied that he had covered all possibilities, he now hurried down to Scarlett.

Having moved the Heavies—with the exception of the Royals—nearer to the camp and completed his instructions, Lucan, watched by Brandling's gunners, now rode with his staff up on to the Causeway to a commanding point to find out for himself where the Russians intended to strike. He remained there until the four Russian squadrons broke away from the main body—which had been stopped by the fire of Maude's and Brandling's batteries—and began to cross the Causeway to the north of Kadikoi. The main mass of Russians began to follow them more slowly.

The Russians had now moved far enough forward across the Causeway to bring their guns within range of the Highlanders. Campbell had drawn up his small force on the hillock near Kadikoi that barred the entrance to the gorge leading to Balaclava, and he now retired them to the rear slope and ordered them to lie on their faces in a line two deep. At that moment the four squadrons came into view across the Causeway with, behind them, just visible from Campbell's raised position, the main body of the Russian cavalry, who immediately came under the accurate fire of a battery on the Marine Heights. Seeing the Russians appear, the Turks, already demoralised by their earlier experience in the redoubts, fired a wild volley and bolted once more, with cries of 'Ship! Ship! Johnny! Ship!' They dashed through the camp of the 93rd, stopping only to loot it as they went, several of them being thoroughly lambasted by a soldier's wife standing guard on her possessions.

Apart from the gunners on the heights above the town, there were now only 550 men of the 93rd, a few Guardsmen hurried up from Balaclava and the invalids between the whole Russian army and the British base. Campbell, who was never at ease unless he was in action, was at his best. Riding calmly along the line he told his soldiers, 'Men, remember there is no retreat from here. You must die where you stand.'

To the approaching Russians, the hillock where they waited seemed to be unoccupied and they were still cantering forward when the Highlanders rose—out of the earth, it seemed—and moved forward to the crest of the hillock. The Russians halted, and from the thin scarlet line came a volley of musketry. The Russians wavered, recovered and began to move forward once more as a second volley was fired. A second time the Russians hesitated and the 93rd, eager to be among them, had to be checked by Campbell. 'Ninety-third! Ninety-third,' he shouted. 'Damn all that eagerness!'

The Highlanders steadied and a third volley was fired, accompanied by shots from the guns. This time the Russians wheeled to their left and galloped off towards Canrobert's Hill to await the main mass, leaving a number of riderless horses and several men killed and wounded—chiefly by the artillery. It was a trivial action and it had only temporarily relieved the threat to Balaclava because the main force of the Russians was still moving up the North Valley and swinging across the Causeway Heights.

While the Highlanders' action was taking place, Lucan had been driven off the Causeway and was heading down the slope to where Scarlett waited with the Heavies.[6] From their position on the lower ground they had not seen what Lucan had seen and what the Scots and the Turks could see, but now, Scarlett's 'Indian' aide, Lieutenant Alexander Elliot, glancing to his left, spotted the tips of the Russian lances as the Russian cavalry began to cross the ridge of the Causeway.

The short-sighted Scarlett had seen nothing, but a moment later, while Elliot was still wondering at the lance tips, the Russians' helmets also came into view and then the men themselves with their horses. At that moment Lord Lucan came thundering down from the Heights and Sergeant-Major Franks with the 5th Dragoon Guards heard one of his staff shout 'Scarlett! Scarlett! Look to your left!'

As it happened, as the eight squadrons of Heavies had formed up near the camp, they had placed themselves directly in the path of the Russians—one squadron of the Greys, one squadron of the Inniskillings and one squadron of the 5th Dragoon Guards in front—not two squadrons as Kinglake suggests—with the second squadron of the 5th and the second squadron of the Greys just behind.[7] No one was in any doubt about what to do. Lucan had been unimpressed by the Russian cavalry when he had seen them in action in the war of 1828 and he sent instructions to Hodge away beyond the left of the British line to charge the Russians with the 4th Dragoon Guards and ordered up the other squadron of the Inniskillings, who were away on the right, then rode back at full speed to Scarlett. For years afterwards there were arguments about who actually ordered the Heavies into action and both Lucan and Scarlett claimed the honour. Blunt says it was Lucan but, in fact, it seemed that Lucan's order was heard and obeyed by the Greys but not by the Inniskillings and the 5th who took their orders from Scarlett. Since both officers were intending the same thing, there was no confusion.

As Lucan rode up to Scarlett he was occupied with sorting

out his men. Expecting the Russian attack to come from the east up the valley, he had been to the south of a small ruined vineyard, in the worst possible position to face an attack from the north, and he was now wheeling and taking ground to the right to avoid the broken walls, tangled vines and unseen holes. The two commanders exchanged a few words as Scarlett explained what he was doing and received Lucan's approval and a promise that he would be supported with the rest of the Heavies.

The operation of taking fresh ground completed, the Heavies were once more facing the Russians—five squadrons, not three as Kinglake asserts.[8] The whole force numbered between five and six hundred, and they faced a mass of roughly 3,500 with a front three squadrons wide. According to Blunt, though without plumes, gauntlets and shoulder scales, they looked as if they were on parade.

By this time the whole of the Russian mass had crossed the ridge at a trot in a solid dark block almost square in shape, and began at a distance of a few hundred yards to take ground to the left with briskness and precision. As soon as they had given themselves room to move, they fronted once more on the tiny group of Heavies and then, to the sound of a trumpet, the huge mass of men began to advance down the slope, shaking the ground with the weight of their numbers. Their speed increased, their ranks opening more with every yard, while all the time, in apparent unconcern, the Heavy Brigade dressed its ranks, the officers of the Greys even with their backs to the enemy. Scarlett sat on his horse, studying the moving mass, then, just when it seemed they would be swept under, the Russian trumpets sounded again and they slowed down and finally halted by a dry ditch.

Ryjoff, the Russian commander, was probably concerned for the obstacle he saw in front and the Light Brigade's camp just beyond, a few of its tents still standing and a few sick and wounded horses still picketed, and the steadiness and indifference of the red-coated squadrons might also have made him feel that

181

they felt safe behind the ditch. As the Russians came to a stop they began apparently to throw out wings whose tips moved forward like horns. This was undoubtedly caused by unalert troopers caught unawares by the abrupt halt, but they looked as though they were waiting to envelop the little body of Englishmen when they moved forward.

It was one of the oddities of this strange battle that, owing to the contours of the ground, in the Light Brigade, only a few hundred yards away on the Russians' right, some men saw what was happening and some did not.[9] Cardigan had kept his first line mounted, but the second line had dismounted, and while Paget only became aware of the little action building up in front of them by sauntering on foot forty or fifty yards to his right, the mounted regiments could see everything, and Captain Morris, wise with the experience of battle, immediately spotted an opportunity for an attack on the halted Russians' flank, and wheeled the 17th Lancers and moved forward.

Never a horsemaster, Cardigan was to prove several times on this day that he was not a cavalry general either. According to Kinglake a bishop or a doctor of divinity would probably have been more competent to seize the right moment for a cavalry charge. He did not possess that special gift to choose the opportunity for action and it never occurred to him that here, right in front of his eyes, with the Russians halted, their flank towards him, was that occasion for glory he had been seeking all through the campaign. While his men instinctively prepared for action, he could only remember that he had been told to hold the position where he had been placed, and he called the 17th back, angrily saying they had been told not to move from where they were.

It was quite obvious by now to Scarlett that he was in danger of being overwhelmed so he sent his brigade major, Captain Connolly, to bring forward his supports on the enemy's left, and to the watchers above it seemed that he was delaying just too long to snatch the opportunity that the halted Russian mass presented. It seemed so to Lucan also. In a fury of frustration, he had waited for Cardigan's expected attack on the Russians' flank but, occupied with the Heavies and with the Light Brigade beyond his reach, he was unable to do a thing to urge him forward.[10] His aides were already busy bringing up the Heavies and he had no one to carry a message and, enraged and impotent, he could only get the Heavies moving before it was too late. More than once he ordered his trumpeter, Joy, to sound the charge, but no one took the slightest notice. The Heavies were about to attack uphill over ground impeded by picket ropes and tents and they were concerned with making sure they were in a compact group.

The observers on the uplands could see the whole scene clearly, the dark mass of Russians with the lines of scarlet-coated men in front of them. Only a few of the Russians were without grey greatcoats and these were wearing the pale-blue pelisse and jacket of hussars. The British soldiers, apart from the Greys in their bearskins, all wore helmets.

Just in front of the Greys now was a little knot of horsemen. Of the first two, one wore a dark blue coat and a helmet, and the other, apparently the staff officer, a cocked hat. As it happened the man with the white beard and moustaches in the helmet was Scarlett, while the man in the cocked hat was Elliot. It had been Elliot's intention to wear a forage cap as orders now permitted but Scarlett had refused to allow it. 'Damn the order!' he had said. 'My staff shall be properly dressed!' And because the chin-strap of his cocked hat was loose, Elliot had stuffed a large silk handkerchief into it to make it more firm on his head. Just behind them waited Scarlett's trumpeter, Trumpet-Major Thomas Monks, and his orderly, Sergeant James Shegog, of the 5th Dragoon Guards, an imperturbable giant of a man with tremendous skill as a swordsman. Scarlett's horse was a thoroughbred bay standing sixteen hands.

While they waited the 5th Dragoon Guards, on the left, were showing signs of setting off on their own and Scarlett had to keep waving them back with his sword. At this moment the distance between Scarlett and the Russians was about 400 yards and Scarlett was well aware that too much time had already been wasted because the Russians were beginning to discharge their carbines. It was a cavalry axiom that a charge should be received on the move because the weight of charging horses had the power to break up a mass, and he could see that the Russians were just beginning to move forward again. Accordingly, he dispensed with all the normal procedure and turned instead to his trumpeter, Monks, and said quite simply 'Sound the Charge.'

.6 Those damned Heavies!

WITH the high notes of the trumpets still hanging on the air, Scarlett began to advance. Normally it was usual for cavalry to advance first at a walk, the speed increasing through the trot and the gallop, but there had been no time for formalities and some of the squadrons were still finding it necessary to pick their way through the impedimenta of the Light Brigade's camp. In a few moments Scarlett was so far ahead Elliot drew his attention to their isolated position. Scarlett simply turned to the Greys and, waving his sword, shouted, 'Come on!' Though they began to make up ground as soon as they were clear, Scarlett was still 50 yards ahead when he scrambled across the ditch and reached the Russians. Because of the bad ground he was not able to get up any speed, while the men following him were cut down to a pace not much faster than a walk.[1]

Directly in front of him was a Russian officer but, judging from his cocked hat that Elliot and not Scarlett was the leader, this man chose him. It was fortunate for Scarlett because he was no swordsman and his poor eyesight was no help. His huge horse crashed past the Russian officer and wedged itself between two troop horses so that he found himself in the middle of the dark mass, whirling his sword with such enthusiasm that he remained untouched. Elliot evaded the Russian officer's thrust and drove his own sword through the Russian's body with such force that it went in to the hilt and, as he went past, whirled the Russian round in the saddle and dragged him to the ground. Shegog and Monks came close behind and, in a moment, because the Russians were still moving slowly forward, they were all engulfed.

The first British casualty of the action was Colonel Darby Griffiths, of the Greys, who was struck in the head by one of the Russian carbine shots as his regiment moved off after Scarlett.

As he reeled in the saddle, his horse swerved, momentarily hampering his men, and Colonel Dalrymple White, of the Inniskillings, was the first after Scarlett's group into the Russian mass. Despite his injury, Griffiths, who had lost his bearskin, was close behind. There had been a long friendship between the Greys and the Inniskillings dating from Waterloo when they had charged side by side in the Union Brigade, and the Greys gave a low moan as they floundered over the ditch and crashed into the Russians, while the Inniskillings went in with a wild cheer, smashing their way into the halted horsemen. Struggling through the remains of the Light Brigade camp, the 5th Dragoon Guards were delayed a little and had several horses brought down by picket ropes, among them those of Captain Campbell and Cornet Neville, but as the three regiments smashed home, the Russians opened their files and as they edged their mounts away the watchers on the heights saw the red-coated soldiers, one body of them distinguished by their bearskins, the other by their burnished helmets, bury deeper and deeper into the dark mass.

Fighting in knots, in some parts of the column the combatants were so close together the horses could not move. One man, whose mount had been killed by a carbine shot as they reached the Russians, scrambled furiously to his feet. 'Bloody wars,' he said. 'This won't do,' and he dragged a Russian from his saddle, killed him, and, vaulting to the horse's back, continued after his regiment; while another, attacked by three men, disabled one, chased away the second and as he attacked the third, his sword point broke off so he had to knock him off his horse with the hilt.

Sword rang on sword, the horses keeping their heads down to avoid the whirling weapons, but there was little chance to use carbine or pistol in the crowded mêlée and even bare hands were used to knock or drag men from their saddles. The noise of equipment and the clash of weapons was so loud it could be heard with the shouts and curses on the ridge. For the most part the Russians fought in silence except for a deep long-drawn sound that was more like a moan than a cheer, and a constant hissing between cages of clenched teeth. Close-wedged in—'it was all push, wheel, frenzy, strike'—Scarlett received five wounds, all of them slight, and his helmet was stove in, but Elliot, wielding a blade of greater length than normal, was fighting not only Russians but his own horse which was lashing out in all directions. He received the point of a sword in the forehead, while another Russian divided his face with a slash. A third cut through his cocked hat and the sabre of a fourth struck him behind the ear. Only the thick doubled handkerchief inside his hat saved his life, and, although he lost consciousness for a while, he remained in the saddle, held there by the closeness of the throng around him, and emerged 'deluged with blood'. Griffiths, without his bearskin, was also covered with blood from his head wound, and Colonel White's helmet was cut through but, though he hardly noticed this, he was able to take stock of his opponents and saw a fair-haired Russian officer of about seventeen fall to the ground with his head cloven in two.

By this time the projecting right wing of the Russians had wheeled completely round and the troopers had their backs to the second line, and the second squadron of the 5th Dragoon Guards smashed into their rear. By now Lucan had reached the spot from which the Greys had advanced and was launching the supports. The Duke of Wellington had always said 'I prefer to appoint an officer to a command who keeps out of the thick of it', and this Lucan had wisely done. He had sent in the charge of the first squadrons and rightly left it to the brigadier in command to lead it while he remained in a position where he could send in reserves. He had already sent an order to Colonel Hodge, of the 4th Dragoon Guards, and was now heading towards the Royals. Still far away on the left without instructions, it was clear already to Colonel Yorke, however, that he was going to be needed. He saw the right wing of the enemy envelop the first line and just as Lucan galloped up, shouting and gesturing, someone cried out 'By God, the Greys are cut off! Gallop! Gallop!' Without orders, the trumpets sounded and, forming line on the move, the regiment leapt forward and plunged into the broken right wing of the enemy mass. On the other flank Captain Connolly, Scarlett's brigade major, had ridden to the second squadron of the Inniskillings who charged the left flank of the Russians across good ground, free from the impedimenta of the cavalry camp. They smashed into the back of the inward-wheeling wing and so tightly did they become locked Connolly found his arms held by the dead body of a Russian who had fallen across his saddle.

The 4th Dragoon Guards, under Hodge, had moved boldly forward to a position on the enemy's right flank behind the extended wing and, using the expression he had used as a boy when coxswain of the Eton boat, Hodge ordered 'Hard all across.' The 4th smashed into the Russian right and drove straight across the mass from right to left, and the chatty Forrest, at last with something to write about that he could truly vouch for, was so busy he 'scarcely saw anybody to recognise them'. Other men of the brigade who had been away from their regiments on detached duties began to join in individually, among them two regimental butchers conspicuous in their white canvas clothing, and a few of those men of the Light Brigade who, able to see what was happening and unable to resist the opportunity of at last getting to grips with the enemy, had sneaked away. The red-coated squadrons seemed to those on the Ridge to have been overwhelmed but now it was noticed that the Russians were actually beginning to give before them. The men at the rear were breaking away and, as the pressure from behind eased, the whole mass began to heave and the next instant it was seen that the column was crumbling.

Apart from the few who had sneaked away to join the charge, the Light Brigade were still sitting in their saddles 500 yards away, their front ranks able to see everything that happened. Chafing at the continued inaction, they had begun to grow excited and muttered to be let loose, and only discipline held them back. Even at this late stage the opportunity to gather a little glory was not gone and if Cardigan had taken up the attack from the Heavies he could have made Balaclava one of the greatest ever of mounted fights, and covered himself with fame. But, nothing but a parade-ground martinet, he merely rode restlessly up and down, cursing his luck as the Russians began to edge away. 'Those damned Heavies,' he said. 'They will have the laugh on us this day.'

Angry as the Light Brigade's opportunity began to fade, from among the 17th Lancers Captain Morris moved over to his brigadier. 'My lord,' he said, 'are we not going to charge the flying enemy?'

'No,' Cardigan replied, 'we have orders to remain here.'

'But, my lord,' Morris insisted, 'it is our positive duty to follow up this advantage.'

'No,' Cardigan repeated, 'we must remain here.'

Morris begged him to allow some sort of pursuit. 'Do, my lord,' he said, 'allow me to charge them with the 17th. See, my lord, they are in disorder.'

Cardigan could only repeat what he had already said. 'No, no, sir,' he said petulantly, 'we must not stir from here.'

In a fury, Morris turned to officers sitting in their saddles nearby. 'Gentlemen,' he said, 'you are witnesses of my request.'

To Private Wightman, with the 17th Lancers, it was clear what was going on. Though Cardigan afterwards denied that Morris had made any request, Wightman saw Morris 'speaking earnestly' to him and heard Cardigan's 'hoarse, sharp' refusal. As Morris fell back, Wightman saw him slapping his leg with his sword, saying 'My God, my God, what a chance we are losing!'

It was already too late, however, and the Russians began to edge away. The Heavies at once began to re-form. Despite the fierceness of the mêlée the officers had never lost control of their squadrons. The Greys had pushed clean through the Russians and Alexander Miller, the adjutant, a man famous for the loudness of his voice, now held up his sword and began to roar 'Rally! Rally, the Greys!' and at once they began to drive together. Cornet Lenox Prendergast, on a mountainous charger that raised him above the heads of the Russians, and White, of the Inniskillings, also had their swords in the air and the scattered groups of men began to form a united front and started to hack their way back through the breaking column. The Royals had not pressed their attack too deeply and Yorke had already rallied his men, and now the other regiments followed suit, their discipline still excellent. With Scarlett at the far side of the Russian mass, it was Hodge who seized the first two trumpeters he saw and caused them to sound the rally. While the infuriated Light Brigade, held back by Cardigan, could only look on, no more than a few isolated men pursued the Russians as they began to move down the valley towards Canrobert's Hill.

Disgusted at Cardigan's supineness, Lucan sent him an angry message. Carried by Lord Bingham, it ordered the Light Brigade to sweep round the Russians' right flank to pick up stragglers. It also pointed out how extremely disappointed Lucan was at not having had the support of the Light Brigade in the Heavies' action and reminded him that, when his divisional general was attacking in front, it was his duty to support him by a flank attack.

As the Light Brigade moved off, the ever-eager John Blunt, no cavalryman and not even armed, was returning from his mission to rally the Turks. He had watched the Heavies' battle and as the Russian stragglers streamed away down the valley to the east he found himself directly in their path. One of them, a gigantic Cossack, charged at him, whirling his sword over his head, and, without a weapon to defend himself, he could only duck and kick his pony into its top speed. The blow fell on the animal's back and his opponent swerved away to be cut down by one of the Heavies. As the pony came to a halt and stood trembling, Blunt dismounted and saw that it was bleeding from a deep gash across the backbone. He relieved it of its saddle but it was so badly wounded he had to have it shot.

As he set off on foot to find Lord Lucan, the Russian cavalry, pursued by heavy fire from Brandling's battery, had now begun to swing northwards and were crossing the ridge of the Causeway Heights with their artillery. Blunt found Lucan pleased with the Heavies' work. The high regard for Russian cavalry Nolan had acquired on his visit to Russia had not proved as sound as the impression Lucan had formed so many years before. Their lack of dash had been borne out by their hesitation at the Bulganak and the Alma and on outpost skirmishes ever since, and the Heavies had fought a very skilful and well-disciplined little action.

Campbell rode up to the Greys as they began to re-form and, to the annoyance of the rest of the Heavies, seemed to consider his fellow Scots were the only troops involved. 'Greys, gallant Greys!' he said, taking off his hat. 'I am sixty-one years old and if I were young again I should be proud to be in your ranks.'

He then turned to Lucan, and declared to him that no one could have done better, while the French also sent a tribute of their enthusiastic admiration, and aides came down from the Ridge with messages of congratulation. Among them was Nolan and, as he rode among the excited men, he could hardly have been pleased by what he heard of the effectiveness of the British swords. They had bounced off the thick Russian greatcoats 'as if they had been indiarubber' while the Russian shakos had been as firm against them as if they had been brass helmets. The weapons of the Greys had even bent. The Russian swords seem to have been even blunter, however, and Elliot's silk handkerchief had been sufficient to save him from a mortal wound, while one trooper of the 4th Dragoon Guards, classed as 'slightly wounded', had 15 head cuts, none of them more than skin deep.

Hardinge, the aide whose message had quite by chance placed the Heavies in the path of the Russians, appeared in front of Russell, his tunic in disorder, the straps of his overalls burst, but flushed and triumphant. 'Did you see it all?' he demanded. 'Was it not glorious?' It was indeed, and the losses had been trivial considering the ferocity of the fight. There were only 78 killed and wounded, among the latter Cornet Neville, whose horse had been brought down as they were pushing through the camp. While he was trying to escape on foot he had been surrounded by Cossacks and received three lance wounds. Two of his men had hurried to his assistance, Private Abbott dismounting and standing over him, holding his horse with one hand and parrying blows with the other. He killed two Russians and hung on until help came, then he carried the mortally wounded Neville on his back to the surgeons.

As the Heavies regrouped and the Light Brigade began to move back there was another of those strange pauses in the battle. What had been a dangerous threat to Balaclava had been changed at once by Campbell's spirited defence and Scarlett's charge. They were no longer in danger of losing the base and the Russians had been driven entirely out of the South Valley. Their cavalry, in fact, had now retreated down the length of the North Valley, and had unlimbered their 12-gun battery at the eastern or bottom end in a line of eight, with a group of two to each side. They still had infantry and artillery on the Fedioukhine Hills on the north side of the North Valley, however, on the Causeway where they still held the captured redoubts, and along the spur projecting into the North Valley.

At this point, according to Kinglake's unctuous account, Raglan's 'swift instinct' decided that the Russian troops along the Causeway Heights had become unsupported and isolated and were likely to retreat on the application of a little pressure, and decided that there was a chance of recovering the redoubts and with them the command of the Woronzoff Road. In fact, the Russians were by no means unsupported and were well within range of the guns on the Fedioukhine Hills, as Blunt was to discover, and it seems more likely that Raglan was occupied with the fact that he was on the point of losing several of his guns, something which his hero, Wellington, had never done. In the minds of Wellington's soldiers the loss of guns had constituted defeat and he began to worry now what to do to prevent the Russians dragging away the captured naval guns from the redoubts.

The divisions of infantry he had ordered forward ought by this time to have been in action along the Causeway but, though the First Division had reached the plain, the Fourth Division was still dawdling. As he had left the plateau, Cathcart had received orders from Airey to recapture the lost redoubts, but he was in his most bull-like mood, and as he stared at the redoubts he was supposed to attack he was startled at their isolation. He couldn't believe his eyes and when Ewart pointed out Canrobert's Hill he said, 'It's impossible that there can be one as far away as that!'

Convinced there must be some mistake, he continued to dawdle in a position approaching the fourth redoubt where he was protected by swelling ground. It was now almost 11 o'clock and three and a half hours since the Turks had been driven off Canrobert's Hill.

There was no need at this point, however, to launch any unprepared attack along the Causeway. The enemy was not moving forward and was not even removing the captured guns.[2] Raglan's later claim that they were was quite wrong, and there was every chance—indeed there was already every sign—that the redoubts would eventually be evacuated because when the 1st Division had begun to appear the Russians had immediately abandoned Three and Four Redoubts, blowing up the magazines. With several hours of daylight left, there was plenty of time to bring up artillery and direct the First Division to move forward with Cathcart's men, but Raglan was not a disciple of Wellington's for nothing. The fact that Wellington had never lost a gun, like so many other of Wellington's achievements, had become a precept of war to him and he was growing impatient. Losing his habitual serenity, he turned to Airey and directed him to send the third order of the day to Lucan—'Cavalry to advance and take advantage of any opportunity to recover the heights. They will be supported by the infantry which have been ordered to advance on two fronts.' This was Raglan's version, though he kept no copy. Lucan's copy read slightly differently. After the word 'ordered' there was a full stop and the word 'Advance' began a new sentence. Either way the message, dashed on to paper in Airey's darting script, remained hopelessly vague.

The cavalry were still watching the approaches to Balaclava and had no view of what was happening in the North Valley, and the two fronts mentioned in the message meant nothing at all to Lord Lucan. There was no sign of any infantry from where he was and he had no idea what was happening now in the redoubts. So much of what took place and was to take place that day is explained by the broken nature of the ground. Men on the Causeway had no conception of what was happening in the valleys while the men in the valleys had no knowledge of what was happening on the Causeway, and only those members of the headquarters staff round Raglan on the Sapouné Ridge had a complete view of the battlefield. But from this position five hundred feet above, the hills and curves of the valley floor were flattened out and Raglan quite overlooked the fact that what was below him was above the cavalry.

Neglecting the golden rule for any general to put himself in the place of the subordinate, he had sent an order that was 'quixotic in the extreme' and quite incomprehensible to anyone who could not see what he could see. To Lucan it seemed it could only be executed if the whole army advanced. An attack by cavalry along the broken ground of the narrow Causeway against the Russian guns and four battalions of Russian infantry would have been disastrous, while an attempt in strength down the North Valley with a swing south would have involved them in an equally disastrous attack over the top of the spur. Like Cathcart convinced that he had not yet received all his orders, it wasn't hard for Lucan to assume that he was to await the arrival of the infantry so that the advance on the two fronts—whatever they were—could be made in unison.

The officer who brought the order seems to have been unable to enlighten him as to what was intended. Aides are supposed to know what their chief is thinking and there was plenty of time, but more than likely, as on other occasions, Raglan simply forgot to make his wishes known. Since there was quite clearly nothing happening now in the South Valley, and knowing Raglan and still determined not to be accused of mistaking orders, Lucan made the aide lead the cavalry through the narrow gap between Number Six Redoubt and the slopes of the Sapouné Ridge into the North Valley where he might see better what was happening.[3] Down the valley and on either side were 24,000 Russians, and he drew his men up again, with the Light Brigade, who had not yet been in action, in front, and the Heavy Brigade, who were still involved in sorting out their mixed ranks, at a point just behind them and to their right. He was in a confident mood and Trumpeter Farquharson, of the 13th Light Dragoons, heard him say to Cardigan as he rode past, 'Well, Cardigan, we have had some fighting this morning. The Heavies did splendidly.'

He was undoubtedly taking a dig at his hesitant brother-in-law but Cardigan was in no mood for jesting. He didn't like their new position and sent Fitz Maxse to point out that there were batteries on each side of them and a heavy battery in front and that the hills were lined with infantrymen. Lucan said he could not help him, he had had his orders, and they remained where they were.

A quarter of an hour passed and still the infantry did not appear. They were not likely to. In the excitement, no one had thought to tell them they were to advance in conjunction with the cavalry and neither the Duke of Cambridge nor Cathcart had received any further orders since they had left the Chersonese.[4]

Twenty-five more minutes passed and Lucan still waited. He still could not see what was happening on the Causeway Heights and no one arrived from the staff to make up for the lack of knowledge of the aide who had brought the message. He still could not believe that Raglan expected him to attack on his own. Again and again—at the Bulganak, at the Alma, in all the skirmishings to the east—his instructions had always prevented him acting on his own initiative. Only that morning, in fact, Raglan had shown that his views had not changed by withdrawing him from his excellent supporting position on Campbell's left to another where his value had been so inadequate the Russians had immediately seized their opportunity to attack. And as he well knew from his personal reconnaissance before the Heavies' charge, the captured redoubts were almost inaccessible to cavalry, way above their heads and in broken ground. Number One was beyond reach on the crown of Canrobert's Hill, which was linked to the Russian-held hills to the east, while Numbers Two and Three would have had to be attacked uphill in the face of that very infantry and artillery which earlier in the day had forced him and his guns to retire.

As he waited for the expected infantry to come up, it never occurred to the men high above him on the Sapouné Ridge that the order he had received could have been unintelligible. It seemed simply that he was dawdling. He had been given the name Lord Look-on and he appeared to be merely behaving in character. Raglan grew more and more angry. He was desperately concerned that he might lose his precious guns. The stump of his arm moved violently, and just as he was growing more and more agitated and in a perfect state to do something rash, someone among the staff called out 'By Jove, they are taking away the guns!' Teams of artillery horses were seen moving along the Causeway but, since the captured guns were not taken away before dark, it is more than probable they belonged to the Russian guns on the Causeway and the spur.[5] Nevertheless, the exclamation was enough for Raglan.

He turned to Airey and gave him his instructions, and Airey translated them in his hasty scrawl into a message, using a pencil on a piece of paper with his sabretache as a desk. He read it back to Raglan who dictated one or two additional words. This was the famous fourth order, of which the original still exists. The paper is thin and the wording, in Airey's pointed scrawl, ran 'Lord Raglan wishes the cavalry to advance rapidly to the front

—follow the enemy and try to prevent the enemy carrying away the guns. Troop Horse Artillery may accompany. French Cavalry is on your left. Immediate.' It was signed 'Airey'.

Calthorpe was the next aide-de-camp for duty and Airey had actually placed the order in his hand when Raglan intervened. The quickest route to the valley was by a narrow track down a precipitous face of the ridge and it needed a good horseman if the order were to be carried quickly to Lucan. Nolan, one of the finest riders in the army, was at hand and bursting to do something to end the stalemate, and Raglan indicated he should go instead. Nolan jumped at the chance and snatched the paper from Airey's hand. For a moment or two longer he was delayed while he received careful instructions from both Raglan and Airey as to what was intended,[6] then, as he turned, Raglan called out to him, 'Tell Lord Lucan the cavalry is to attack immediately.'

Riding a troop horse of the 13th Light Dragoons, Nolan hesitated only a moment, then he swung away and began to scramble down the cliff at breakneck speed.

17 There are your guns!

DRIVEN by his obsessions about cavalry, Nolan was also possessed of a nervous excitement that was always likely to lead him wrong, and he had been under considerable mental strain all morning, especially when he had seen Cardigan fail to take his opportunity before the Heavy Brigade's charge. Nothing, he had always said, could withstand the speed and power of light cavalry, yet he had been forced to watch them remain idle while the heavy men on heavy horses that he so despised had carried away all the laurels.

Suffering from an anguished fear that once again opportunities would be allowed to slip by, he was frantic with impatience. He had reconnoitred the movements of the enemy along the Causeway Heights but otherwise his contribution to the battle had been slight and he was dying to do something. Yet so impulsive was his personality and so 'wild a devotion to one idea' did he hold, he could never be a safe courier for Raglan's schemes,[1] because his enthusiasm had never been tempered by personal experience in a cavalry action. Though most people had been pleased enough to listen to him, a few had disagreed strongly, but here, now, in front of him in the plain, was a perfect opportunity to prove his ideas right. Many years before, as an instructor at Maidstone Barracks, he had drawn on the wall of the quartermaster's store a hypothetical plan of a situation cavalry might have to face. There had been guns to the right and left and ahead,[2] and before him now was exactly the same situation, and in his obsession he still could not—as he could not on that earlier occasion—imagine anything but success.

It had always been his belief, as he had written in one of his books, that despite the improved fire of the present day, volleys could never be repeated 'sufficiently quick' to inflict a loss on cavalry if their attack was delivered at speed, and he was in no doubt whatsoever as to the outcome of an attack.

*

Higginson, the adjutant of the Grenadier Guards, moving down to the plain, had passed Nolan returning after carrying his message of congratulation to Scarlett, and had felt even then that he was 'in the stress of some great excitement and had lost self command', and now Fred Maxse, the brother of Cardigan's aide, saw him riding down to Lucan 'eager and full of life . . . anxious and determined to make him do something with the cavalry', and he recalled how indignant he had been at the little the cavalry had done in the Crimea and how bitter he had been against their divisional general.

While he was descending the slope, Lucan was engaged in watching the Russians on the Fedioukhine Hills, who were probably nearer to him where he sat with his division than were the only troops he could see on his right—those posted along the spur just to the north of the Causeway. The Russians on the Fedioukhines appeared to him to be making threatening movements, and because of this he had retired the 4th Light Dragoons behind a small knoll and faced them north-east to deal with any attack coming from that direction. With him again by this time was the indefatigable Blunt who saw everything that happened.

He had still been on foot when he had found Lucan, who had accordingly directed his orderly to catch him one of the Russian chargers which were cantering about riderless. After several attempts a large horse was brought up and though Blunt didn't much like the look of it, the orderly recommended it as a good mount and he climbed gingerly into the saddle. Though it had a hard mouth, it seemed steady enough and gave him no trouble, and Lucan sent him off with another message to Rustum Pasha. When he returned he and Lucan and some of his staff rode to the top of a small hillock between Redoubt Number Four and Redoubt Number Five from where they could see the Guards and other regiments still arriving from the plateau. Assuming that these were the infantry with whom he was to act, Lucan sent off several of his staff with messages to the cavalry and all who were left with him were Charteris, his orderly and Blunt.

The Light Brigade were by their horses, dismounted now, the officers swapping biscuits, hard-boiled eggs and rum. Paget, who had had differences in the past with his second-in-command, Major Douglas Halkett, decided that this was not the time for disagreement and offered his flask. He had just lit a cigar when Nolan was seen approaching and the order came to mount. Private Wightman, waiting in the ranks of the 17th, saw the aide, whom they all knew well by sight, arrive at a gallop, 'an excitable man in an excited state'. He emerged through the interval between the Lancers and the 13th Light Dragoons who were on their right, his horse blown and lathered. To Private Pennington he seemed 'eager for the fray'.

'Where is Lord Lucan?' he demanded.

Morris pointed out the divisional commander who was near the Heavies, then, because he, too, had no idea what was happening in the redoubts, he asked, 'What is it to be, Nolan? Are we going to charge?' Beside himself with delight, Nolan was already off in the direction of Lucan, 'You will see, you will see,' he flung over his shoulder.

He reined in alongside Lucan and handed him the order. Lucan opened and read it. Like the third order, it was completely obscure and terse to the point of being useless. Like everyone else in the cavalry, he could still see nothing of what was happening in the redoubts.[3] From where he sat, not a single enemy soldier was in view beyond those on the spur and the Fedioukhine Hills, and he read the order carefully while Nolan waited impatiently beside him. To Lucan the order seemed quite absurd.

Certainly the French cavalry was on his left. Everybody could see the Chasseurs d'Afrique, sent forward by Canrobert, moving up in their rear but nothing in the message indicated what they were about to do. Indeed, they appeared to be advancing in the direction the front ranks of the Light Brigade were facing, and it seemed that once more someone else, not them, was to have a chance at the enemy. In fact, Cardigan's aide, Lockwood, Mrs. Duberly's admirer, impatient and angry at Cardigan's hesitation, had turned to Fitz Maxse and observed acidly that it looked as though the French would get the chance of the next attack while the Light Brigade would again be foiled.

Lucan studied the order once more. It was vague in the extreme. In his position 'to the front' could only mean down the valley. From his own reconnaissance he knew the Russians were in the redoubts, but so far as he could see, they were not carrying away any guns from them. It surely couldn't mean that, against all the usages of war, he was to attack the artillery down the valley with cavalry; the whole of his small force was not sufficient for what Raglan seemed to be asking of it. In this message also there was suddenly no reference to infantry, and it was a known axiom that when charging artillery cavalry should have support as they were unable to capture guns on their own. He read the order again with much consideration—even consternation. It said 'Immediate', which seemed to indicate that there was no time to send to the Sapouné Ridge for clarification.

As one French authority commented, the order was 'in a not very military form', and there was plenty of room for misinterpretation. But, when he was approached, there was no enlightenment from Nolan, who was behaving in a manner that was 'excited and theatrical'. According to Fortescue, one of the greatest of military historians, Lucan was 'acknowledged to possess more than ordinary ability, but his warnings of the previous day had been neglected, his perfectly correct disposition —carefully concerted with Sir Colin Campbell—had twice been upset by superior order, with results that must almost certainly have been fatal if the Russian cavalry had known its work; and now had come a fresh staff officer with an order which, not in itself too clear, had been further obscured by that staff officer's excitability'.

What follows has often been called a fierce argument and was suggested by Kinglake and all who followed him as the reason why Lucan failed to get a reasonable answer from Nolan. Blunt, however, says only that it was a 'discussion' and suggests that Lucan did not lose his temper. He indicated the pointlessness of advancing against guns with cavalry and Nolan, blinded by his own theories and glad to hit at the hated Lord Look-on, snapped back triumphantly. 'Lord Raglan's orders,' he said, 'were that the cavalry should attack immediately.'

Lucan was even more bewildered. A new demand had now been made. Up to now the word 'attack' had not been used and Nolan's manner was becoming insolent.

He stared about him. Twice that morning he had been painstaking about getting his orders clear so that there should be no accusation of misunderstanding them and now he tried a third time.

'Attack, sir?' he demanded. 'Attack what? What guns, sir?'

In a sentence that was to have tragic results, Nolan flung back his head, threw out his arm towards the bottom of the North Valley and 'in the most disrespectful but significant manner' cried, 'There, my lord, is your enemy! There are your guns!'

For a hundred years and more, historians have been trying to decide what Nolan meant. Kinglake, who wrote eight volumes of history, trying hard all the time to salvage Raglan's reputation, claimed that the gesture was merely a taunt and not an attempt to give guidance, yet he pointed out elsewhere that it was always Raglan's habit to see that his aides gave just such guidance as Nolan appeared to be giving now. Judging by the observations of the men who knew him, there seems little doubt that from the moment he left Raglan's side Nolan had been under a complete misapprehension as to what was to be done.

Calthorpe, who liked him, considered him over-bold and it is more than likely that he was so excited at the possibility of bringing about the light cavalry action he had dreamed of for so long he had not paid sufficient attention to what Airey had told him. It is also likely that he had assumed all along that what was to be attacked was the cavalry he had watched with such fury from the Ridge as they were allowed to escape before the Light Brigade only a short time before. Nolan was well aware of the opportunity which had been lost and had suffered agonies at Cardigan's inaction and he had jumped to a completely wrong conclusion. If he read it, even the message he carried was unlikely to indicate anything else to him because he had not read the third order and there is nothing to indicate that he thought other than what his gesture indicated.

According to officers who watched the scene, Lucan should have put him under arrest at once for his behaviour to a senior general. He had been angry with Raglan for a long time and now he had been handed an infamous and futile order which seemed to indicate he was to take his division to certain destruction—and in an insolent manner—by a mere captain!

Nevertheless, a firm believer in the chain of command, once again—according to Blunt, who was alongside him—he held his temper in check. He appeared, Blunt said, 'to be surprised and irritated at the impetuous and disrespectful attitude and tone of Captain Nolan and looked at him sternly, but made no answer'. Watched by Brandling's gunners, who could see everything that happened, after some hesitation he turned his back and, followed by Nolan and his staff and still glancing in bewilderment at the message,[4] rode across to Cardigan who was sitting in the saddle in front of the 13th Light Dragoons. The two men had detested each other for years and ever since the campaign had started Lucan had been plagued by Cardigan's idiocy, while Cardigan had smarted with resentment at the way Lucan had taken away from him what he had always considered was his independent command. Not speaking, they had more than once exchanged cold letters criticising each other but, on this occasion, with so much hanging on their actions and watched by Nolan and their staffs[5] they behaved absolutely correctly towards each other. Holding the message in his hand, Lucan informed Cardigan of its contents and ordered him to advance down the North Valley with the Light Brigade, while he himself followed in support with the Heavy Brigade.

From the ranks of the 13th Light Dragoons James Lamb noticed that Cardigan looked 'sort of queer' as he glanced in the direction they were to go but there was little discussion about the meaning of the message. There would not have been much point. It would have revealed nothing. Neither of them could see what Raglan could see, and Nolan, still there to enlighten them,[6] had made plain what was intended.

For once Cardigan made no issue of the matter but he did point out the dangers, as he had done not long before. 'Certainly, sir,' he said, behaving with his usual formal manner towards his commanding officer, 'but allow me to point out to you that the Russians have a battery in the valley to our front, and batteries and riflemen on both sides.'

Lucan shrugged his shoulders. 'I know it,' he said, 'but Lord Raglan will have it. We have no choice but to obey.' Cardigan argued no further and Lucan instructed him to advance 'very steadily and keep his men well in hand'. It was his intention that they should move cautiously and he told Cardigan that, to narrow the front of the brigade, he wished the 11th Hussars to move back to form a second line between the 17th Lancers and the 13th Light Dragoons and the two regiments of the rear line, which would thus become a third. This would mean that the brigade was in a more compact form and that after the impact of the first line there would be successive lines to keep up the pressure. Cardigan reacted angrily, because the 11th Hussars were his own regiment and he was anxious to see them in the van.

Lucan ignored him and he turned away, as well aware of the suicidal nature of the order as anyone. 'Here goes the last of the

Brudenells,' he said aloud. As they parted company, Colonel Shewell, of the 8th, driven by his dour covenanting sense of duty from his sick bed, had just appeared, galloping up at the last moment, determined his regiment should not go into action without him. 'Hello,' one of his men said. 'Here comes the colonel! How about the Old Woman now?' Shewell's first reactions were typical. Noticing at once that some of the men had taken out their pipes and were smoking, he insisted on them putting them away. 'The thing is inconceivable,' he snorted, and when, a few moments later, he thought he saw them again trying to smoke, he insisted on their names being taken. Among them was Sergeant Williams, who, despite his protests of innocence, was ordered to give up his sword, belt and carbine and fall out.

As Cardigan rode across to his men, Paget, uncomfortable after Shewell's anger, was beginning to worry about his cigar. He thought he might be setting a bad example, yet he had no wish to throw away an excellent smoke. While he was trying to decide what to do, Cardigan arrived. 'Lord George,' he said, 'we are ordered to make an attack to the front. You will take command of the second line, and I expect your best support—mind, your best support.' He seemed excited and repeated the last sentence twice very loudly so that Paget, faintly irritated by his insistence, replied in kind.

'You shall have it, my lord,' he said, and, guessing like the rest of them what lay ahead, decided he might just as well keep his cigar. Cardigan now galloped back to his troops, who were still drawn up in two lines, the first comprising the 13th Light Dragoons, the 17th Lancers and the 11th Hussars, the second the 4th Light Dragoons and the 8th Hussars, less one troop which was acting as escort to Lord Raglan under Duberly. With the 8th was Jemmy, a rough-haired terrier, a pet of the officers' mess which followed them everywhere. They were 673 strong, scarcely one effective regiment, and in Roger Fenton's photographs, with the present-day fashion for facial hair, they look

205

surprisingly of the 20th century. The officers have the air of confidence that comes from wealth but there was no lack of pride in the bearing of their men. They were a well-assorted lot: Morris an ardent, intelligent, studious soldier of great experience; Lord George Paget, a son of Wellington's cavalry leader at Waterloo; Shewell, renowned as an example of Victorian piety; Douglas, tall, handsome, a friend of Paget's and for a long time the long-suffering second-in-command to Cardigan. Captain Oldham, recently put under arrest by Lucan, was in command of the 13th Light Dragoons.

The mixture was much the same in the Heavies behind, from the harassed, unambitious, depressed, complaining, snobbish Hodge, with his miniature stature and his worry that he would be 'caught in a brevet' and become a general at the cost of his lieutenant-colonelcy, to Yorke, of the Royals, brisk and keen-eyed for an opportunity. There was the usual mixture of junior officers, too, from the easy-going Forrest to the modest and painstaking Sir William Gordon and the intelligent, industrious Portal; from the blasphemous to the pious like Edward Seager, whose sabretache contained his wife's and his children's pictures, the hair of one of the children, and his mother's gift of a prayer book and testament; from the lightweights to the heavyweights like Alexander Dunn, of the 11th, whose sword was more than the regulation length, and Major Low, of the 4th Light Dragoons, another vast man of 15 stone and a great swordsman, with the long yellow moustaches of a Viking, who was to penetrate farther down the valley than any other man; from the worried Percy Smith who, not yet having had the opportunity to look for the lost iron wrist-guard for his crippled hand, was about to advance on the enemy virtually unarmed, to the irrepressible youngsters Cornet Fisher, whom nothing ever depressed, the fair-haired boyish Cornet Archibald Cleveland, a nephew of the recently dead Major Willett, who had been on the point of selling out when he had inherited a fortune at the outbreak of war but had elected to go with his men instead, and Cornet

Clowes, who had the 'dignified composure of a very big dog . . . noticing a very little one'.

Their men were much the same and far from being the product of the rookeries of the poor. Photographs of the survivors taken years later show them as neatly dressed decent men full of self-respect. There were the usual rogues, of course, but there were several who were the sons of officers too impoverished to buy them their commissions and were trying to win them the hard way, several who were to become wealthy, several who were to be awarded the Victoria Cross, and several who left colourful accounts of what they were shortly to endure. Many of them, neglected like old soldiers before and since, were to end their days in the workhouse or on charity of other sorts, but two, Private Pennington and Private Spring, the deserter, were to enter the theatre, Pennington to become famous as an actor; another, Corporal Kilvert, was to become the mayor of Wednesbury; another an official with the United States War Department in Washington. They ran through the erudite types like Trumpet-Major George Loy Smith, of the 11th, Private Melrose, of the Lancers, an expert on Shakespeare, and Private Wightman, brought up and educated within sound of the trumpet, through the whole gamut of impertinence, roguery and rigidness. There were good-looking Sergeant-Major Fowler, of the 4th Light Dragoons, Sergeant-Major Charles Wooden, of the 17th, an unpopular man of German extraction who still spoke with a strong accent, ex-India men like John Lee and like Penn, who had exchanged from the 3rd Light Dragoons immediately on his return to England so he could go back East. There were the ambitious like Trumpeter John Brown, who was to end his life a colonel, the sober like William Fletcher and Christopher Spain, whose brother, with the 4th Dragoon Guards, had died of cholera, and Peter Marsh, of the 17th; and at the other end of the scale the knaves like William Kirk, a lively, aggressive character with a taste for liquor, the deserter, Spring, who like a few others had left his regiment—not because he disliked the army but because he felt he could do better in another—and the hard-swearers like Private Dudley, and the dregs like Hodge's Private Burbidge, 'a terrible old drunkard'. There were several sets of brothers and they were all irreplaceable. Himself a newcomer, Pennington was well aware that he was surrounded by many men who had served fifteen years with the colours and by few who had served less than six or seven.

They were not looking at their best, however, because draggled plumes had been discarded, and busbies, jackets and overalls were patched and discoloured by the hard wear they had had since their arrival in the East. There were rents in sleeves and jackets and some of the gold lace was tarnished, while their shirts were 'rotting off their backs'. They were largely in blue, the Lancers—always a drabber unit since they had been raised by one of Wolfe's lieutenants at Quebec and their uniform had been designed as a gesture of mourning for Wolfe—the darkest block, their death's-head badges hidden under the oilskin covers that cased their square-topped lance caps. The shakos of the dragoons were also cased and shoulder scales and epaulettes had long since been left off. Because of the cold, the pelisses of the 11th were worn as extra garments, but the 8th had only their jackets, their pelisses having been lost en route east. Only occasional touches of red stood out—on busbies and on the overalls of the 11th and the collars and cuffs of the 4th Light Dragoons—while the white facings on the two remaining regiments hadn't seen pipeclay for some time and were grey and stained.

The horses were gaunt, hangdog and half-starved and, suffering from want of grooming and good forage, had a shaggy, tucked-in look, while the squadrons as a whole had a shrunken appearance after the sickness which had depleted their ranks. Morale was high, however, and they were itching to be at the enemy. A private of the 13th Light Dragoons, who had been acting as butcher, had been found drunk at the beginning of the battle and had been arrested and placed in the guard tent, but now he broke out and rejoined the ranks of his regiment, while a Welshman named Hope, of the 11th, also a prisoner in the guard tent, mounted a riderless horse of the Greys.

Other men hurried up, sensing that something was about to happen—cooks, invalids, men on special duty, some without all their equipment, their jackets unbuttoned. They came from all angles, a man of Paget's regiment who had been killing for the commissary in shirtsleeves and a red nightcap and carrying a naked sword, and Private John Veigh, of the Lancers, who had been slaughtering down at Balaclava. He also had been drinking and came thundering up at a gallop on the troop horse of a dead Heavy. He had stripped the dead man of his belt and arms and donned them over his white canvas smock frock, with his canvas trousers tucked into his boots, and he now carried two swords. His shirtsleeves were rolled up above his elbows, and his face, arms and hands, as well as his clothes, were smeared with blood so that he presented a gruesome figure. But he formed up alongside Wightman's right-hand man, John Lee, the old soldier who had served in India, shouting that 'he'd be damned if he was going to be left behind . . . and so lose the fun'. Lucan asked him where he thought he was going and he replied cheerfully that he was 'going to have a slap at the Russians'. Lucan laughed and said, 'Go in then, and fight like the devil.'

As Lucan rode back to the Heavies, intending to accompany them, Blunt, preparing himself to face death with his chief, was making ready to follow him when Lucan stopped him and told him that he was not to take part. At the same time he gave him Lord Raglan's order, telling him to take care of it. Lucan was a precise, careful—even fussy—man and, like Blunt, he was well aware that the cavalry were heading towards destruction. But he was a good soldier and he knew that when presented with a difficult or dangerous order the middle of a battle was not the time to question it. Sometimes it was necessary for a commander to sacrifice a unit for the safety of the army and it was not his place to argue. The only thing he could do—the one thing that is always drummed into every soldier, whatever his rank, from the first day of his service—was to obey the order first and question it afterwards. This was what he was preparing to do, but he was also taking care that the evidence should be safeguarded, even in the event of his own death, so that, if the action turned out as he clearly expected it to, he could not be later accused of misinterpreting it.

As they made ready to move off, his aide, Walter Charteris, a son of Lord Elcho, and Lucan's nephew, was near Blunt. A clever and unassuming officer who had often been kind to the inexperienced young linguist, he seemed beset with a presentiment of death. He asked Blunt to lend him a pocket handkerchief and when Blunt told him that the one he had in his pocket was not very clean, he replied that it would suit his purpose. As Blunt handed it to him, he drew his sword from its scabbard, twisted the handkerchief into a loop round its hilt and his wrist to strengthen his hold and, after brandishing the weapon, said, 'This will do, Blunt.' Then he added in a melancholy tone which Blunt never forgot, 'But I doubt if I shall ever return it to you.'

As Lucan and his staff approached the Heavies, Blunt rode up the slope of the Causeway a short distance from Redoubt Number Five to a position where he could watch the advance. He saw the Light Brigade taking up its position and recognised Cardigan at the head of the first line. Nolan was still at hand and he now moved up to Cardigan and had a short conversation with him.[7] Even now he could not resist reminding him of the Light Brigade's failures. According to Cardigan he even hinted that they were afraid.[8] They were together for a few minutes and if Nolan was really clear of the direction of the intended advance it seems highly unlikely that he did not mention it then. But he had no idea of what was in Raglan's mind and, as they parted, he drew his sword with a flourish and Wightman noticed that he seemed 'greatly excited'. The blood came into his face in a way that Wightman always remembered, then he fell back a little way behind Cardigan and to his left, near to Maxse and on the right of Captain Morris, who had taken post in front of his own left squadron. He was clearly determined not to miss this opportunity for glory. 'Led away by some mad desire for distinction', instead of returning to Airey as he should have done, he did what he had done so often before, the thing Wellington had so much deprecated, and placed himself in a position of prominence at the front of the line.

Cardigan had now moved forward to a point two horse lengths in front of his staff and five lengths in front of the right squadron of the 17th Lancers. Behind him were ranged George Wombell, his orderly officer, Fitz Maxse, who had been on the sick list but had insisted on taking his duty, and Mrs. Duberly's admirer, Lockwood. His position had placed Cardigan directly in front of Private Wightman, who noticed that his brigadier was calmer now in the face of the enemy than he ever normally was on parade. Wightman thought, in fact, that he looked the ideal cavalry leader, with his stern face and soldierly bearing. He was a tall man and always rode 'sort of stiffish', and his long military seat was perfection on the thoroughbred chestnut, Ronald, with the white stockings on the near hind- and forelegs. Wightman knew the horse well because his father, Cardigan's old riding master, had broken it in for him. He was in the full uniform of the 11th Hussars, but he wore his pelisse not slung but like the others— because it was cold and he was still far from well—like a patrol jacket, its front a blaze of gold so that his slim waist was accentuated to give him a dashing appearance.

At the last moment, two Sardinian officers attached to the French, Major Govone and Lieutenant Landriani, also decided it was an opportunity too good to be missed, and they took up a position to the right of Cardigan and Maxse, while from the ranks of the Heavies Sergeant-Major Franks saw the haughty young commissariat officer who had annoyed him so much over the green coffee beans at Varna bridle a horse and snatch up a sword and take his place in the line.

As the last shouts of the troop officers died away, there was another of those strange hushes that kept falling over the battlefield of Balaclava. Neither gun nor musket spoke on either side as the men settled themselves in their saddles and fidgeted nervously with their equipment. Behind the Light Brigade, Lucan had formed up the Heavies in three lines. In front were the Greys and the Royals, with the Inniskillings behind, and the 4th and 5th Dragoon Guards forming a third line. They were slightly to the right of the Light Brigade, with Lucan out in front, in a good position to maintain control of his two brigades. Scarlett was to his left. The time was eleven-twenty.

Then the silence was broken as Cardigan spoke in his strong, hoarse voice, 'The brigade will advance. First squadron of the 17th Lancers direct.' He then turned his head to his trumpeter, Britten, of the Lancers.

'Sound the Advance,' he said, and wheeled his horse to face the dark mass at the end of the valley that they all knew to be the enemy.

8 We've a long way to go!

His heart thumping, Private Pennington heard Cardigan's words with amazement, suddenly aware of the madness on which they were embarking. Though he could see little of the enemy, he knew they were on both sides of them and ahead with their infantry and guns, and from the moment he heard Cardigan speak he 'had no hope of life'. He wasn't the only one. Lieutenant Thomas Hutton, of Paget's regiment, thought that a child could have seen the trap, and a man near Trumpeter Farquharson said 'Many of us will not get back to the lines again,' while a private of the 8th Hussars, binding his sword to his hand with a twisted handkerchief like Charteris, 'felt his blood thicken and crawl, as if his heart grew still and quiet like a lump of stone' within him.

But pride and the discipline of their regiments held them and, like so many other young soldiers before and since, they fought down their fears. As Britten sounded the Walk, the brigade began to move forward across a heavy patch of ploughed land, the silence broken only by the jingling of bits, the clink of equipment, the snorting of horses, and the low rumble of hooves. Despite their depleted ranks, and the fact that the regiments of the front line were led only by captains, the brigade made a brave show and they held themselves proudly, advancing with confidence over the turf, without doubt the finest horsemen in Europe, drilled and disciplined to perfection, and eager to show the Heavies what they could do. Cardigan, at their head, for all his faults, made a bold and brilliant figure. He knew little about strategy or tactics, but if there was one thing he could do it was handle regiments on parade, and his men were on parade against the enemy. All that was asked of him now that he had his men aligned and on the move, was to behave like a soldier, and no one was more fitted to show physical courage than the narrow-minded Cardigan. He rode stiff-backed, his sword at the slope, tall and upright in the saddle; according to Wightman 'steady as a church'.

Just as the brigade began to move off, Lucan saw that Cardigan had done nothing about moving the 11th and he sent an aide down to John Douglas, their colonel, with instructions to drop back behind the 17th Lancers,[1] and Paget, in the second line, not knowing what was happening, was puzzled to see the usually exact Douglas allowing his men to lose their alignment with the regiments on their right. It caused no confusion, however, and the movement was made as the brigade advanced. The walk changed to a trot, the brigade taking up roughly one-fifth of the width of the valley. Between the front line and the second there was a difference of about 400 yards, with rather less between the second and the third, so that the operation, as Lucan had visualised when he had arranged the Heavies in three lines behind to follow in support, was not one attack but a succession of attacks.

By this time, the Russian artillerymen on the Fedioukhine Hills and the Causeway Heights were staring, startled. They could not believe that this magnificently drilled force trotting down the long valley between them really intended to attack the battery at the end, exposing itself to cross-fire every bit of the way. The Russians on the spur, in fact, certain that they were to be the object of the brigade's attention, had formed square to receive the expected assault.

The cheerful spectators round Raglan on the Sapouné Ridge, surrounded by their lunch baskets and wine and untouched by the struggle in the plain, watched as though in a box at the theatre, all of them gay and enthusiastic and eager to see the Russians driven off, and it was only after the Light Brigade had covered a matter of 200 yards and, instead of inclining to their right towards the redoubts, continued straight down the valley that the error became apparent. They were charging the wrong guns!

There were gasps of horror but the tenseness of the moment

was to be followed by yet more. The pause in the battle suddenly ended as on both sides of the valley the Russians came to life and their guns and the riflemen crouched behind every bush[2] and along the spur flanking their path woke up and began to pour their fusillades down on the advancing horsemen. 'A most fearful fire opened on us', Portal wrote, and Lucan's aide, Walker, who had been away with a message and was hurrying to rejoin his chief, felt like crying. 'I do not think cavalry were ever before, or will be again, exposed to such raking fire,' he said.

It was at this point that the first instance of melodrama occurred. Kinglake made much of it and since then practically every historian who has ever written about the charge has faithfully followed his description, despite a surprising absence of witnesses. Certainly, as Kinglake described it, the incident was far too good to leave out but, when studied coldly, a great doubt about it creeps in. While the spectators on the Sapouné Ridge were still digesting the horrifying realisation that the brigade was heading in the wrong direction, they saw Nolan, riding beside his friend, Morris, in the front line, suddenly put spurs to his horse and begin to gallop ahead of the brigade. One soldier riding near him had noticed a triumphant smile on his face as they had moved off and Morris now decided that his excitement and enthusiasm had gone to his head and, aware of the distance they still had to cover, called out a warning to him. 'That won't do, Nolan,' he shouted. 'We've a long way to go and must be steady!'

Nolan did not look back. According to Kinglake, he continued to spur across the leading files of the brigade from left to right, waving his sword and shouting words that no one could hear as he passed in front of Cardigan. Kinglake's claim was that at this late moment he had realised what his rash words and gestures had brought about and was trying to put things right by turning the brigade towards the captured naval guns on the Causeway Heights. He said he based his view of what happened on a diagram drawn for him by an officer who was watching nearby, but he never named or produced his witness and, as Nolan was dead within seconds, no one ever knew what he really intended.

With a crash, one of the first shells fired from the Fedioukhine Hills exploded between him and Cardigan and a fragment of metal tore into his chest, exposing the heart. The sword dropped from his hand but his arm remained high in the air, and, with his legs still holding him in the saddle, the horse wheeled about and began to gallop back towards the advancing brigade. Kinglake— and here again one suspects him of using his imagination a little —wrote that 'what had once been Nolan' retained his strong military seat for some time while an unearthly and appalling cry broke from his crushed lungs, and the dead horseman, his arm still held high, a weird cry coming from his throat, disappeared through the ranks of the 13th Light Dragoons. Then, as his muscles finally relaxed, he fell at last from the saddle, the first man to die.

It is a highly dramatic recital but Wightman from his position just behind Cardigan left a more prosaic version. He claimed that it did not happen as Kinglake described and, though the sword arm, after the weapon had fallen from the nerveless fingers, did remain upraised and rigid, he said, all the other limbs so curled in on the contorted trunk in the spasm of agony the men behind wondered how Nolan's huddled form kept the saddle. From his position directly behind Cardigan he saw all that happened and he insisted later that he never saw the horse cross Cardigan's front, stating categorically, even after reading King-lake's version, that it was only the convulsive clutch of the dying man's bridle hand at the shattered chest that caused the horse to swerve out of line. In other words the move to the right was made *after* Nolan's death not before. Private George Badger, in the front line with the 13th Light Dragoons, and almost knocked over by Nolan's swerve, and Fitz Maxse, whose fractious stallion shied as it was passed so close by Nolan's uncontrolled horse that the two animals almost collided, took exactly the same view. But the incident was dramatic and horrifying and later seemed to contain a kind of awful justice.[3]

As the brigade swept past the body of the aide, however, everybody had eyes only for Cardigan and the order 'Draw swords' was greeted with a cheer. Cardigan didn't turn his head. He was staring straight down the valley, his eyes on one gun for every inch of that dreadful ride. Though he had heard Nolan's fearful cry, he did not suspect he was dead and was under the impression only that he had ridden ahead of him and tried to shout orders to his troops. His disgust was such that, as he advanced into the increasing smoke and flames, this and the taunt against his men—the only things his narrow mind could absorb—kept him from being afraid.

The Russians on his right and left had been slow to bring their full fire to bear but now they were wide awake and battery on battery of guns and rank after rank of riflemen along the spur were pouring shot, shell and bullets at point-blank range among the advancing men. At first only an occasional horse had crashed to the ground, flinging its rider down, and the pace had remained steady, but, as the fire intensified and more men and animals fell in heaps, the pace began to quicken. Cardigan was well in control of his brigade, however, and as the speed increased Wightman, almost directly behind him, saw him turn his head to his left towards Captain Morris and shout hoarsely, 'Steady, steady, Captain Morris,' reminding him that it was his right squadron which was directing the pace and the course of the line. Again and again Wightman heard his sonorous voice, even when they began to suffer heavy casualties, and were eager to force the pace, calling 'Steady, steady, 17th Lancers.' Close behind the trumpeter, Britten, he heard the Trot sounded but failed to hear the Gallop, which was probably not blown because several survivors insisted that the brigade continued to advance at a trot. The Charge was certainly never sounded, because Britten was mortally wounded long before the horses had reached their full speed.

As the advance continued, the watchers on the ridge held their breath. 'Stop,' one man cried. 'Stop, it's madness!' And Henry Clifford, the tears streaming down his face, was consoled by an elderly French general. 'What are they going to do?' he said. 'I'm old and I've seen many battles, but this is too much.'

Only the fact that some of the shells burst too high[4] prevented complete annihilation but the end of the valley was now a white bank of smoke, laced with tongues of flame as the battery there crashed out. Cardigan chose what he considered to be the position of the centre gun and rode steadily for it, not looking back, his bearing helping the men behind him to hold their ranks with such steadiness. As the shells smashed down men and horses —'it thinned us like a sickle through grass', Maxse said—the lines began to expand and contract like the bellows of a concertina. As the horses crashed to the ground the men on either side were opening out to pass them, then closing up again to keep the ranks tight, riding as though on parade. 'Close in,' the officers and NCOs were shouting. 'Close in to the centre.' But with each volley that screamed across the plain the lines grew shorter and shorter.

Though by this time they had still been riding only for a matter of minues, to the men in the shattered ranks the time already seemed hours. They managed to raise a cheer or two but as the furious enfilade brought down more men and horses the yells became wild and broken. Even at this moment of stress, however, the bonds of discipline and obedience were still strong and control was never lost. 'Close in, close in,' came the constant command of squadron and troop officers, but the order was scarcely needed, for men and horses alike sought to keep touch with their neighbours, and as the terrified horses began to force the pace it became impossible for Cardigan's staff to hold back the men behind them.

When the inner squadron of the 17th Lancers broke into a canter, anxious to get out of the murderous fire and into the guns as the lesser of the two evils, Captain White—'both his spurs in hard'—found himself almost alongside Cardigan's bridle arm. Cardigan checked him at once with his outstretched sword, laying it against his breast as he told him sharply not to ride ahead of his commanding officer and not to force the pace. Apart from these commands, Cardigan neither spoke nor showed any other sign that he had a brigade behind him, and advanced down the valley, looking steadily ahead every inch of the way. 'By God,' one of the 13th said, 'he's a wooden man.'

By now, however, it was becoming impossible to hold the horses back and they began to thunder into a headlong gallop, 'every man feeling convinced', Cornet Wombell said, 'that the quicker they rode through the awful showers of grapeshot, musketry and shells . . . the better chance he would have of escaping unhurt'. 'I longed to be at the guns,' one of the men behind him said, and even the old regimental rivalries took hold. Arthur Tremayne, of the 13th, just before his horse fell dead beneath him, heard someone shout, 'Don't let those bastards of the 17th get in front,' while the 17th were yelling, 'Come on, Deaths! Come on!'

By this time, Cardigan had had to extend his horse to the charge to avoid being ridden down, and along the ragged lines there ran 'a sort of grunt of satisfaction as the spurs went home and the swords came to the Right Engage'. They had not been long at their new pace when Trumpeter Brown of the 17th was shot through the thigh. Even while he was catching his breath in pain his horse was brought down. Captain Webb had his shin pulverised and Cornet Cleveland's horse was hit twice. Wightman's right-hand man, Lee, an old soldier whose time was nearly up, was caught by a shell-burst. He managed to touch Wightman's arm and, with a smile on his worn face, quietly said 'Domino, chum,' and fell out of the saddle. His grey mare kept alongside Wightman for some distance, but she was treading on her own entrails now as she galloped, and finally she dropped out of sight with a shriek.

Wightman's left-hand man was his friend, Peter Marsh, and

beyond him Private Dudley was cursing loudly. As a shell swept down four or five men on his left, he turned to Marsh. 'Did you notice what a hole that bloody shell made?' he asked, and Marsh turned on him angrily. 'Hold your foul-mouthed tongue,' he snapped. 'Swearing like a blackguard when you might be knocked into eternity next minute.'

Round shot, grape and shell, and musketry volleys from the spur were mowing men down in whole groups now, and as the steady advance Lucan had ordered became a charge, the Heavy Brigade, still moving at a solid trot, were being left behind. As the distance between the two brigades had widened, in an attempt to hold the connection between them, Lucan had ridden farther and farther ahead of the Heavies. The splendid doomed squadrons of the Light Brigade's first line were now beginning to enter the smoke at the end of the valley and, well in front of Scarlett, Lucan had just passed the fourth redoubt, straining his eyes after Cardigan's men, when he realised that the Heavy Brigade was also in danger of being destroyed. The Russian guns had the range to an inch now and as the Heavies also came under the withering cross-fire which was tearing the Light Brigade to pieces he was wounded in the leg and his horse hit in two places. Charteris, fulfilling his presentiment, was killed at his side, and Paulet had the cover cut from his cap, while MacMahon had his horse wounded by grape.

Glancing back as he approached the level of the third redoubt and the spur, Lucan saw that his leading regiments, the Greys and the Royals, were now also sustaining heavy casualties. 'The batteries . . . began cutting us up terribly', wrote Hodge, and in the Royals alone 21 men were killed, wounded or dismounted, and their commanding officer, Yorke, was disabled for life with a shattered leg. Walker, still trying to take his place with Lucan, saw seven or eight horses of the Greys knocked over by a single shell, and in the ranks of the 5th Dragoon Guards three men, Troop Sergeant-Major Russell, Troop Sergeant-Major Franks and Trumpeter Baker, were riding together when a shell sloshed into the body of Russell's horse. The horse was blown to pieces and the shock lifted the other two chargers off their feet for a moment. But though Russell went over the horse's head, he was on his feet again immediately, none the worse, caught Franks's stirrup, ran a little way, then caught a riderless horse and rejoined the advance. Another shell knocked down six horses and men at one go, three of the riders brothers named Kelly, but none of them suffered more than bruises; while another man, Moses Plumpton, a Lancashire youth, was buried under three horses from which he was later dragged out unhurt.

Their losses by this time were higher than in their own charge earlier in the day and Lucan, who was far from being a coward, was now forced into another of the terrible dilemmas that seemed to be his lot. Should he risk the loss of a second brigade or should he withdraw them? He came to a decision that showed that his moral courage was as strong as his physical courage. From what he could see, the only use to which the Heavy Brigade could now be put was to protect the Light Brigade against pursuit on their return. Knowing perfectly well what the spiteful tongues at headquarters would make of it, he turned to Paulet, still riding alongside him, and said, 'They have sacrificed the Light Brigade; they shall not have the Heavy if I can help it.' His trumpeter, Joy, sounded the Halt and the Heavies were ordered to retire. Hodge was by no means sorry.

Scarlett, who was sixty yards ahead of his men, did not at first realise what had happened and, thinking that instructions had been misunderstood, he ordered his trumpeter to stop the rearward movement. The Heavies halted once more and faced about towards the bottom of the valley, as though on parade, until Lucan set them in motion rearwards again and finally pulled them back until they were out of range, but still sufficiently far forward to make the dreadful journey back over their own dead a little easier for the survivors of the Light Brigade. 'It was a miracle that any of us . . . escaped unhurt,' Walker decided.

With the Heavies was Maude's battery, which had been led by Shakespear down the valley after the Light Brigade until it became obvious to him, too, that they could do nothing to help, and Brandling, who was now up on the Causeway. In the South Valley, unaware of what was happening in the North Valley, he had ridden up to the Heights with his trumpeter out of sheer curiosity and, seeing the Light Brigade moving off, had galloped back at full speed. 'My God,' he said, 'Mount! Mount! There's a bad business over there. They have sent the Light Brigade into the heart of the enemy position!' Bringing his guns up to the Causeway, he had immediately engaged the Russians in Number Two Redoubt until he started suffering casualties and was theatened by Russian cavalry and had then moved back to where the Heavies had halted, all but one gun still on the Balaclava side of the road on the south slope of the Heights.

The Heavies sat in their saddles still troubled by the Russian fire, their eyes on the rolling bank of smoke down the valley and the last glimpse of the Light Brigade before they vanished. The ordered lines were still under control but they were very short now. Captain Jenyns had had three canister shots through his rolled cloak, then the end was torn off by a piece of shell which bruised his knee, and Sergeant Albert Mitchell, riding on the right of the line, was spattered by the blood and brains of Corporal Aubrey Smith, the son of a major, as he was hit in the face by a round shot. His riderless horse continued, still trying to close in, jostling the others and causing confusion.

By this time Wightman had been struck by bullets in the right knee and shin and his horse had three wounds in the neck. 'Fall out,' Marsh begged him, but, despite the blood pouring down his leg, he refused, pointing out that in a minute or two they would be into the enemy. As he drove his spurs home he saw the head of Sergeant Talbot carried off by a round shot, but for another thirty yards the headless body kept the saddle, the lance still at the charge under the right arm.

Discipline rather than courage kept the Light Brigade going.

Cardigan was still moving in fine style but his thoughts were less with his men than with himself. Maxse swore admiringly that he rode down the valley more or less 'in a state of phantasmagoria of self and never saw or thought of anybody but himself doing his duty as a leader well'. His shallow brain still could not reject the affront Lucan had offered by demanding that he move the 11th Hussars or Nolan's insult and the impertinence he believed he had shown in trying to lead the brigade.

In Cardigan's mind was the one idea of Nolan's insolence; fixed in the mind of Paget, in the second line, was the memory of Cardigan's stern demand. 'Your best support, mind, your best support,' he had insisted, and, anxious to carry out his promise, Paget, by shouts and gestures, had increased his pace, directing his line with the 4th Light Dragoons. He had slowly caught up with the 11th Hussars, while the 8th Hussars, on his right—still accompanied by the dog, Jemmy, and held firmly to the correct pace by their colonel, Shewell—were advancing at a steady trot and despite Paget's yells to them to close in were falling farther and farther behind and inclining to the right.

Both the 8th Hussars and the 11th had now fallen back so far, in fact, that Paget found he had lost the 8th completely; his front rank was almost level with the rear of the 11th, so that together they now made up the second line, while the 8th formed the third. Still smoking his cigar, he was riding with his trumpeter, Crawford, and his orderly, Parkes, and had not yet unsheathed his sword. 'Come, my lord,' Parkes chided, 'it is time you were drawing your sword. We are on top of the guns.'

As they rushed into the cross-fire Lieutenant Hutton had his sleeve ripped by a bullet and was struck on the right thigh with such violence he thought his leg had been carried off by a cannon shot. Though 'it was awful work on a blown horse' with a wound in the leg, he decided to carry on, determined to stick to his regiment and on his horse if he could, and not trust to the mercy of the Cossacks hovering on their flanks. He yelled to his squadron leader, 'Low, I am wounded, what shall I do?'

'If you can sit on your horse,' Low shouted back, 'you had better come with us! There's no use going back now! You'll only be killed!'

With the 11th Hussars on their left, Sergeant-Major Loy Smith was spattered by fragments of flesh as the arm was torn off a private just in front. Another man also lost his arm and yet another was struck full in the chest, then a shell burst overhead, mortally wounding Lieutenant Houghton in the head. As they neared the battery Smith saw the infantry on the spur on his right, drawn up in a square, send a volley into them. 'The very air hissed' as the shower of bullets passed through them, he noticed. His cuff was scorched by one of them, and two more men fell out, one with his jaw shattered, the other shot through the neck. The second line was hardly more than a party of skirmishers by now and there was little left of the first line to support, but Cardigan was still leading, and now Wightman saw his sword was in the air. He turned at last in the saddle with his final command, 'Steady, steady, close in,' and just at that moment the Russian battery in front of them fired its final salvo.

The flashes from twelve guns lit the smoke with a flare of red and to the second line it was as though what was left of the first line had simply ceased to exist. Cardigan's charger shied violently at the blast as a torrent of flame seemed to roar past his right, and for a while he thought it had torn off his leg. He was on top of the guns now, however, and, wrenching the excited Ronald back on to course, he drove into the smoke and, choosing a space between two guns, charged into it, the first man into the battery.

9 Look out and catch a horse!

THAT last salvo from the twelve bronze cannon had wrought the final destruction of the two leading regiments. A splinter of shell or a spent round shot struck Fitz Maxse's foot and he saw one of the Sardinians, Landriani, go down, horse and man. Wightman's captain, White, also crashed to the ground as Cardigan disappeared. Then the next moment Wightman himself was in the smoke. A shell burst immediately over his head with a crash that all but stunned him and he felt his horse take a gigantic leap into the air, though he never knew or saw what it cleared. Private Melrose, who had given so many Shakespeare recitals to his comrades, had noticed that the day was the anniversary of Agincourt and had just shouted in an ecstasy of excitement and patriotism 'What man here would ask another man from England?' when he, too, was smashed down. Captain Oldham, commanding the 13th and recently under arrest for losing his sergeant, had been riding a fractious horse which had bolted ahead of the others in the excitement and one of the shells blew off the animal's hindlegs and knocked over several others. He jumped up unhurt, his sword and pistol in his hands, but was knocked over almost immediately by a musket ball.

From the scattered remnants of the 13th Light Dragoons Sergeant Mitchell saw Russian gunners diving under their guns and running for their lives, then a shell hit his horse, carrying away its shoulder and part of its chest. As he was flung sprawling, it exploded a little distance away and only the fact that he was on the ground saved his life. Private Badger, wounded and knocked silly as his horse was brought down, recovered consciousness to see Oldham lying nearby. He called Badger across and told him to take his personal treasures, but as Badger moved towards him another bullet struck him and he fell back dead, still clutching the watch and purse he was holding out. Badger turned away and, seeing Cossacks advancing, caught the stirrup of a straggler of the 13th, but, unable to run with his wound, had to let go. As the Russians had stopped by the body of Oldham, however, he was able to escape.

Cornet Cleveland, of the 17th, engaging a dismounted gunner, had his already wounded horse run through the leg so that he could hardly get it to move, and, attacked by three Cossacks, he wounded the first, received a lance thrust through his cartouche box from the second and a prod in the ribs from the third. Penn, the veteran of India and Afghanistan, speared a gunner and, as he had seen native troops do, wisely left his cumbersome lance in him, then he rode at a Russian officer, who bolted. Penn almost decapitated him with a swing of his sabre and, dismounting, cut off the Russian's belt and took his knife and sword. Troop Sergeant-Major John Berryman's horse had stopped dead at the guns, and, slightly wounded himself, he dismounted to find its off hindleg broken. While he wondered whether to shoot it, Captain Webb rode through the smoke in a daze of agony with his shattered shin, asking what he should do. Berryman advised sticking to his horse and caught hold of a riderless charger to join him. As he swung into the saddle, however, it was hit in the chest and Berryman crashed to the ground.

Wightman, the smoke so thick about him he could not see an arm's length around him, no obstacles, no adversary, no gun or gunner, was beyond the battery before he knew for certain he had reached it. There was a small group of Lancers fighting a little way on his left and he now saw Cardigan some distance ahead, as though he had increased his speed. At that moment Maxse, faint from his injury, appeared from the smoke and crossed his front. 'For God's sake, Lancer,' he yelled, 'don't ride over me!'

'See where Lord Cardigan is,' he went on, pointing. 'Rally on him!' And Wightman was hurrying to support his brigade commander when a Cossack came at him from the smoke and sent his lance through his right thigh.[1] His temper up, Wightman went for him bull-headed, but he bolted. Wightman overtook him, drove his lance into his back with a thump and unhorsed him just in front of two Russian guns which had been captured by Sergeant-Majors Lincoln and Smith, of the 13th Light Dragoons, and a few other men. Lincoln's horse had been one of the first to go down and he had caught another, which he always believed was Nolan's. Nearby, Colonel Mayow, the brigade major, was struggling with a big Russian officer and Wightman saw him neatly tip off his shako with the point of his sword then lay his head open with a cut.

As the first line crumbled into a mêlée, the second line was closing in fast, their pace steadied by Paget's insistence on their keeping their alignment and dressing, and, even as their own men crashed down, they found they were having to avoid the casualties of the first line, dead and wounded men writhing on the ground or endeavouring to crawl to safety, or screaming horses plunging and struggling against appalling wounds. Many of the men were friends, some of them unhurt and stumbling frantically back through the smoke towards where they thought safety lay, weaponless in many cases, their lance caps or shakos gone, their uniforms torn. Horses, some of them uninjured, others with shattered jaws and torn flanks, were behaving as they had been taught to behave and were trying to force their way back into the ranks. With a rider in the saddle and a hand on the reins they had behaved without undue panic—Paget's horse was wounded but showed no fear—but the riderless animals endeavoured to do the only thing they knew and take up their station as troop horses alongside other horses. Mad with fear, eyeballs protruding, the blood from their wounds reddening the lather round their mouths, they ranged themselves alongside Paget, alone in front of his regiment, making dashes at him, trying to gallop with him, and he soon found himself in the middle of seven riderless animals which surged against him, covering his overalls with blood. They came so close to unhorsing him he was forced to use his sword to drive them away.

227

Despite the shouting and the rumble of hooves, the officers were still in control, their orders distinct, holding their men together by sheer discipline. However precious they might be, these gorgeously uniformed young men were behaving like soldiers now. 'Close in to the centre,' they were shouting. 'Back the right flank! Keep up, Private Smith! Left Squadron, keep back! Keep back! Look to your dressing!'

*

As the second line thundered down on the now silent guns Lucan, watching with Scarlett from the head of the valley in an agony of anxiety, became aware of another of the strange and sinister silences that marked the battle. The guns down the valley had stopped as their gunners had begun to fight for their lives and, as the third line, the 8th Hussars—still under the firm control of Shewell and still holding their pace to a trot— vanished into the smoke, the valley became empty. Except for the scattered dead and the torn carcasses of horses, the few wounded or unhorsed men stumbling back up the slope and the riderless chargers trotting aimlessly about, nothing could be seen, and the guns on the flank stopped too. Over the bottom of the valley the smoke continued to hang like a pall, and a long time passed—a very long time, Clifford noticed—before it was split by men staggering out or a horse broke into view.

A matter of fifty men only from the first line had survived. Sergeant Mitchell, trapped with one leg under his dead horse, saw the 4th coming up and shouted, like Maxse, 'For God's sake don't ride over me,' then dragged himself out among the flying bullets coming from infantry on the flanks who were picking off the dismounted men. As he grasped his sword, a man called Pollard flung himself down behind his horse, shouting that it was good cover, but Mitchell thought it safer to make their way back and they stumbled out of the battery. At the other side of the guns Wightman was still looking for someone to rally on. Sergeant O'Hara had gathered a group of Lancers to him and directed them against the Russian gunners while another twenty under the command of Morris, who by the course they had taken had passed beyond the left of the battery, had found themselves, on emerging from the smoke, confronted by a solid mass of Russian horsemen drawn up behind the guns. They were already drawing their horses' heads towards their bridle arms to allow free use of their swords as Morris turned in the saddle. 'Now, remember what I have told you, men,' he yelled, 'and keep together,' and without a second's hesitation he led them on their blown horses into another charge.

The Russians received the charge halted, and the handful of British, like the Heavies earlier in the day, broke through them. The Russians scattered 'like sheep' and retreated in disorder, followed by the Lancers, but, almost at once, a large body of Cossacks swept down on the struggling group and the 17th were forced to wrench their horses' heads round and retreat themselves, fighting every inch of the way, every man swinging his weapon in the centre of a group of Russians who prodded at him with their lances. Morris was not with them. Hurling himself at the Russian commanding officer, he had run him clean through the body up to the hilt of his sword and, as the officer fell from his saddle, Morris, unable to withdraw his sword, found himself helpless. While his men swept past he was leaning down from his saddle, secured to the dead man by the wrist knot round his hand. As he fought to free himself, he received a sabre cut above the ear which carried away a piece of bone, and was knocked unconscious by another which went through the acorn of his forage cap and penetrated the skull. He didn't remain unconscious long, however, and as he came round he found his sword, which was still attached to his hand, had somehow been wrenched free from the body of the Russian. He had hardly gripped it, however, when he was surrounded by Cossacks who were thrusting at him with their lances and his temple was pierced by a lance point which lifted the loose piece of bone. In great pain and convinced he was dying, he finally gave up his weapon to a Russian officer who appeared, knocking up the lances.

Nearby, another officer of the 17th was a prisoner also. Lieutenant Chadwick had found his starved horse so weakened by wounds and loss of blood that, on arriving at the battery, he could not make it move an inch farther. He defended himself against Cossacks and dragoons who attacked him but a Russian lance point in the neck knocked him from the saddle. Wombwell was also a prisoner. He had had his horse shot from under him and a stray horse he had caught had also been shot. While he was standing exhausted and weaponless, surrounded by Cossacks, Morris was pushed towards him, his face covered with blood, but far from defeated.

'Look out,' he said to Wombwell. 'Look out and catch a horse.' At that very moment several loose horses came by and Wombwell, dodging between the clumsy lances, grabbed one of them and mounted it. Morris, who had been robbed of all he possessed by his captors, also broke away and, dodging into the thickest smoke he could find, also caught a riderless horse. But, weak with loss of blood, he was unable to climb into the saddle and was dragged along by the horse until he fell unconscious once more.

What at first had seemed a minor victory for the remnants of the first line had changed by this time to confusion, and Colonel Mayow, the brigade major, forcing his way from the mêlée, saw another body of Russian cavalry preparing to attack in force. Realising that the scattered Lancers would be destroyed, he tried to rally them. 'Seventeenth, Seventeenth, this way, this way,' he roared, collecting the few survivors about him, together with the dozen men who were all that were left of the 13th Light Dragoons. At their head, he charged out of the battery, driving the Russians before him, until he was 500 yards farther down the valley and in sight of the bridge. As the Russians halted he looked round for support, and one of the men with him grinned and pointed out that 'the Busby-bags were taking their time.'

*

As the fragments of the first line stared about them for help, the second line crashed through the smoke into the guns. Most of the 11th Hussars, like the 17th, had outflanked the guns because Douglas had noticed that the valley curved to the left and he had seen a group of Russian horsemen at the entrance to a gully and had thought he might trap them there, but the 4th Light Dragoons went between the great weapons, the 8th Hussars, still at their steady trot, pressing on in their right rear. The smoke, dust and confusion were such that Paget never saw the battery until he was among the guns, then one of the officers gave a 'View halloo' and they were hacking and cutting in a ferocious hand-to-hand combat.

Tossing aside his cigar, Paget realised he had lost his second-in-command, Halkett, his trumpeter, Crawford, and his orderly, Parkes. Then he heard Parkes shouting 'Where's my chief?' and yelled back, 'Here I am, my boy, all right,' but as they made their way towards him Crawford's horse collapsed and Parkes's horse was also hit. He saw a Lancer prodding at a dismounted Russian and shouted to him to leave him alone but the Lancer was wild with excitement and loath to obey. Near him, Trumpeter Farquharson caught a glimpse of one of the 13th defending himself against five or six Cossacks, every one of whom he unhorsed before sloping his sword and joining the second line, and Major Low carving away at the Russians, eleven of whom he killed with his huge sword.

The Russians were still fighting to get the guns away and as no one had any spikes Lieutenant Warwick Hunt dismounted and tried to unhook the traces. Hoarse now with shouting, Paget called to him to get back on his horse and the Russians were driven aside by wildly plunging animals or cut to the ground by sabres. Though Paget did not remember it, he accounted for one with his sword, while Lieutenant Joliffe pistolled several more, and Paget finally found himself in control of the battery.

Pausing only to accept the surrender of a much-decorated Russian officer, John Douglas, with the 11th, had swept far ahead of Paget's men and was farther down the valley, charging the lancers he had seen. As the attack disintegrated into a new mêlée, Roger Palmer, all unaware, had his life saved by Jowett, the man he had found asleep on outpost duty, who cut down a Russian as he put a carbine to Palmer's head and was about to pull the trigger. The Russians were giving way everywhere now and in the battery, the cry went up: 'Fourth Light Dragoons, to the assistance of the 11th!' Just as they reached the fight, Trumpeter Farquharson's horse was hit and a Russian gunner, attempting to cut him down, missed and opened the animal's breast with his sword. As the horse sank beneath him, Farquharson killed the gunner, but when he looked round the skirmish was over and he was alone, running about in the smoke trying to find his way to safety.

Breaking clear, the 11th had come to an abrupt halt as they found themselves facing a fresh great mass of Cossacks and hussars. These were the men the 17th had faced, and Douglas, feeling that the whole mass of the Russian army was in front of him, shouted to his men to retreat. As they tugged at the reins, and swung away, the Russian mass trotted forward. Trumpeter Farquharson was still trying to decide which way to go when a man of his regiment rode up, wounded in the arm and almost fainting. Farquharson tore a strip from his overalls and tied it tightly above the wound and the man rode off; then his sergeant-major, the handsome Fowler, appeared and, after asking where the regiment was, also disappeared. Then he saw the 11th, only about 70 strong now, moving back under Douglas. They had swung instinctively into an orderly group under what officers remained.

The vast mass of Russian horsemen were now only a few hundred yards away and Farquharson heard Douglas call for his men to halt. The 11th Hussars checked their retreat at once with the same steadiness they had shown throughout their whole headlong dash, and the few British horsemen fronted as if they had been on parade, and for a moment or two faced the Russians as they advanced.

Douglas was all for another charge, but as the 11th approached the Russians wheeled and galloped away, despite the odds of 20 to one in their favour. A few stragglers from the first line joined the little group of Britishers and they followed the Russians almost to the aqueduct, one of the Russians falling from the bridge in his haste to cross. The Russians finally halted on a slight slope and faced about, and for a while, almost in silence, the two groups stared at each other, the horses' noses almost touching. They remained like that for some time, the weary Englishmen on their exhausted mounts, with their hearts in their mouths; then the Russian officers woke up and, calling to their men to follow, tried to drive their horses at the British front rank. Their men failed to show the same resolution and the British kept their mounts close together, parrying the thrusts that were made at them with their swords. Dragging out pistols, the Russians began to fire at them, while the Cossacks on the flanks doubled round to their rear, and there were scuffles in which several of the British were killed. Thinking that with adequate support they might even now drive the Russians from the field, Douglas started looking round for help and not far away behind him he saw a body of lancers who had swept out of a valley leading to the Tractir Bridge.

'Rally, men,' he shouted to them. 'Rally, men of the 17th Lancers!'

But Cornet Palmer, whose eyes were keener, pointed out that the lance pennants and headgear were different. 'That's not the 17th Lancers,' he said. 'That's the enemy,' and Loy Smith decided they hadn't many minutes of life left to live.

20 Has anyone seen Lord Cardigan?

YOUNG Blunt had watched the beginning of the tragedy from his position on the hills, then, his Russian mount becoming restive at the gunfire and constant trumpet calls, he decided with sinking heart to ride back towards the cavalry camp in the South Valley. It began to dawn on him, however, that he was losing control of the horse and suddenly it swerved round and began to gallop at breakneck speed towards its Russian friends beyond the Woronzoff Road. Blunt's hands became sore with heaving at the reins and he grew worried as he saw himself carried into the Russian ranks. Fortunately the horse's mad career came to an abrupt end. Frightened by the Russian shells bursting nearby, as it reached Redoubt Number Five it attempted to leap over its narrow trench, stumbled and threw Blunt on to its parapet. As he got to his feet to scramble into the redoubt he saw a Turkish soldier rushing forward to help him killed by a shell splinter, and the horse struggling to its legs, to gallop away across the North Valley in the direction of the Fedioukhine Hills.

Redoubt Number Five, where Blunt now sheltered, had only been garrisoned since the charge of the Heavies when Rustum Pasha put 200 men into it. Several of them had been killed and wounded by the fire from the other side of the valley and Rustum Pasha had had his horse wounded. He was understandably bitter and asked why Raglan had failed to act on the information he had sent him through Lucan and Campbell.

Cathcart was coming up at last, however, but it was already far too late, and the only thing that could be done for the Light Brigade was what Lucan was doing: try to help them on their return. Also realising that help was needed, the Chasseurs d'Afrique had gone into action. A force with a record of courage and skill against the Arabs in North Africa, they were originally irregulars but were now all Frenchmen mounted on Algerian horses, and their commander, General Morris, having seen the fate of the Light Brigade, ordered them to attack the batteries and the infantry on the Fedioukhine Hills. They crashed over the scrubby ground in the loose formation they had learned in their campaigns in North Africa and the Russian artillery immediately retreated to where their infantry had formed square. At a cost of 38 killed and wounded, they had driven the Russians from the allied end of the north side of the valley so that when the Light Brigade reappeared they would not have to suffer a harassing fire from that point.

Down the valley the survivors of the 11th had now been joined by the 4th Light Dragoons. Paget had been looking anxiously for his brigadier, and as he and his men emerged from the smoke they saw the 11th Hussars, not far away, chased by what seemed to be six times their own number. As they rallied to the hussars, someone pointed out that they were being attacked in the rear themselves and, turning, Paget saw the same force of lancers Douglas had seen. He noticed, however, that the Russians were showing the same disorderly hesitation they had shown against the Heavy Brigade and remembered his father's often-repeated advice about keeping control of cavalry when in difficulties.

Dragging at his reins, he shouted at the top of his voice, 'Halt front! If you don't halt front, my boys, we're done,' and as the men swung about he turned to Low. 'We are in a desperate scrape,' he said. 'What shall we do?'

Though their numbers were now small, the men were still responding well to orders, either from their own officers or the officers of other units, or even from sergeants and corporals, but there was no central direction from a general.

'Has anyone seen Lord Cardigan?' Paget demanded.

No one had. Cardigan's knowledge of what was expected of a cavalry leader was very limited, as he had proved once already that morning. He had dashed through the guns untouched, still unaware of the condition of his brigade, and like so many others his view of what was happening was obscured by the smoke so that he had passed through it without any real knowledge of the bitter struggle beginning to take place behind him. He rightly felt it was a general's duty not to engage the enemy hand-to-hand but to find a position where he could use his experience to direct the fight, but, as he emerged, about 100 yards away he saw a large body of Russian cavalry and he was alone. Ronald, his charger, was wild with excitement by this time and almost out of hand and before Cardigan could control him he had been carried almost into the Russian ranks. For a while they stared at each other, Cardigan on his blown, excited horse, the Russians startled by the sudden appearance of this splendid horseman, his crimson and blue uniform glittering with bullion.

By an extraordinary coincidence, one of the Russian officers opposite him, Prince Radziwill, was a man he had met at functions in London, and it probably saved his life. Instead of cutting him down the Cossacks were directed to capture him alive, and there was a brief struggle in which Cardigan received a slight wound in the thigh and a lance through his pelisse that almost dragged him from the saddle. He managed to drag his horse round, however, and as he galloped back towards the shelter of the smoke he was seen by Corporal Thomas Morley, a Nottingham man in the 17th Lancers, and several others who had lost their officers and were riding past him to right and left. Morley 'had no impulse to join him' and no one else seems to have had either, and, reaching the battery, Cardigan emerged at the other side of the guns almost where he had first entered. As he had swept back into the smoke the fight in the battery had died away and the second line had driven out and were at that moment, with Douglas and Paget, halted between the advancing Russian mass and the lancers, who had swept across their rear, wondering where Cardigan had got to.

As Cardigan passed back through the battery there was no sign of anyone and the smoke still hid the dead gunners and the wreckage of his brigade. He could see no sign of his men, only the dead and dying and the crippled horses struggling on the slope of the valley and small groups of unhorsed and injured men making their way to the safety of the British lines. Of his staff Maxse was wounded and Wombwell and Lockwood had disappeared. Although he must have noticed the soldiers Morley had seen riding past him, he claimed he assumed his men had retired without him and it seemed to him now that his duty was done. The sounds of combat behind him were drowned by the guns and the muskets firing at the small groups of wounded and unhorsed men, and the idea that there were men in the smoke looking for his leadership never occurred to him. He made no attempt to find them or to rally anyone.

He had led the brigade down the valley 'like a gentleman', with a calm indifference to danger, and now, feeling that as a general his position was a special one, to avoid any undignified appearance of a hasty retreat he rode back very slowly, most of the time with his horse at a walk. He was not a lovable character, but his courage was never in question, and by the same lucky chance that had got him to the bottom of the valley untouched when two-thirds of his men had been hit he rode back again through the fire from the Causeway Heights, which was still screaming among the survivors, and again remained untouched.

*

While Cardigan was occupied with his retreat, his men were still struggling in ones and twos and small groups to extricate themselves. The 4th Light Dragoons and the 11th Hussars under Paget had decided that there was little hope for them. Their horses were blown, and, though they were still held together by discipline, many of them were wounded.

'Threes about,' Paget shouted, one eye on the lancers across their path to safety, and he saw his officers with their swords in the air shouting for a rally. As they jammed spurs to their stumbling horses, the Russian lancers, their weapons at the Carry, edged back to their right with the same hesitation the Heavies had noticed, so that their front was at an oblique angle away from the British. Then, still uncertain, they halted again. The British, little more than a rabble now, were allowed to slip past, beating away with their swords the thrusts of the lances. Among the last of them, Paget was hoarsely shouting 'Left shoulder forward!' to try to face the Russians squarely, but no one heard him and, as they shuffled past, his sword contacted at least four Russian spears. Though the Russians, still apparently bewildered, jabbed at him, they did no more, probably because they were becoming aware of the danger they were in from their own guns on the Causeway which were now firing on friend and foe alike. Loy Smith, however, heard a harsh Russian order as he passed and thought several men were lost. Certainly Sergeant-Major Bentley was cut off by three Cossacks, and Lieutenant Dunn swung round and dashed back into the fight to rescue him, going on to the aid of Private Levett, who was also being attacked.

But if the Russians had behaved with anything like common bravery—'like English ladies', was the suggestion—the British would never have escaped. As it was, the survivors of the little group were able to begin the painful drag up the slope, sweeping up as they went Lieutenant Percy Smith, who had found himself facing three lancers without a weapon. He had ridden the charge unarmed without his hand guard but had escaped injury and now, trying to reach safety, as one of the three Russians hesitated, he brushed aside the lance of the second with his arm at the cost of a scratch, and as the third pointed his lance at his chest, he dug in his spurs and leapt over the Russian's horse. As the Russian went down, the lance point caught Smith but did little damage and he was rescued by Paget and the 11th Hussars as they came by.

As the Russian artillery fire increased with this bigger target to aim at, Loy Smith felt his horse limp and someone called out that its leg was broken. He kicked his feet free from the stirrups and, jumping clear as it fell, started running. A few men were galloping past and, afraid of being knocked down, he inclined to the left, the bullets kicking up the dust around his heels. Hearing galloping he saw Russian lancers following him, but two of his men were behind and he decided to turn and fight it out. The Russians surrounded the other two men, however, and as he saw the lances go down he decided to keep on running.

Not far away, Private Pennington was also dodging bullets. His black mare which had somehow managed to keep her condition throughout the campaign had been struck in the hind-leg after about a mile of the ride down by a bullet from the Causeway that lamed her so badly she was useless, and, feeling horribly alone, he had watched the rest of the brigade ride past. A bullet passed through his right leg while a shot from the left tilted his busby over his right ear, then the horse went down with a crash. As he scrambled to his feet, bleeding but conscious of no pain, bullets were kicking the earth up all round him and he could see disarmed men being speared by groups of Russian lancers who had come down from the slopes of the hills and were sweeping across the valley.

Trumpeter Farquharson had caught a riderless horse of the 17th by this time but, just as he was mounting it, it was hit and fell to the ground, knocking him senseless. Recovering his wits as a large body of Cossacks rode by in chase of the 11th, he found himself being prodded with a lance. It only tore his overalls, however, and as the Cossacks passed on he took to his heels again, dodging the shot that still bounded across the valley from both sides. Eventually he caught his third horse, a Cossack pony, and, mounting it, set off again up the valley. A Russian hussar made a cut at him with his sword but he parried it and, as he rode past, he made the Russian yell as he caught him in the right cheek.

As the scattered groups of survivors made their way slowly to safety, their rear was covered by Shewell and the 8th Hussars, still accompanied by Jemmy. They had been reduced to the size of a squadron by the time they reached the guns. Captain

239

Tompkinson had already fallen and Private Hanrahan, hit in the head, had sunk over his saddle bow, one leg sticking out so that his spur kept jabbing Lieutenant Phillips's horse. As he had finally slipped from the saddle his horse had gone down, and a moment later a deep 'Oh'—'something between a groan and a shriek'—came as Lord Fitzgibbon was hit. Nevertheless they had reached the battery still in excellent alignment, only to find it already silenced by the 4th Light Dragoons. One man took a swing at a gunner who was trying to prod at him with his sponge staff and cut his hand clean off, then a hussar swiped at him and he cut him across the neck with a slash that almost sickened him.

Shewell began to rally his men immediately, and as they lined up someone shouted to Sergeant Riley that he was out of his place, only to realise that 'his eyes were fixed and staring, and his face was rigid and white as a flagstone'. He was dead, though still sitting in the saddle. Dead also was Sergeant Williams, the man who had been put under arrest by Shewell. Giving up his sword and carbine, he had arrived at the guns without a weapon to defend himself.

As they drew together Shewell demanded 'Where is Lord Cardigan?' and as they waited a few men of the 17th Lancers and the 13th Light Dragoons under Mayow appeared with a large body of Russians in pursuit. Mayow galloped up to Shewell and also demanded 'Where is Lord Cardigan?'

As they tried to decide what had happened to him, Shewell noticed a force of Russians across their path to safety and the cry went up that they were cut off. With the men rallying instinctively to the senior officer, Shewell, a conscientious and single-minded man, attempted to wheel his little force into line, shouting 'Threes about!' But his men had lost their numbering and there was a moment's hesitation before he gave the order to charge. A poor swordsman, he gripped the reins in both hands, put his head down, and drove his horse like a thunderbolt at the Russian commander. The Russian's horse shied away and Shewell burst past him as his men hacked their way through, as though 'cutting through a thickset hedge with a billhook'. Pennington, running for his life, saw them approaching. He had unbuckled his belt and gripped his sword and was hobbling back stiff-legged when he heard the hooves behind him. Sergeant-Major Harrison was leading a grey horse whose rider had been killed; an officer shouted 'Come on, my boy!' and Pennington managed to mount. As they forced their way past the Russians, he found he was bearing to the left and losing touch and he was careful to keep the pursuing Cossacks on the side of his sword arm so he could hold them at bay.

Behind him, Sergeant-Major Berryman, recovering his senses after having had his second horse shot under him, looked up to see Captain Webb halted, unable to ride with the pain of his shattered shin. He was lifting him from the saddle when Sergeant Farrell, of the 17th, and Private Malone, of the 13th, appeared, followed by Private James Lamb, who had crouched behind his dead horse watching Russian riflemen firing at the riders until they were chased away by the Chasseurs d'Afrique. None of them had water bottles so, taking a chance with the Cossacks and the riflemen who were shooting at the unhorsed men, Lamb went back down the valley searching among the bodies until he found a calabash half-full of water on the saddle of a dead horse. They all drank, then Berryman and Farrell began the long trudge up the valley with Webb, while Lamb went with Malone to the help of another wounded man.

As they struggled up the slope, Wombwell came by and his conversation with Webb sounded as if Webb had been injured on a football field. 'What's the matter, Peck?' Wombwell asked, using Webb's nickname.

'Hit in the leg, old fellow,' Webb said. 'How did you escape?'

As they reached the French they saw General Morris riding past, shocked and angry. 'It is not war,' he was saying furiously. 'It is not war.'

While all this was taking place, Cardigan was still riding slowly up the valley. On the way he passed Sergeant Mitchell who, like the rest up since 4 a.m. and without food since the night before, was stumbling exhausted to safety. He had dragged from under his horse a man of his own regiment only to find he was dying and, as the smoke began to clear, he saw he was surrounded by dead and crippled horses. Joining up with a group from the 8th and 11th Hussars, he had just reached the slopes of the Causeway when Cardigan came past, urging him to hurry.

As he reached Maude's battery, Cardigan halted and, pointing to the tear in his overalls where the lance had gone through, wryly told Shakespear he would not now be able to keep the cold out at night. Shakespear produced a flask and after a drink Cardigan rode up on to the Causeway. He was beginning by now to realise what had happened and when he met Cathcart, still accompanied by Ewart, he burst out indignantly. 'I have lost my brigade,' he said, but, situated where they were, Cathcart and Ewart had not even seen the action and could only stare back at him; and Mitchell saw him turn his horse's head towards the valley again, as though at a loss what to do, and ride down it a little way on the north slope of the Causeway.

The Russians were taking prisoners by this time. Trumpeter Farquharson had got clear of the battery at last and been swept up by Douglas and Paget as they cut their way through. Seeing the Scots Greys in the distance, he was beginning to feel safe when a cannon ball, which he saw coming every inch of the way, hit the Russian pony he had captured on the head, killing it instantly. As it fell, he was surrounded and taken prisoner by the Cossacks who were following. Wightman was also a prisoner. He had finally rallied on Paget's orderly, Parkes, who was supporting an injured Trumpet-Major Crawford with one arm and slashing at the Russians surrounding them with the other. After losing their horses, they had been joined by Private Edden, also of the 4th, whose horse had been shot, and, coming across the mortally wounded Major Halkett, they were about to pick him up when the Cossacks appeared. In the scuffle, Edden and Wightman cut their way free, but the other two were captured and dragged down the valley past the body of Halkett, who was dead by this time, his body stripped naked except for his jacket.

Wightman now joined a friend of his, Private Mustard, and Private Fletcher, of the 4th Light Dragoons, who had been so far past the guns they had been able to see the Tchernaya. But they were all wounded and their horses had also all been wounded several times. Wightman had read in the regimental library of a heavily pressed officer in some ancient battle who had told his commander 'We have done enough for honour' and he felt it applied to them, too. They turned back to the guns and, forcing their way through group after group of enemies, fell in with Wightman's friend, Peter Marsh.

It was then that they heard the rough Nottingham voice of Corporal Morley, roaring 'Coom 'ere, coom 'ere, fall in, lads, fall in!' With shouts and oaths he had rallied some twenty men of various regiments. A body of Russian hussars blocked their way but Morley, still shouting oaths, led them straight at them and they went through them 'as though they had been made of tinsel paper'. Wightman's horse had taken a bullet in the shoulder, however, by now, and he was having hard work to push it along and, as they rode into the fire of the infantry on the Causeway which was hitting Russians and British alike, more of Corporal Morley's party fell. Wightman's horse was riddled with bullets, while another struck him on the forehead and another in the shoulder. As he scrambled from underneath the dead horse, a Cossack came at him and stabbed him several times with his lance in the neck, shoulder and back and under his ribs, and as he struggled to his feet, trying to draw his sword, drove the lance through the palm of his hand. Wightman only escaped death by blinding the Russian with a handful of gravelly soil, but by this time he was surrounded again and in no shape to resist.

Not far away, his commanding officer, Morris, regaining his senses yet again, became aware of a Cossack approaching him with the obvious intention of killing him and, forcing himself to his feet, he once more sought shelter in the slow-drifting smoke. As another loose horse passed, he caught it and this time was able to mount it. Just as he turned it up the valley, however, it was killed by the cross-fire and pinned him to the ground as it fell. Once again he lost consciousness.

Paget and Douglas, with their group and, following them, Shewell's men, trailed by a bleeding Jemmy, who had been twice wounded in the neck by shell splinters, began to labour painfully back up the valley. Fitz Maxse was clinging to his horse's mane, almost fainting with pain and able only to use his left stirrup. He had cut at two Russians as he had passed through the guns and one had pointed a pistol at him but he was too preoccupied to notice whether he fired. As he rode back he was worried that the man with the pistol would 'pot him' and, to be on the safe side, he had dragged out a 'rotten old pistol' belonging to his brother Fred. The Russian was not waiting for him and instead he pointed the pistol at a Russian cavalryman who was chasing him. It misfired.

The retreat was a worse ordeal than the advance. 'The fire . . . going back was more severe than before', Portal noticed, and both riders and horses were exhausted and hardly any of them were unhurt. Portal's own horse was killed by a splinter just as he reached safety. Men were still crouching over their dying chargers, loath to leave them, while all around them others, wounded and bleeding, staggered along, dragging injured mounts. Those with horses still able to move gave them up to the wounded, Captain Rodolphe De Salis, of the 8th, leading his charger with a wounded private in the saddle. Among them all formation had been lost and when the eager Mrs. Duberly, now happily established on the Ridge, saw them appear below her, she asked, 'What can those skirmishers be doing?' Then she realised what she was seeing. 'Good God!' she said. 'It is the Light Brigade.'

The pace was terribly slow and they had a mile to cover, some men carrying others on their backs, or helping them to limp along, while the Russians kept swooping down to cut off isolated men, take prisoners and spear the wounded as they lay on the ground. Cornet Clowes, his horse down and weak with loss of blood, decided to pretend to be dead until they had passed but then he noticed they were spearing everyone, dead or alive, and he decided instead to take a chance and ran for it. Among the wreckage of the brigade, in what Paget called 'a scene of havoc', men were running, limping and crawling to safety, while horses with shattered legs struggled to rise then, in their agony, rolled back on their trapped riders.

Lieutenant Percy Smith, bleeding from his two slight wounds, saw Lieutenant Chamberlayne, of his regiment, by the body of his favourite horse, and he told him that since he might get a new horse but never a new saddle and bridle, to concern himself with rescuing them. Chamberlayne did so and, carrying the saddle over his head, probably owed his life to the fact that the Cossacks took him for one of their own pillagers and allowed him to thread his way through them unharmed. Lieutenant Edward Phillips, of the 8th Hussars, also owed his life to a saddle. His horse shot, he had fought off a group of Russians attacking a private who had been wounded in both hands, then he found one of his men dead on the ground, his horse standing alongside, its saddle twisted under its belly. Unable to right it, he unfastened the girths and used it instead to stand on to mount the horse's bare back.

Whenever the stumbling men and riders clotted together the batteries on the Causeway Heights sent a shell towards them. There were dozens of riderless horses, Captain Winter's wounded by grape, its rider last seen in the guns wielding his sword, one of the first to reach the British lines. Sergeant Mitchell, still struggling back, saw two officers' chargers which seemed a little mad and tried to catch one but without success. By this time he had reached the ploughed land up the valley and to his horror he saw the Greys not far ahead of him having to retire again from the shellfire. As Cossacks began to approach, he moved over to where he could see a few Chasseurs d'Afrique and fell in with an unhorsed Grey, who had been blinded. Bandaging his head, he led

245

him up the valley to a point near Number Four Redoubt, where they were given rum by an infantry officer before setting off again.

Pennington was one of the first to reach safety. As he approached the Heavies, the Russians who had been harassing him fell back and rode away down the valley. Bullets were still kicking up dust around him but they were spent now, and the first person he saw as he passed through them to safety was a sergeant of the 13th—more than probably Mitchell—and without a word they shook hands, knowing how lucky they were to have escaped. He was helped from the saddle and, grateful for his life, made a point of kissing on the nose the grey mare which had saved him. The hungry Mitchell's first act was to go to his tent and cram his mouth with a handful of biscuit.

Loy Smith, still struggling up the valley, saw an officer of the 17th in front and called out, 'This is warm work, sir,' and when the officer turned he saw it was Morris and that his face was a horrifying mask of blood. As he had recovered his senses yet again, he had worked his leg free from the dead horse lying across it and, this time, had set off on foot, staggering up the valley as fast as he could go. With Morris just ahead, Sergeant-Major Smith inclined to the right. On top of a little hillock he saw three Russians, one dead and two badly wounded, and he noticed that they belonged to the Russian 11th Hussars who had been hit by French artillery when they had been firing over the Light Brigade at the beginning of the battle. He couldn't resist taking a button from the tunic of one of them, then he ran among the riderless horses, rejecting the wounded ones until he found an uninjured animal of the 4th Light Dragoons which he mounted and rode up the valley.

Step by step, exhausted bleeding men stumbled in, each group cheered and greeted by handshakes. The unhappy Heavies watched them pass 'by ones and twos . . . such a smash was never seen'. Wounded troop horses were standing all over the plain, unable to move because of wounds. One cantered by, its broken hindleg swinging round and round, and there was a wounded grey with one of the Chasseurs d'Afrique lying across its neck, its shoulder covered with his blood as he rode about looking for a surgeon to attend two of his comrades. A wounded man creeping along on his belly was rescued by a sailor wearing a dragoon's brass helmet, and another fell dead from the saddle as his blown horse came to a stop. Far behind, Morris saw the body of Nolan and, remembering that the aide had been the first to fall, decided he was finally safe and collapsed by the side of his friend.

Cardigan, meanwhile, had picked up Cornet Yates, of the 11th Hussars, a recently commissioned ranker. To the gunners round Brandling's single gun his horse as he appeared looked exhausted, but though he seemed to have been 'knocked about', he was cool and collected. He sheathed his sword and undid the front of his tunic, then, as though talking to himself, observed that the Russian lances were 'deuced blunt; they tickle one's ribs'. Aware for the first time that he was carrying a revolver—in those days still a new weapon—he dragged it out and said 'And here's this damned thing I have never thought of until now!' Replacing it, he re-drew his sword and, pointing to the Chasseurs d'Afrique, unaware of what they had done, observed 'It's time they gave those dappled gentry a chance.'

Just at that moment, Shewell and Mayow were leading up the survivors of the 8th Hussars together with those few men from the other regiments who had joined them. Hearing the cheer from the Heavies that greeted them, Cardigan wheeled his horse and set off across to them at the gallop, and took up a position in front of them to lead them in at the walk. The moment his back was turned, Mayow indicated him, shook his head and made signs of disgust. Some of the first line had seen him, down the valley, heading back alone into the smoke round the guns and were aware how soon he had set off back again; and more than one of the 8th Hussars had seen the mortally wounded Lieutenant Houghton riding slowly up the valley as they had ridden down.

Since he very much resembled Cardigan in stature and colouring and was wearing the same uniform and riding a similar horse, they had imagined the brigade commander had never even reached the guns. These men also began to point to him and make jeering signs to the Heavies, throwing out low comments on him as they passed. Shewell, with Cardigan, saw nothing of what was happening and, to the embarrassment of Brandling's gunners, Cardigan, unaware of the ridicule behind his back, smiled and waved his sword self-importantly to acknowledge cheers that were addressed to the 8th.[1]

Almost immediately behind the 8th, crossing the valley towards the Causeway, were the 4th Light Dragoons under Lord George Paget, whose horse was failing so that he had to use the flat of his sword on its flanks. As he had ridden back he had overtaken Lieutenant Hutton who, despite his wound, had remained with the regiment and had disabled several of the enemy in the guns. As he made his way back, however, he had been shot through the other thigh and was struggling along on a dying horse which was suffering from eleven wounds. As Paget reached him, he asked if he could be given a little rum, and Paget fumbled a flask out of his holster and passed it across.

Level with the Heavies were the Chasseurs d'Afrique and as he saw them moving forward 'turned out like bandboxes' Paget, dusty and dry-throated and, like Cardigan, unaware as yet of the good service they had done, thought it might have been better if they had 'taken a turn' with the Light Brigade. Higginson of the Guards, who had watched the charge in horror from the top of the valley, saw the shocked look on Paget's face.

'God alone knows what has happened to my poor regiment,' Paget said in a voice that was racked with too much shouting. He had lost every one of his trumpeters and two out of three sergeant-majors and he thought the 13th and 17th were annihilated. He was excited and furious with Cardigan, furious enough in fact to write later an official complaint about his conduct, considering it his duty, after demanding his best support, at least to see him out of trouble instead of disappearing, apparently indifferent to his fate.

He halted alongside Brandling's gun in almost the same spot Cardigan had halted. He was hot and angry. 'It's a damned shame,' he said loudly, staring at the Guards. 'There we had a lot of their guns and carriages taken, and received no support, and yet there's all this infantry about!'

Cardigan had left the 8th by this time and was riding up to greet the 4th, and he called out a sharp admonition—'Lord George Paget! I am surprised!'

Paget lowered his sword in a sullen salute and, without speaking, turned his horse and rode after his men.[2]

Cardigan followed. The only thing that was in his mind beyond the sense of pride at having done his duty was still disgust at Nolan's insult and his insubordination at trying to lead the Brigade. He was so obsessed by the thought that as he met Scarlett he at once broke into a condemnation of Nolan's actions. 'What do you think,' he said angrily '. . . of the aide-de-camp . . . riding to the rear and screaming like a woman?'

Scarlett had better information than Cardigan. 'Don't say any more,' he advised. '. . . I have just ridden over his dead body.'

As they talked, more wounded and unhorsed men appeared, stumbling nightmares with their uniforms torn by lance thrusts or covered with blood from head wounds, their faces marked with pinprick injuries where splinters of stone thrown up by bursting shells had cut the flesh. The last to arrive was Private Badger, stumbling in with his uniform soaked with blood from the wound in his side.

Meanwhile Ewart, leaving Cathcart at last, had ridden along the north side of the Causeway. A party of retreating horsemen told him that a staff officer was lying badly wounded behind them, and as he descended into the valley he found Nolan dead, and then Morris, almost unconscious with terrible wounds on his head. A little farther on was a Heavy with his jaw smashed and when Ewart asked him his regiment he could only point to his buttons which indicated the 5th Dragoon Guards. Riding back to Number Four Redoubt, now re-occupied by Turks, Ewart persuaded them to help, and between them they lifted Nolan, Morris and the dragoon, but, as the Russian fire began to fall among them again, the Turks dropped their charges and bolted. A message had by now reached the 17th Lancers, however, and Surgeon James Mouat and Sergeant-Major Wooden ran forward. Wooden was later said by his enemies to have deliberately thrown himself from his horse during the advance but there could have been little truth in the story because now he and Mouat carried Morris to safety through the plunging shellfire. The letter Nolan had written for his mother was found in his pocket and put on one side for posting home. As they laid him down once more, Sir William Gordon, nearby, who had received five sabre wounds in the head, was being attended by surgeons. Hardly able to keep himself in the saddle, he had lain across his horse's neck, trying to keep the blood out of his eyes, and had ridden out of the valley at a walk, even managing to escape through a gap when a body of Russians got across his path. His horse, shot through the shoulders, fell dying as he was lifted from the saddle.

Blunt, once more without a horse, had walked down from the Causeway to meet the survivors as they limped in. On his way he met a group of Guardsmen standing round the body of an officer whom he recognised at once as Nolan. The face was almost black and the chest was lacerated and covered with blood.

While he was watching, the Duke of Cambridge appeared and asked 'Who is that?' When Blunt told him, the Duke rode on, saying, 'Poor Nolan! Poor Nolan!'

Poor Nolan indeed, Blunt thought bitterly. The aide had been a great favourite at headquarters but during his visits to the cavalry camp Blunt had too often heard him busily disparaging Lucan. Feeling tired and hungry—he had had nothing to eat except a biscuit given to him by a Turkish soldier as they crouched under fire in the redoubt—he walked back towards Kadikoi. As he went, he saw the party carrying Morris, who had known his uncle in India and had always been helpful to him, but Morris was so faint he didn't recognise him. He was carried past Brandling's gunners, covered with blood and crying out 'Lord have mercy on my soul!' in his agony.

As the survivors began to form up, Cardigan appeared, and the belief, springing from the sight of the wounded Houghton and Cardigan's vanishing act at the guns, that he had never reached them—a belief that was to plague him for the rest of his life—cropped up at once.

'Hello, Lord Cardigan,' someone greeted him, 'were you not there?'

'Oh, wasn't I, though?' Cardigan replied. 'Here, Jenyns, didn't you see me at the guns?'

Captain Jenyns, one of the few survivors of the 13th Light Dragoons, answered that he had been near Cardigan as he had entered the battery, and Cardigan turned again to his brigade.

'Men,' he said, 'it was a mad-brained trick but . . . no fault of mine.'

An undefeated voice answered him. 'Never mind, my lord, we are ready to go again.'

To the sound of farriers' pistols putting the wounded and dying horses out of their misery, the roll was taken. It was a sad record as the names were called. Many were not answered, but the fate of a few was known—Cornet Montgomery, hit by a cannon ball as he had defended two of his men from Cossacks; Houghton, mortally wounded by a shell splinter; Clowes, cut across the shoulders by grape and a prisoner—but in many cases, like that of the frantic Cornet Goad, of the 13th, injured earlier in the day and searching for his brother, a captain in the same regiment, there were no particulars at all. Among the survivors was Jemmy, the terrier, who lived to return to England.

Of the 673 men who had charged down the valley, only 195 had returned. The 17th Lancers could muster only 37 troopers and the 13th Light Dragoons only two officers and eight mounted men. Five hundred horses had been destroyed. The losses for the day were small compared with Wellington's Peninsula standards or with the Alma and Inkerman which followed, but they were enough. Despite Raglan's care for his horsemen, his light cavalry had virtually ceased to exist, and it had taken no more than twenty minutes to destroy them.

IT was over. That catastrophe everyone had been expecting for so long had come about at last. Springing from obsessions, it had started with Cardigan's preoccupation with his independence and Raglan's concern for his cavalry, and the restriction placed on Lucan had set off Nolan's impatience for action which, as Campbell had predicted, had more than anything else provoked the disaster.

No one was clear yet, however, what had happened, and while the shattered remains of the Light Brigade still crawled back up the valley, Lord Raglan and General Canrobert, surrounded by their staffs and onlookers, descended to the plain to find out.

As the roll-call ended, Lord Cardigan rode up to them. Raglan's 'marble calm' had deserted him for once. He was quivering with rage and Russell noticed how his head shook and how he gesticulated with the stump of his arm.

'What do you mean, sir,' he said, 'by attacking a battery in front, contrary to all the usages of war and the customs of the service?'

Cardigan was not worried. 'My lord,' he said, 'I hope you will not blame me; I received the order to attack from my superior officer in front of the troops.'

Raglan's interview with Lucan was not much more helpful, and Brandling's gunners were witnesses of the angry exchange. Raglan greeted Lucan icily, flinging at him at once the accusation he had been expecting.

'You have lost the Light Brigade,' he said. His argument was academic because within a matter of weeks he would have lost them anyway through his own ineptness and the supineness of the commissariat.

While the farriers' pistols continued to put out of their misery the crippled horses, the shaken Mrs. Duberly watched as wounded and dying soldiers crawled past her to safety, and a distraught officer showed her the piece of grape which had killed his horse. Wives went in search of their husbands' bodies, washing them and wrapping them for burial in blankets or discarded greatcoats, and men went in search of friends. Hearing of Nolan's death, Brandling rode down the slope and found his body, noticing how the gold lace and blue cloth round the gaping wound in his chest was burned and scorched. Fetching several of his gunners, they scooped a shallow grave and from the body took Nolan's watch and scabbard and the letter Morris had written to his wife and given to Nolan to keep. In the wrong belief that Morris was dying, it was handed over for posting and Morris was at first reported dead. Lucan was anxious to recover the body of his nephew, Charteris, and his son, Bingham, also upset by Charteris's death, went out to bring in his cousin's remains. He took his watch and sword and a few other things but the valley was now covered by fire and he had to leave the corpse where it had fallen.

The surgeons were busy amputating Captain Webb's leg and sewing up the ghastly sabre cuts on the heads of Morris, Gordon, Elliot and others. Cornet Neville, mortally wounded in the Heavies' charge, was requesting with his last breath that his father be told of the bravery of the man who had carried him to safety, and in addition to the Distinguished Conduct Medal and the pension that went with it Private Abbott received a grant of £20 a week for life from Lord Braybrooke. A lancer was dying of thirteen lance wounds in chest and stomach while another, who miraculously survived, had had two horses shot under him, suffered six lance wounds, several sabre cuts, bullets through his lance cap, saddle and lance staff and had had his sword bent almost double in its scabbard by a bullet.

Resentful of criticism from anyone who had not ridden with them, the unwounded were discussing their narrow escapes, a few of the more excitable talking themselves into a prominence they didn't deserve. One hunting enthusiast thought the charge 'more exciting than the longest run in Leicestershire' but he was doubtless showing off a little and the pious Seager's view, 'That any of the Light Brigade returned . . . was through the great providence of God . . .' was nearer the mark.

Some men had had as many as three horses shot under them, and Corporal Harry Powell, of the 13th, had had his jacket slit from top to bottom, 'as though by a sharp knife', by a bullet which had grazed his throat and hit the right top button. Penn was showing the Russian officer's sword from which he had broken ten inches of the point against the Cossacks on the ride back, others weapons with fragments of brain, skull and hair attached. Veigh, the butcher, came in still wearing his butcher's smock and still smoking the short black pipe he had had in his mouth when he had left. He had cut down six Russians and lost his horse but he was unwounded, and he also had done so well he had earned a Distinguished Conduct Medal. He was to die of cholera in India. The butcher of the 13th, who had sneaked out of the guard tent was not only let off the charge against him but, on Lucan's instructions, also received a Distinguished Conduct Medal.

For Spring, the deserter, wounded eleven times, the charge proved his undoing. In the reduced brigade, he was soon spotted and was later turned over to the 17th Lancers for punishment. Corporal Morley was boasting of his heroism, fully expecting a medal, and when he didn't get one he left the Service and joined the Northern forces in the American Civil War, ending up as a captain and an official in the War Department in Washington. Still bitter, he spent his old age trying to get himself the Victoria Cross.

A few had disappeared off the face of the earth. The husband of Mrs. Duberly's maid was one and so was the admiring Captain Lockwood, who had been noticed by Fitz Maxse well down the valley. As the Light Brigade had begun their painful retreat, however, he had appeared in front of Lord Lucan demanding to know, like so many others, where Lord Cardigan had got to. He had obviously followed him down the valley and, trying to keep close to him, had followed him out of the smoke and up the slope again. Lucan had assumed that he had not yet been down the valley and told him that Cardigan had ridden off some time before and he set off again towards the guns and was never seen again.

Lenox Prendergast and other wounded were being prepared for the journey to Balaclava and the dreadful hospital of Scutari. Among them was Pennington, who was one of the few to survive its horrors and return to the Crimea. Years later, he posed for the central figure in Lady Butler's picture of the charge and once found himself appearing before other survivors in a stage presentation of the battle in which, to his disgust, actors representing lancers wore *busbies*.

After seeing the body of Nolan and the agony of Morris, Blunt had set off towards the cavalry camp where he found Lucan on his cot with his wounded leg stretched out. As he expressed his sympathy, Lucan said 'It's nothing serious, Blunt. I shall be all right in two or three days,' and added 'I shall want tomorrow one or two copies of the commander-in-chief's order.'

Cardigan had thanked the leader of the Chasseurs d'Afrique for his help and then sought out the dying Trumpeter Britten and Maxse, whose injury had proved less of a wound than a crippling bruising that prevented him from walking. By this time he was beginning to suffer from delayed shock. He had been proud of his brigade and an infantry officer who saw him at this time said he had 'never seen a man looking so grieved'.

The reaction was setting in everywhere now. It was possible to hear the church bells in Sebastopol ringing out in celebration of a victory, and a few of the Light Brigade were noisy from the rum on their empty stomachs. They were still hungry, and many had lost their belongings. What hadn't been smashed had been stolen by the Turks or the Cossacks. No fires were lit because the Russians had opened a cannonade on the infantry positions and Lord Raglan was anxious about his flank; later in the evening the

the brigade moved nearer to Sebastopol. They had to show more vigilance than ever now though, because of the Russians established along the Causeway, and their tents were left standing to deceive them, so that they had to cower in the open air, many of them without the greatcoats or blankets which had been strapped to the horses now lying dead down the North Valley. A few of the animals found their way back to the lines and a few men who had hidden under rocks and bushes stumbled in, but it was a sorry night and it had all been so pointless, of course, because the guns Raglan had thought were being moved had only just been taken away to be displayed in Sebastopol's Theatre Square to lift the spirits of the garrison. Two of them were seen in Novocherkassk by a British officer serving in the Russian Civil War in 1919. In the Heavies' lines, Hodge's servants got brutally drunk, so he took his bed into Forrest's tent and slept there, while Paget—because of the change of position—did not get his men settled until 10.30 p.m.

In none of the many letters and diaries that the survivors were beginning to write by lantern and firelight did anyone indicate that they felt they had been expected to attack the redoubts. Nor did they blame their leaders, and there were none of the cries the French were in the habit of setting up after a military disaster —'Nous sommes trahis!' Indeed, Tremayne thought the men were simply 'glad they had not let the Heavies have all the day to themselves'.

But no one was feeling happy either, and they were bitterly aware of failure in face of the Heavies' success. Though they didn't know it, their failure was to be remembered generations after the Heavies' success was forgotten, and to have ridden with the Light Brigade in later years was enough to make them privileged men. Pennington dined on it for years and when he was introduced on stage to people like Gladstone and Princess Louise it was not as the famous actor he had become but as a man who had ridden in the charge.[1]

When the Victoria Cross was instituted later in the war nine were awarded to the cavalry for the day's work. They could hardly be said to have conducted themselves like badly led men. But that was still in the future and, as they angrily wondered why they had been allowed to destroy themselves, the arguments were beginning, and everybody was looking round for someone to blame. There were no recriminations from Lucan against Cardigan, however, and it was significant that Paget, already aware that there would be a lot of bad blood over the affair, noticed that Cardigan for once did not blame Lucan.

A few people considered that Cardigan had exceeded his instructions and as usual led too fast and some, not knowing he had never been allowed it, thought Lucan should have shown initiative and ignored orders. A few of his critics including Raglan claimed he should have made a reconnaissance but, as Blunt and Brandling's men had seen, he had twice ridden with his staff on to the Causeway. A few, like Seager, took a cynical view. 'The man who carried the message . . . is killed, so I suppose the blame will all be laid to his account', but no one blamed the old quarrel between Lucan and Cardigan, and on the whole no one had much doubt where the real blame lay. 'Never was such a mad order given,' Jenyns thought, 'Nolan is the man to blame.'

'We think it is a judgement on him for getting us in such a mess', was the opinion of Portal, who considered the order 'the maddest and most extraordinary ever given to cavalry'. Calthorpe considered Nolan had died 'from an act of over-daring and courage', and said 'he appeared totally to have misunderstood his instructions . . .'. Blunt recalled the constant criticisms of Lord Lucan and Nolan's boast after the Alma that he would have pursued the Russians to the very gates of Sebastopol, while Paget, who thought it wrong to have chosen Nolan to carry the fatal order, considered him 'brave, unconciliatory and headstrong', and felt that his constant disparagement of the cavalry made him totally ill-suited for so grave a mission. He called him bluntly 'the madman who was the chief cause of the disaster'. Windham, Cathcart's aide, who knew Nolan well, hit the nail most squarely on the head. 'His whole object', he wrote, 'appears to have been a charge at the Russians at any cost . . .'.

Thanks to Kinglake, the argument was to occupy the minds of historians for over a century afterwards but in the minds of the men who knew Nolan there was never any question but that, as he had promised, he was snatching at the chance he had been seeking the whole campaign. Russell, like a good newspaperman, was alert for scandal, and he very quickly came to the conclusion that Nolan had been killed as he rode in front of the line, cheering them on. Certainly it is hard to believe that Nolan wasn't fully aware of what he was doing. Kinglake's version of his death, written years later, exonerates Raglan by making it appear that Nolan knew what the brigade was supposed to do and was endeavouring to put right a mistake made because Lucan had been too impatient to question him.

But Kinglake was writing at the request of the Raglan family and the Light Brigade's charge was the most disastrous of all Raglan's errors, and there were too many people who were watching who never saw the incident he described and too many others who said quite firmly that it did not happen. According to several witnesses there had been plenty of opportunity, if Nolan knew the real direction to be taken by the Light Brigade, to get the matter straight. He had been with Lucan when he rode across to Cardigan and he was also seen to talk to Cardigan himself for a minute or two, and sat alongside his friend Morris for some time while they waited for the forward movement to begin.[2] It is hard to believe the two friends did not discuss what was to happen, yet Morris, too, to the end of his life—he died in India soon afterwards of heatstroke said to be caused by the sun on the silver plate which had to be inserted in his skull—continued to believe, as he had in the beginning, that Nolan was merely spurring ahead in his wild excitement and was intending to charge the guns down the valley. His cry, 'We have a long way to go', indicates what he was expecting to attack.

As for Cardigan, he believed Nolan had moved across the front of the brigade, but despite Kinglake's attempt to put into his mouth the assertion that he had galloped across his front, his written statement said only that he believed Nolan had turned and gone to the rear. Henry Clifford had watched the charge—and it must be remembered that the watchers on the Sapouné Ridge could not only see everything that was taking place below but could even identify the individual officers—and he had noticed nothing odd about Nolan's behaviour. When he met Cardigan on the road to Balaclava four days later, in fact, Cardigan told him quite firmly that Nolan had been galloping off in the direction he had pointed—to the Russian guns down the valley.

Fred Maxse wrote home of him '. . . all the cavalry lay this disastrous charge on his shoulders and say he left no option to Lord Lucan', while his brother Fitz and Wombwell, who were riding two horse lengths behind Cardigan and in a better position to see than Kinglake's unknown officer, wherever he was, had no doubt at all about what had happened. Fitz Maxse, whose horse, like Private Badger's, had almost collided with Nolan's as he swerved, was so incensed, in fact, when he read Kinglake's story,[3] he felt constrained to put it right with a letter to The Times. He had no recollection, he said, of Nolan's 'divergence in the line of advance . . . either by deed or gesture until after he was killed'. A letter to his brother Fred was even surer. 'Nolan', he said, 'was killed close to me and Kinglake's account is . . . absurd [this word heavily underlined] as to Nolan wanting to charge any other guns but those which he did.'

Most men felt that only death had saved the aide from a court martial. Armed with a dangerously inept order he had allowed his obsessions to overcome his common sense. In his eagerness to get the Light Brigade into action, he had probably never listened to his instructions, and his finger pointing down the valley indicated what he firmly believed. He had often said that cavalry should be thrown into a charge at the utmost speed and that there should be a man in front with drawn sword to indicate the direction, and he was doing exactly that, trying against the steady pace Lucan had ordered to hurry them on in the direction he was indicating. And if he *did* intend to ride to the guns down the valley because he thought that was where he was supposed to ride, it demolishes utterly the argument that if only Lucan had been less consumed with dislike for him and had questioned him more closely, he would have learned the true course of the brigade.

Lucan, who had previously barely noticed Nolan, had been in no doubt about what he was expected to do. If a man has to do something he suspects will bring disaster and disgrace, and takes pains to preserve the evidence he believes will prove him innocent, it is unlikely that he hasn't also taken the trouble to get clear in his mind first what it is he is expected to do. The elaborate precautions he and his staff took showed that he was expecting disaster and, if he survived, trouble; so it is unlikely that he did not question Nolan carefully to make sure yet again that he should not be accused of misunderstanding orders. If Nolan had the facts wrong to start with, however, he could have questioned him till he was black in the face. He would still have got the same answer.

*

With the uproar subsiding, Lucan, not allowing his wound to be reported, decided to face Raglan and have the matter of the charge out. As he told Russell, he was quite satisfied with his charge (the Heavies') whatever Raglan might think of the charge he had initiated (the Lights'), and his men had behaved magnificently, despite Raglan's old-womanly fears. The discipline and courage of the Heavies had been visible to everyone and the Light Brigade's charge, to quote Fortescue, had been 'no headlong rush of reckless cavaliers, but an orderly advance of disciplined men . . .'. He knew he was on firm ground and he angrily threw back at the commander-in-chief the accusation that he had lost the Light Brigade.

His anger startled Raglan, who could not reply with any safety *what* he had ordered. It is an indication of the way headquarters was run that, although Lucan had taken the precaution of retaining *his* copy of the order, no one at headquarters had a copy of either the third or the fourth order.[4] Raglan sidestepped the issue.

'Lord Lucan,' he said. 'You were a lieutenant-general, and should therefore have exercised your discretion, and, not approving of the charge, should not have ordered it to be made.' It was tantamount to a confession that the order was a dubious one and Lucan was not slow to seize on it. He had endured neglect and restraint, he said, and had been given orders like a junior officer. He had asked on several occasions for latitude and been firmly told he had none, and Lord Raglan, after sending him 'confused and random orders' throughout the battle, had not appreciated what he, Lucan, could not see. He *could not* have seen because even the people on the Heights, like Ewart and Cathcart, had no idea that anything at all untoward was taking place in the North Valley. The order was not even verbal but had been written down by Airey, far too hastily, in his careless, plunging hand with little regard for the man who would have to act on it. Indeed the order is barely readable and it had been delivered by the one man who was unlikely to give a reasoned explanation. Yet Queen's Regulations, which Lucan knew well, laid it down firmly that orders brought by aides-de-camp had to be obeyed as if they were brought personally by the general officers to whom they were attached, and Wellington himself had said that a private dragoon could be the bearer of a written order as well as a staff officer, 'but for this consideration: that a staff officer is supposed to know somewhat the views of the commander who sends the order, and therefore can be appealed to in the case of a doubt as to the purport of the order'.

When Lucan left headquarters, Portal noticed he was 'dreadfully cut up' and had tears in his eyes. Running into Paget, he said the blame had been laid on him and observed of Raglan's orders, 'A man might just as well put a bullet through his head as disobey them.' In this, of course, he was quite right. As one man put it, 'No consideration would have saved Lucan's reputation if he had refused to carry out the instructions brought by Nolan.'

His voice like an old crow's after all the shouting he had done, Paget was bitter that, after all the sneering against them, they should be blamed for something that was no fault of their own, but there were other things to do besides complain. It was necessary to call in all horses lent to staff and other officers to mount the dismounted men, and a truce had to be arranged to discover what they could about the men in the Russians' hands. Captain Fellowes, DAQMG to the division since Morris had left to command the 17th Lancers, was sent down the valley accompanied only by a trumpet-major carrying a white flag and sounding every two or three minutes. They were met by two officers whom Fellowes addressed in French, pointing out he had seen many bodies lying about and asking if they could be buried. An older and more senior officer appeared. 'Tell your general,' he said angrily, 'we are enemies, but we are Christians,' but when Fellowes produced letters from Russian prisoners, he promised to give the names of survivors.

It turned out that there were thirty or forty of them, among them Lieutenant Chadwick, of the 17th, Cornet Clowes, of the 8th, and one of the Sardinian officers. The Russian also handed over a bloodstained paper from the body of Captain Goad, of the 13th Light Dragoons, who had last been seen sitting about 150 yards from the guns, holding his revolver and wounded in the face. The Russian said the charge had been against all military law, but it had not failed to impress them, too, and as long afterwards as 1908 at a banquet for a British commission in Russia an old man recalled it with emotion.

At that moment, however, the prisoners were being driven forward by lance butts or dragged along at the tail of a horse. Wightman was on the back of Fletcher who was shot through the head and—though Wightman didn't know it—already dying.

Once they were handed over by the Cossacks to regular troops, they were much better treated and they were given vodka and conveyed in carts beyond the Tchernaya. One man had 36 wounds and others were terribly mutilated by sword cuts to the face and head.

General Liprandi showed surprise at the height of some of them. 'If you are a light dragoon,' he said in English to the six-foot-two Parkes, 'what sort of men are your heavy dragoons?' He would not believe they had been sober—'Come now, men, what did they give you to drink? Did they not prime you with spirits to come down and attack us in such a mad manner?'—and Private Kirk, of the 17th, who had been at the vodka, jumped up at once. 'By God,' he exploded, 'if we had so much as smelt the barrel we would have taken half Russia by this time,' and Sergeant-Major Fowler, who had been run through the back by a lance and was sitting in a corner, rose stiffly, a fine dignified soldier, his wound already mortifying, and checked Kirk for his impertinence.

'Except for the vodka that your men have given some of them,' he said to Liprandi, 'there is not a man of us who has taken food or drink this day.'

*

On 27 October Lord Raglan visited the cavalry camp, and though the men ran out in their shirtsleeves to cheer him, he gave no indication that he was pleased.

'How I longed for him to do so as I walked by his horse's head', Paget wrote his wife. 'One little word. "Well, my boys, you have done well!" or something of the sort, would have cheered us all up.'

If Raglan could find no praise, Lucan could. In his despatch he was generous to his command. He paid high tribute to Scarlett and, despite his dislike for Cardigan, did not hesitate to compliment him. He referred to the Light Brigade attack as 'very brilliant and daring' and said that Cardigan had led it in 'the most gallant and intrepid manner'. They were hardly the words of a man possessed of ungovernable hatred.

He had left a lot of uneasiness behind him at headquarters, however, and some of the opinions about the camps were now being heard. They were forceful enough. Loy Smith, an able, intelligent man, blamed Raglan without hesitation. The charge could have been avoided, he claimed, if he had shown 'more forethought and discretion'.

'Had a few battalions of . . . infantry been posted in the redoubts to support the Turks,' he said, 'and more . . . artillery brought into action, the day would have ended differently.' Hamley, of the artillery, thought the same—that the disaster was due to Raglan's 'strange purpose' of using cavalry alone and beyond support and for his 'too indistinct order'. Hodge, huddled in Forrest's tent, considered bluntly that the Light Brigade had been 'murdered'.

The men were low in spirits, and Raglan's second thoughts were uncertain. Lucan's anger had left him shaken. It was clear his own part in the affair would be under scrutiny and he had written a private letter to the Duke of Newcastle, Secretary for War, in which an attempt was made to make Balaclava sound like a victory. The blame for the disaster was laid firmly on the cavalry commander who, he claimed, had made 'a fatal mistake'.

'The written order sent to him by the quartermaster-general,' he went on, 'did not exact that he should attack at all hazards, and contained no expression which could bear that construction.'

Despite this letter, however, that evening he sent Airey down to the cavalry camp to try to talk Lucan round. Lucan was waiting for him and he was in no mood to be calmed. He had been accused of being responsible for something which was clearly the fault of the staff, but he had to admit Airey was no unskilful diplomatist and he had a very great interest in the matter himself, since it had been he who had translated Raglan's orders into the fatal and vague written command.

Airey pointed out that that no one was to be blamed. 'You may rest satisfied,' he said, 'you will be pleased with Lord Raglan's report.'

Even as he was speaking, that report was being completed. It had become clear that something cautious would have to be said officially which would not incriminate headquarters but would yet not be stiff enough to annoy the prickly and self-righteous Lucan. Raglan trod as lightly as he could and in his official despatch, written on the 28th, he wrote 'from some misconception of the order to advance, the Lieutenant-General considered he was bound to attack at all hazards'. He did not inform Lucan what was in the despatch but he showed it to Cardigan, with whom he was now riding regularly once more.

Perhaps Raglan was trying in his way to make the blame as light as possible but what he had said by no means exonerated Lucan. And it is by no means unlikely that he was trying to avoid trouble, knowing full well that when the facts were known it was more likely to come his way than any other. A general order to the army four days later, designed to calm everyone, could hardly be said to express the dissatisfaction he had shown to Lucan. It paid tribute not only to Campbell but also to the 'brilliant conduct of the division of cavalry, under the command of Lord Lucan', and congratulated Scarlett and the Light Brigade on their actions.

The early reports of the battle that reached England were doubtful and based largely on surmise, and the comfortable English middle classes, wading through the columns of their newspapers, found the first indication of disaster—alongside adverts for Rimmel's Toilet Vinegar, Jackson's Patent Preparation and Moxon's Effervescent Magnesium aperient—in a despatch from the Ambassador to Turkey, who had received the news from the captain of a ship which had left Balaclava on the 26th. 'Three regiments of English cavalry,' it said, 'exposed to . . . cross-fire

. . . suffered immensely.' Harsher news came via the Paris *Moniteur* which stated that 400 men had been lost. A garbled message dated 28 October said 'Our cavalry advanced too far, got near a masked battery and were somewhat cut up', and *The Times*, inevitably, came nearest the truth with a cable dated 30 October—'800 cavalry were engaged, of whom only 200 returned. The 17th Lancers were almost destroyed.'

It was *The Morning Chronicle* which brought the first indications of blunder. Alongside Raglan's despatch and the lists of killed and wounded, *The Morning Chronicle*'s correspondent wrote 'By an imbecile command . . . the flower of the British army were . . . led to butchery . . . Never was more wiful murder committed than in ordering an advance to such . . . certain destruction . . . The popular voice has united in subscribing this great calamity to Captain Nolan.' He referred to Lucan's 'well-earned reputation for prudence' and went on, 'On the day of Alma, when victory had crowned the brave efforts of our infantry, and when the complete rout of the enemy, the loss of his artillery, and perhaps the fate of Sebastopol, hung on a dashing cavalry pursuit, then our own force was deemed insufficient; but now, in a miserable skirmish, this very force was despatched against formidable batteries, a cavalry twice superior in number, and an unknown force of infantry.'

Russell added his measure in *The Times*. Of Nolan he said, 'He entertained the most exalted opinions respecting the capabilities of the English horse soldier.' Properly led, he went on, he had felt 'they could break square, take batteries, ride over columns of infantry . . . as if they were straw'.

It was pretty strong stuff and laid the blame squarely on Nolan's shoulders. But letters from men who had taken part were beginning to appear, too, now—'We all knew that the thing was desperate before we started . . . The Light Brigade was greatly damaged, and for nothing'—and *The Daily News* was stating that the order to the cavalry was not purely verbal as was at first thought, but was in writing. Even as it said that Nolan could not have been to blame, Nolan's friends were rushing to his defence with the same line of thought, and the indignant middle classes, already beginning to suspect that something was horribly wrong with the aristocratic handling of the war, began to ask how, if Nolan carried a written order, could a mistake have been made at all.

22 They will tell us we have neglected our regiments

THE newspapers containing Raglan's despatch did not arrive in the Crimea until a month after the battle, by which time Balaclava had been forgotten in new disasters. The cold weather had started killing off the horses within three days of the charge and, while trusses of hay lay on the beach or floated in the harbour of Balaclava, they were being allowed only three pounds of barley daily and were so weak they could not labour seven miles and back through the mud with what could be found.

Lucan's temper continued to make him unpopular but he did not shirk his responsibility. Fussy and self-righteous, but dedicated and determined where his men were concerned, he was constantly badgering headquarters about forage and provisions.[1] What he said was right enough and Portal was writing home of 'miserable-looking brutes, covered all over with mud and dirt' and of men with 'their clothes all in patches . . . begrimed with mud . . . some even already with no boots and bands of hay tied round their feet', men who had not tasted bread in many cases since July. Paget, who had been on the point of retiring from the army when the war had started, took the opportunity now to resign his commission, and 38 other officers of various branches of the Service, 'profiting by his example', also sent in their papers.

The battle of Inkerman on 5 November when the Russians had made another attempt to drive away the British and been repulsed with losses that made Balaclava seem a mere scuffle, had thinned out the ranks of the senior officers. George Brown was wounded on board the *Agamemnon*, De Lacy Evans was severely bruised, Cathcart was dead and the Duke of Cambridge was on board the *Retribution*, said to be suffering from strain. Cardigan, too, was sick and anxious to go home, but still creating difficulties by turning down his colonels' requests to move their horses which were up to the knees in mud, because he felt it would spoil the arrangements of his camp. He had not appeared at Inkerman until the battle was over.

On 14 November, by which time the state of the cavalry camp was 'beyond anything beastly' with mud a foot deep and Hodge wishing he were back in foggy London, a tremendous gale struck the peninsula to complete the ruin. Hospital marquees vanished, leaving sick and wounded men without shelter. Tent poles snapped, barns and sheds were stripped of their roofs and torn down plank by plank, stone by stone, and the air was filled with flying blankets, coats, tubs, tiles, bedclothes, tables and chairs —even mud—and the heavy arabas were upset and men and horses rolled over and over. While Raglan's house, with smoke streaming cheerfully from its chimneys, was eyed enviously by his miserable army, the officers and men were up to their knees. Russell's tent went down and Hodge's tent took wings as the sleet and snow came down in showers, and Lucan was seen in the mud in the ruins of his establishment. Saddlery and accoutrements were blown away and forage destroyed and the horses were like drowned rats. Many were dying and several men were dead of exposure, and Walker, sent by Lucan to headquarters to find out what was to be done with the sick and wounded, was never more thankful of shelter in his life.

The position was critical. The army had got itself into a mess from which it took a whole year to extricate it, and Hodge was longing for the end of the war. There was no food for the horses and little for the men, no shelter, no medicine and no order, and Hodge was blaming Lucan for 'his mulish obstinacy'. But Lucan could do nothing beyond share his men's hardships, and he was already in a bad mood when the newspapers arrived and he read what was said about him. No one in the cavalry believed the nonsense about 'misconception of orders',[2] least of all Lucan, and he decided angrily to write a letter home 'so that the English public should know the facts of the case'. On 30 November his letter went—as usual through the proper channels—

to Raglan. It was an impressive epistle, but his friends saw the danger. 'It is clever,' Sterling said, but he added, 'I never knew a case of a man defying his commanding officer who did not come off second best.'

He was right, and on three occasions Raglan sent Airey down to suggest that he withdraw the letter. But Lucan had had enough. He had already withdrawn several letters without much noticeable change in the set-up and he had no reason to believe that his treatment this time would be any different. Unwisely, he refused, and the letter was sent off on 18 December, but with every one of his points well covered by a letter from Raglan that kicked all the props from his argument. It was inevitable that the government would take a poor view of his quarrel with his senior officer and by 27 January, when Newcastle replied to it, other factors were entering into the question. The government itself was in trouble.

*

The army by this time was dying on its feet. Balaclava was 'one great pigsty', the stench of misery and despair hanging over its tideless waters like a miasma. Piles of amputated arms and legs, the sleeves and trousers still on them, could be seen dimly through the water into which they had been thrown, and corpses rose from the mud and floated on the scummy surface to become entangled with ropes and anchor chains. The sick arriving in Scutari were suffering from malnutrition[3] and Hodge was reduced to sorting for food through a sack of onions. 'Nice employment for a lieutenant-colonel of cavalry', he thought.

By 5 December Lucan had had to report that the cavalry was quite useless. The horses were dying in dozens of starvation, cold and wet, and the last humiliation came when he had to tell his colonels that they had been ordered to give up 500 horses a day to carry provisions from Balaclava to keep the infantry alive. 'This, then,' Hodge mourned, 'is to be our end.'

That fine cavalry Raglan had been so eager to preserve had been destroyed by his own carelessness and neglect. His letters home had given little idea of the condition of the army. Up to the end of the year almost all he had said was that 'the ground was still in a lamentable state' and his references to the weather were detached. When he wrote on 13 January that every man had received a second blanket, a jersey, flannel drawers, socks and an extra coat, although they had probably arrived in the Crimea, they had certainly not reached the troops.

The army was disgusted. Portal, who had never yet seen Raglan, could not understand why he did not ride among his men. 'All agree', he wrote '. . . that not once since we landed has Lord Raglan shown one spark of military knowledge'. 'We all feel he does not care two pence what becomes of us,' Strange Jocelyn said. The cavalry were bitter. While they called themselves 'The Butcher Boys' because of their new duties and made light of their own sufferings, they were angry as they saw their horses die. By this time there was not only no hay but the feed bags had rotted in the wet and, while thousands of them lay unused at the bottom of ships' holds in Balaclava, the corn had to be placed in the wet mud for the horses, many of which were so wretched they didn't even try to eat it. 'When all our men's things are destroyed,' Hodge said, 'saddlery gone, and horses killed, they will tell us we have neglected our regiments.'

His bitterness found an echo throughout the army. When Lord Raglan was made a field marshal, Windham observed sourly that he hoped he would use his baton 'to flog matters on a little faster' and Henry Clifford said tartly 'He has more to thank the army for than it has him.' He saw 900 sick taken down to Balaclava and knew that about 100 of them would never see the next day. 'Field marshal', he wrote, 'must sit heavy on his shoulders...'

On 16 December, with a dead or dying horse every ten yards of the road to Balaclava,[4] he wrote 'Here comes one of the miserable remains of the Light Brigade . . . Which is most to be pitied, the man or the horse? The man thinks nothing of the brute he is on . . . He can only get what forage it can carry up on its back . . . to keep it alive with . . . it has been tied up all weathers without any covering but its saddle, which has not been taken off for days because that reopens the dreadful sore back under it. It can't go out of a walk and he will soon have no further trouble with it . . . he says he wishes he had been cut up in the Charge of the Light Brigade . . . and then all would have been over.'

Soldiers' widows huddled over their graves and Jocelyn, almost shoeless, watched the horses standing knee-deep in slush and snow, the cutting wind freezing their emaciated bodies as they broke loose in search of non-existent food and shelter. 'As the wretched officers and men cowered . . . there wandered daily before them a grey horse growing more and more like a spectre, dying literally by inches . . . falling more and more often from weakness, less able to rise each time until . . . he lay down for the last time.' All Cardigan could think of was to double stable hours to keep the animals' circulation going, and when told that the exposure would kill the men instead, he said 'Ah . . . but we can't replace the horses.'

Lucan was by no means unaware of what his men were suffering. He later bitterly detailed to an army board[5] every minute of a private soldier's day and, with half the cavalry sick or dead, it was a formidable list. But the middle classes back home knew nothing yet of this and, already regarding with distaste the appointment of so many titled officers to command, were by this time in full cry.

Cobden's statistics, Dickens's caricatures and Bright's lay sermons had worked hard during the forties at their indignation but, though the aristocracy had withstood them as they had withstood the recent European revolutions, they had left anger and resentment. The middle classes didn't so much object to the aristocracy running the country, they only asked that they should be fit to, and the complaints began after Inkerman when the generals started coming home and began to talk. Sir George

Brown, Evans, Paget and others had already arrived—though Paget, when he was cut in the London clubs, soon decided to return. Cardigan, after a last quarrel with Lucan about late returns and the orderlies who had to make the arduous daily journey to his yacht, and a last complaint to Raglan about him, was home too.

'No loss either', Portal wrote. Angry and embittered after Balaclava and ready to blame anyone, he had already informed his family that he considered him 'one of the greatest old women in the British Army . . . He has as much brains as my boot. He is only equalled in want of intellect by his relation, the Earl of Lucan . . . Without mincing matters, two such fools could not be picked out of the British Army to take command . . . But they are Earls!'

Cardigan had visited Mrs. Duberly before he left with a long tale of woe. His health was gone, he said, his command had gone and even if he had a command, he added, still dreeing his weird about independence, he wasn't allowed to command it. 'My heart and health are broken', he ended. He showed sufficient concern to stop in Scutari to pay a visit to Captain Morris and other wounded survivors of his brigade but he had soon recovered his spirits and was now showing off round London with frightful bombast.

Even the Duke of Cambridge was home, much to the annoyance of the Queen, who felt that a member of the Royal Family should have set an example by sticking it out,[6] and looking at him, listening to Cardigan, the middle classes felt they had plenty of ammunition, and now they were after Raglan himself.

On 8 November, after Inkerman, Russell had written to The Times 'I am . . . convinced that Lord Raglan is utterly incompetent to lead an army through any arduous task . . .' and the leader writers were saying '. . . the noblest army ever sent from these shores has been sacrificed to the grossest mismanagement', and blamed lethargy, aristocratic hauteur, official indifference, favour, routine, perverseness and stupidity. Armed with Russell's vitriolic despatches, Delane, the editor, attacked the aristocratic rule of the army, while furious officers were encouraged to write bitter letters. 'Our state here is shocking!' Windham wrote '. . . and on my honour as a soldier . . . I believe the fault is in our rulers here, not in the Duke of Newcastle.'

Even Raglan's following of Wellington's habit of mentioning no one in his despatches but his generals and their staffs—most of whom were well connected—was held against him and it was felt he was interested only in his titled friends. While junior officers and NCOs brought forward by their divisional commanders were ignored, Raglan's five nephews, all of them in comfortable staff jobs, received rapid promotion. There was even bitterness among the Guards. 'The list of CBs amazes me', wrote Higginson, while Sterling commented 'If I only had a bit of interest or was Lord Tom Trumpeter . . . !' and the middle-class officers began to ask if they were ever to be noticed.

It was very clear that before long someone would have to be thrown to the wolves and by 23 January John Arthur Roebuck, QC, 'Tear-'Em' Roebuck, Member of the growing and class-conscious Sheffield, that man of forceful speech who had been so quick to advocate the use of the sword the previous year, was demanding an inquiry.

The country was eager for the heads of a few aristocratic officers and Lord Lucan, by his letter, virtually offered himself as the first. On 27 January Newcastle wrote to Raglan recalling him. The Horse Guards were right behind him. They had put forward Raglan's name as commander-in-chief and a criticism of Raglan was a criticism of them, too. A sacking, by implication, laid the blame elsewhere with the unthinking emotional public.

Once again Lucan was unlucky. Two days after Newcastle had sent off his letter the House of Commons divided on Roebuck's motion that a committee be appointed to enquire into the condition of the army and the conduct of those departments of the government whose duty it had been to administer to its wants. The aristocratic Lord Aberdeen fell, to be replaced as it happened by the most arrogant of them all, Lord Palmerston. But it made no difference to Lucan. He had lost by 48 hours.

By this time the cavalry had almost disappeared. 'Poor brutes,' Portal said of the horses, 'it is horrid to see them shivering and shaking, with clothing a mass of ice . . .' With the men taking to any cheap liquor they could find to alleviate their misery, Hodge was noticing that his hair was becoming thin and grey, and to the information that they were to receive a medal for their battles it was said 'Maybe one of these days we'll have a coat to stick it on.'

Roger Fenton, the photographer, arriving soon afterwards, saw one of the 17th Lancers, who pointed out his regiment . . . 13 men, 'their horses a sad spectacle, rough, lanky, their heads down, their tails worn to stumps and most of them showing great patches of bare skin . . .'. Animals which had starved to death after trying to gnaw each others' tails, and even the spokes of gunwheels, lay dead in the mud and snow of the gullies, with the ravens and wild dogs round them, while those still living looked 'more like costermongers' donkeys'. Eighty pounds was considered their full load on transport duties—not much more than a large child. The skeletons of 25 October were still lying where they had fallen, covered with rotting saddles, a man's skull sticking up here, feet and hands with scraps of uniform still attached starting out of the ground there. When Paget returned he found that the ten regiments of cavalry in the Crimea numbered no more than 400 men and the Light Brigade had 44 horses, of which twelve were unserviceable. The 17th Lancers had not a single serviceable horse and the 8th Hussars had three. A few stables had been constructed by this time from the wreckage of sunken ships and Lucan had endeavoured to provide a horse hospital. He was as unlucky as ever. The situation was a poor one, and they were washed away by the rain and several horses drowned, and they were so close and damp glanders broke out and almost every animal put into them was lost. To those who didn't know him he was a hard, unfeeling man and there were still occasional angry disputes with his officers, but Paget had understood him as, curiously, he had seemed to understand Cardigan. His staff, even the unmilitary Blunt, had accepted his faults, knowing how hard he worked for his division, while Mayow, who had never had 'a bed of roses' under him, said of him 'he not only thought of his cavalry by day, but he dreamt of them at night'.

By 31 January, with a spell of warm weather that made Hodge think of May, they were hearing of Lord Cardigan's doings in England. The shops were full of prints of him, 'jumping a gun, and sticking a Russian en passant in mid-air', but 'no one had a good word to say of him'. They all suspected he had no intention of returning to the Crimea and felt it was better that he should not.

Although the cavalry were still in desperate straits things were actually beginning to look better when Lucan's recall arrived on 12 February, and some of the surviving horses, their tails almost eaten away, tough old ribs showing through flesh that was covered, it seemed, with nothing but skin that was hairless with mange, were beginning to hold up their heads and even their stumps of tails in the warmer sun. Feeling that all along he had only done his duty, the recall shook Lucan and he was startled that his excellent letter should have backfired in this manner. In his distress he rode down to see his friend Campbell.

'We were startled', Sterling wrote, 'by the entry . . . of Lord Lucan, in a flurry, just recalled home on account of his row with Lord Raglan . . . It is a terrible blow to him.' It was indeed, and he sent for Hodge and Douglas, of the 11th Hussars, with whom he had always got on well, and informed them of the news.

'I pity him,' Hodge said, surprisingly after his earlier dislike. 'He has been uniformly kind and civil to me, though I think he is not the man to command, being obstinate and headstrong.' The news was received in his division with mixed feelings, according to how paths had crossed. He had not gained one whit of popularity—Cornet Fisher wrote 'It is quite a relief to get rid of

277

Lord Lucan. Poor old man, he was a horrid old fellow'—but there was a lot of sympathy. Forrest, who had so often lambasted him, was unexpectedly kind. He attributed his downfall to his irritability and obstinacy and suggested—with a great deal of shrewdness—that he had made many enemies by his manner. 'He will, though, I think,' he added, 'come out of any investigation better than our old friend Lord Cardigan.'

Portal, whose opinion of him was changing, was looking forward to the 'grand disclosures' he would make when he arrived in England: 'He will spare nobody . . . and put the saddle on the right horse.' Remembering the Dobrudja, his desertion of his brigade after the charge and a few other things, he was particularly looking forward to seeing Cardigan given his just deserts. The opinion in the cavalry camp generally was that Lucan was a hardly used man with many bitter foes at head-quarters, where even his insistence that his camp was in a dangerously exposed position had been ignored until Paget had made representations, as the son of Raglan's old comrade, and had got the thing done at once. On the whole, though no one was sorry to see the back of him, the cavalry thought he had had a very raw deal.

He took leave of his staff and said goodbye to Campbell and Canrobert—but noticeably not to Raglan—and left the Crimea on 14 February. Four days later at Constantinople he bumped into Paget, on his way out again. He had always impressed Paget by his sense of truth, the emphatic way he spoke, and the indefatigable way he performed what he considered his duty—as hard on himself as on those under him and full of consideration for their welfare despite the roughness of his tongue.

'A worse-treated man never existed,' Paget said. 'He read me all the correspondence, but seemed consoled by the feeling exhibited towards him by the cavalry . . . for it is very strong.' Roger Fenton, warning his publisher not to worry about Cardigan as before long he would 'have a very different account of his conduct from that which he has himself given', said of

Lucan, he is 'no great favourite, but the officers all sympathise with him and say he is badly used and that he had no chance but to act as he did'.

He arrived in England on 1 March. He had saved all his correspondence as commander of the Cavalry Division and, certain of the outcome, he sent his son, Bingham, to see Lord Hardinge, to demand a court martial. To his surprise, it was refused. He appealed to the House of Lords and sent in another demand for a court martial but this, too, was refused. Lord Panmure, the Secretary for War, was absolutely against it. No one wanted any dirty linen washed in public and, though the government was after Raglan's blood, it had no wish for anyone to add to its load. Lucan was labouring under difficulties. Though he had kept Raglan informed of all his own moves, Raglan had not had the courtesy to do the same for him and he had learned of the contents of the commander-in-chief's letter only on arriving in England. His letter to The Times impressed the cavalry. 'A most excellent letter we all think it', Portal wrote to his family, and his speech in the Lords was received in the Crimea with enthusiasm. The reports arrived about the time when there was a minor panic among the cavalry at the news —false fortunately—that Lord Cardigan was coming out to command them.

'Lucan's answer seems to clear him', Sterling wrote. 'He is a man of considerable ability but Cardigan was thought to be a favourite of Lord Raglan. His lordship always seemed disposed to put him in an unfair position towards Lord Lucan.'

The speech served to solidify the belief that the disaster to the Light Brigade was not Lucan's fault. One man thought he came out of the mess 'with flying colours' and that on Raglan alone fell the responsibility. Another said 'I always hated him, but . . . for heaven's sake let a man have fair play—here is this unfortunate man catching it over head and ears because he obeyed an order given by the thick-headed Raglan . . .' The Times was criticised[7] for attacking him and in his diary Greville blamed Raglan without

279

hesitation. 'He wrote the order,' he said, 'and it was his business to make it so clear that it could not be mistaken.' It had not helped though. The aristocratic members of the Lords considered him a traitor to his own and their interests and it was inevitable that they should not support his application for a court martial.

There was nothing more he could do. He had been unlucky all along the line. The time had not been ripe for his denouncements and only back in Ireland did he get any satisfaction with an address of welcome from his tenantry and a painting of himself from the County of Mayo. He had suffered enormous unpopularity. After his speech in the Lords a pamphlet had been published by Anthony Bacon, the man whose place he had taken years before as commander of the 17th Lancers and who inevitably had little love for him. In a bitter and sometimes nonsensical pamphlet in which he even had the gall to call Cardigan 'a superior tactician' he condemned Lucan not only for inefficiency and for being out of date but also for not leading the Light Brigade himself. In spite of his friends' wishes that he should ignore it, Lucan plunged into a correspondence with Bacon, which only served to increase his unpopularity. When he was given the K.C.B. and, in November, 1855, appointed colonel of the 8th Hussars, The Times wrote scathingly of him.

To his fury he had seen the useless Cardigan appointed Inspector-General of Cavalry and invited to Windsor and, when Napoleon III and his Empress visited London, had read of him commanding the cavalry at the review on the horse he had ridden in the charge. Slowly, however, things began to improve. Nolan was long dead and so now was Raglan. He had fought four battles, three of which were noted for their muddle, while the fourth—the only one in which he made any effort to direct his troops—had ended in blunder. He had died after an attempt to storm Sebastopol had ended in abject failure, saying 'I shall never return home. I should be stoned to death.' Even Cardigan's glory was diminished. A court action fought over that old accusation that he had not ridden to the guns, while it left his courage unsullied, showed his indifference to the sufferings of his men, and E. H. Nolan (no relation to the aide), whose history of the war was quite as vast and considerably less wordy than Kinglake's, wrote 'Never was an officer more unjustly blamed than Lord Lucan.' As Forrest had predicted, he had come better out of the affair in the end.

The board set up to enquire into the causes of the army's sufferings had had to clear him, because it was proved conclusively that the sufferings were due to the system, and Russell had begun to pick up the cudgels on his behalf.

'He was "an indefatigable officer",' he wrote, '. . . and had as little to do with the "glorious" Balaclava bungle as I had.' His summing up came nearest of all to the crux of the matter. He felt that justice had not been done to a 'very rugged, violent and ardent officer who was hit because he had left himself no friends—and he had bought none!—and whose recall was a very high-handed exercise of authority to cover with a false appearance of "vigour" the weakness of those who made him a victim of their own shortcomings'. He noticed that, while Cardigan continued to rail at Lucan, Lucan refrained from saying anything about Cardigan; yet—inevitably perhaps—no one attributed to him the many traits of generosity and nobility which Cardigan's sycophantic friends hurried to attribute to him.

He was promoted full general, made Gold Stick, and colonel of his old regiment, the 1st Life Guards, in 1869. By 1887, by which time the bitterness had faded, his position in the House of Lords had changed to that of a respected elder, and Higginson, a general himself by this time, was impressed by 'his dignified acceptance of a responsibility from which a man of less firmness of character would have shrunk'. He left him convinced that 'besides the great qualities expected from every cavalry leader, he possessed that high sense of responsibility which calls for respect . . . from those under his command'.

On the occasion of Queen Victoria's Jubilee, he was created field marshal, and since field marshals never retire, when he died in 1888, alert and active to the end, he was the oldest soldier in the British Army. His coffin was carried on a gun carriage by the Chestnut Troop of the Royal Horse Artillery and escorted by a hundred non-commissioned officers and men of the Life Guards.

He had had to wait a long time for recognition but he had got it at last.

Sources

Adye, Gen. Sir John Recollections of a Miltary Life 1895
Airlie, Countess of With the Guards We Shall Go 1933
Anglesey, Marquess of One-Leg 1961
Atkinson, C. J. History of the Royal Dragoons 1934

Bacon, Gen. A. The British Cavalry at Balaclava 1855
Barrett, C. R. B. History of the 13th Hussars 1911
Bell, Maj. Gen. Sir George Soldier's Glory 1956
Best, Geoffrey Mid-Victorian Britain 1971
Blunt, Sir John Papers

Calmont, Rose E. Memoirs of the Binghams 1915
Calthorpe, Hon. Somerset J. G. Letters from Headquarters 1858
Cardigan, Countess of My Recollections 1909
Cardigan, Earl of Eight Months on Active Service 1855
Clifford, Henry Letters and Sketches from the Crimea 1956
Compton, Piers Cardigan of Balaclava 1972

Daniell, D. S. Fourth Hussars 1959
Duberly, Mrs. H. Journal Kept during the Russian War 1856

Evelyn, George Palmer A Diary of the Crimea (Ed. Cyril Falls) 1954
Ewart, Lt. Gen. J. A. The Story of a Soldier's Life 1881

Farquharson, K. S. Reminiscences of Crimean Campaigning and Russian Imprisonment 1883
Fenton, Roger Photographs and Letters from the Crimea 1954
Fisher-Rowe, E. R. Letters during the Crimean War 1907
Forbes, Archibald Camps, Quarters and Casual Places 1896
                    Colin Campbell 1895
Forrest, Gen. William Charles Letters
Fortescue, Hon. J. W. History of the 17th Lancers 1895
Franks, Sgt. Maj. H. Leaves from a Soldier's Notebook 1904

Gibbs, Peter *The Battle of the Alma* 1963
Gowing, Timothy *A Voice from the Ranks* 1884
Greville, Charles *Memoirs*, Ed. Lytton Strachey and Roger Fulford 1938

Hamley, Sir Edward *The War in the Crimea* 1891
Henderson, R. *A Soldier of Three Queens* 1866
Hibbert, Christopher *The Destruction of Lord Raglan* 1961
Higginson, Gen. Sir George *71 Years of a Guardman's Life* 1916
Hodge, Lt. Col. E. C. *'Little Hodge'* (Letters, Ed. Marquess of Anglesey) 1971

Jocelyn, Col. J. R. J. *The Story of the Royal Artillery* (Crimean Period) 1911

Kinglake, A. W. *The Invasion of the Crimea* 1863–1877

Lamb, James *The Charge* 1856
Leader, R. E. *The Life and Letters of John Arthur Roebuck* 1897
Legge Pomeroy, Maj. Hon. Ralph (Ed) *The Story of a Regiment* (5th Dragoon
    Guards) 1924
Longford, Elizabeth *Wellington, The Years of the Sword* 1969
Lucan, Earl of, and Bacon, Gen. A. *Correspondence in reference to the Pamphlet
    Entitled The British Cavalry at Balaclava* 1855
Lucan, Earl of *English Cavalry in the Army of the East* (Divisional Orders and
    Correspondence) 1855
Lunt, Col. James *Charge to Glory* 1961
Lysons, Gen. Sir Daniel *The Crimean War from First to Last* 1895

MacMunn, Lt. Gen. Sir George *The Crimea in Perspective* 1935
McNeill-Tulloch *Commission's Report into the supplies of the British Army
    in the Crimea* 1856
Maude, Capt. G. A. *Letters from Turkey and the Crimea* 1896
Maxse, Frederick Augustus and Henry Fitzhardinge *Berkeley Papers*
Mitchell, Sgt. Albert *Recollections of One of the Light Brigade*
Mollo, John and Boris *Uniforms and Equipment of the Light Brigade* 1968
Morley, Thomas *The Cause of the Charge* 1892
                The Man of the Hour 1892
Moyse-Bartlett, Col. H. *Louis Edward Nolan, and his Influence on the British Cavalry* 1971
Murray, R. H. *History of the 8th King's Royal Irish Hussars* 1928

284

Nolan, E. H. Illustrated History of the War Against Russia 1857
Nolan, Capt. L. E. The Training of Cavalry Remount Horses 1852
                Cavalry, Its History and Tactics 1853

Paget, Lord George The Light Brigade in the Crimea 1881
Parry, D. H. The Death or Glory Boys 1899
Pemberton, W. Baring Battles of the Crimean War 1962
Pennington, W. H. Sea, Camp and Stage 1906
                Left of Six Hundred 1887
Portal, Captain Robert Letters from the Crimea
Powell, Cpl. H. Recollections of a Young Soldier during the Crimean War 1876

Raglan, F. M. Lord, Crimean Papers
Russell, W. H. The British Expedition to the Crimea 1877
                The War to the Death of Lord Raglan 1855
                The Great War with Russia 1895

Seager, Lt. Edward Letters
Shadwell, Gen. L. Life of Colin Campbell, Lord Clyde 1881
Small, E. M. (Ed) Told from the Ranks 1897
Sterling, Lt-Col. Anthony The Highland Brigade in the Crimea 1897

Tait, Mrs. W. J. (Ed) An Officer's Letters to his Wife during the Crimean War 1902
Taylor, James A History of the 19th Century
Thomas, Hugh The Story of Sandhurst 1961
Tisdall, E. E. P. Mrs. Duberly's Campaigns 1963
Tremayne, Capt. Arthur Letters
Turner, E. S. Gallant Gentlemen 1956

Wake, Joan The Brudenells of Deene 1953
Walker, Gen. Sir C. P. B. Days of a Soldier's Life 1894
Warner, Philip The Crimean War—A Reappraisal 1972
Whynyates, Col F. A. Coruna to Sebastopol 1884
Wightman, J. One of the Six Hundred 1892
Williams, G. T. Historical Records of the 11th Hussars 1908
Williamson, Brig. H. N. H. Farewell to the Don 1970
Windham, Lt. Gen. Sir. C. A. Crimean Diary and Letters 1897

Wolseley, Field Marshal Viscount *The Story of a Soldier's Life* 1903
Wood, Field Marshal Sir Evelyn *The Crimea in* 1854 *and* 1894 1895
Woodham-Smith, Cecil *Florence Nightingale* 1950
                          The Reason Why 1953

Blackwood's Magazine
British Army Review
Cavalry Journal
Fourth Hussar Journal
Hampshire Gazette
Journal of the Society for Army Historical Research
The Nineteenth Century
Public Record Office, War Office, H.Q. Records, Crimea (W.O.28)
Punch
Quarterly Review
Sheffield Telegraph
Strand Magazine
Daily News
Morning Chronicle
Morning Post
The Times
Thirteenth/Eighteenth Hussars' Journal

Notes on Sources

As the affairs of the cavalry in the Crimea have been so well chronicled, the text of this book doesn't need to be encumbered by a great many notes. They are therefore included here mainly for controversial incidents or opinions, in the case of new material, or where the source is not obvious from the text.

CHAPTER 1 : *The sick man of Europe* (*pages 17 to 21*)

1 MacMunn

CHAPTER 2: *Uneducated as soldiers* (*pages 22 to 27*)

1 Higginson
2 Thomas
3 As Fortescue said, purchase was 'illogical, iniquitous and indefensible and, being so, was heartily accepted by the British public'. Although it was all too often abused, it prevented regiments becoming the closed shops of the aristocracy and there was a great deal more snobbery when it was abolished.

CHAPTER 4: *The English Murat* (*pages 36 to 41*)

1 Pennington
2 Best

CHAPTER 5: *Such ignorance they displayed* (*pages 42 to 51*)

1 Moyse-Bartlett
2 Moyse-Bartlett
3 Evelyn
4 *Hampshire Telegraph*
5 When the band of the Lancers had been broken up, two bandsmen deserted and were found in the orchestra pit of a notorious music hall. Escaping the patrol sent to pick them up, they were last heard of in a travelling menagerie.

CHAPTER 6: *We expect to be in it red hot* (pages 52 to 65)

1 Journal of Society for Army Historical Research
2 Blunt
3 Walker
4 Paget
5 Franks, Anglesey
6 Duberly
7 Walker, Duberly

CHAPTER 7: *He neither feels for man nor horse* (pages 66 to 73)

1 Cardigan decided not to take the Lancers because he felt their spears would be too conspicuous. Although he had known for a whole day he was going, it still took him six and a half hours to get off. 'How long will it take to move the whole British force?' Mrs. Duberly wondered.
2 Russell
3 Raglan papers.
4 Powell
5 Duberly
6 Walker
7 Duberly

CHAPTER 8: *In a state of mutiny* (pages 74 to 87)

1 *Hampshire Telegraph*
2 Among the first to die was a son of Napoleon I's Marshal Ney whom Napoleon III had sent out as a suitable reminder of Napoleonic glory.
3 Sterling
4 Nolan's diary, quoted by Kinglake
5 Franks
6 It was believed to be the work of saboteurs and the French bayoneted a few. 'They do things better than we do,' Paget said.
7 Walker
8 Most of the story of the troubles in the 5th Dragoon Guards comes from Franks's account and there is no reason to doubt him because he was proud of his officers. The regimental history quite naturally skates over the incidents and, despite what Hodge and others had to say, doesn't

even show Le Marchant as commanding officer. It goes so far, in fact, as to state that the 5th D.G. were never attached to the 4th, contrary to the statements of Hodge, Temple Godman, Franks and others to that effect.

CHAPTER 9: *The eye-tooth of the Bear must be drawn (pages 88 to 97)*

1 Walker
2 Raglan papers

CHAPTER 10: *A pleasant march, though rather hot (pages 98 to 111)*

1 Walker
2 Walker
3 Greville
4 Private Spring, in a magazine account
5 Powell
6 Russell

CHAPTER 11: *The infantry will advance (pages 112 to 122)*

1 One remarkable round shot passed clean through 14 or 15 men so that they lolled forward on each other like broken dolls.
2 Raglan also had a conspicuous telescope fitted with a rifle stock so that he could hold it with his single hand.
3 Russell

CHAPTER 12: *They ought to be damned (pages 123 to 134)*

1 Russell
2 Kinglake
3 J. R. J. Jocelyn
4 Walker
5 Pennington

CHAPTER 13: *Wait till I get a chance (pages 135 to 153)*

1 Russell
2 E. H. Nolan

3 Grigg (quoted in Small)
4 Since it was also known as the Black River to the troops it would probably be more correct to call it the Chorniye.
5 Lucan to Board of General Officers at Chelsea
6 Sterling
7 Farquharson, Portal, Fisher, Whynyates
8 She couldn't share her husband's tent because it also contained three other officers.
9 Paget
10 Russell
11 Paget, Kinglake and others

CHAPTER 14: *The poorest fun I know of (pages 154 to 166)*

1 Hodge, Godman
2 Blunt, Russell
3 Blunt
4 Wood, Russell
5 The whole of the plateaux and hills was covered only with thistles.

CHAPTER 15: *Those Turks are doing well (pages 167 and 184)*

1 Forrest and others
2 The Russians sent officers in British uniforms into the French lines and vice versa.
3 Because it was cold he insisted on Russell borrowing his cloak. 'I shall not want it tonight,' he said. Nor did he the next night nor ever after. It is now in the National Army Museum, London.
4 Maxse papers
5 Paget, Whynyates, Godman, Portal and others
6 Whynyates. Lucan's movements and the movements of the Heavies were all seen by Brandling's gunners from their position on higher ground. They are borne out by other eye-witnesses.
7 Whynyates, Godman
8 Whynyates
9 Morley, Paget and others

10 Contrary to what Kinglake says, it seems quite clear from the accounts of
eye-witnesses like Blunt, Morley and others, and from Lucan's message to
Cardigan (see Chapter 16) about making a flank attack, that it was at this
point that he expected Cardigan to move. He could not have expected a
flank attack *after* the Heavies' charge because—again according to eye-
witnesses—the Russians after their defeat did not, as Kinglake says, move
straight back up to the Causeway but withdrew for a distance down the
South Valley first and then swung over the Causeway, so that an attack on
them at this point by the Light Brigade would have been not on their
flank but against their rear. ('A pursuit', Morris called it, while Blunt
couldn't possibly have found himself in their path had they merely
turned in their tracks.)

CHAPTER 16: *Those damned Heavies!* (pages 185 to 197)

1   Godman
2   Hamley, Russell
3   Morley and others
4   Russell, who was told by Cambridge and Cathcart
5   The Russians said later that only a diversion was intended.
6   Calthorpe

CHAPTER 17: *There are your guns!* (pages 198 to 212)

1   Kinglake
2   Henderson
3   Franks, Lucan and others
4   Whynyates
5   Whynyates
6   Whynyates
7   Wightman, Blunt, Whynyates and others
8   Lady Cardigan

CHAPTER 18: *We've a long way to go!* (pages 213 to 224)

1   Douglas, who told Paget
2   Account by Parkes

3   Maxse papers, Wightman, Badger account (in *Midland Evening News*)
4   Walker

CHAPTER 19: *Look out and catch a horse!* (*pages* 225 *to* 233)

1   According to Joseph Grigg, of the 4th Light Dragoons (quoted in Small), the Cossack lance had a tuft of black hair at the end hiding a small hook which cut the veins when withdrawn.

CHAPTER 20: *Has anyone seen Lord Cardigan?* (*pages* 234 *to* 252)

1   Whynyates
2   Whynyates

CHAPTER 21: *You have lost the Light Brigade* (*pages* 253 *to* 268)

1   As late as 1906 he was autographing copies of his autobiography with the words 'who rode in the famous charge'.
2   Wightman, Whynyates and others
3   Oddly enough, even the diagram supposedly drawn by Kinglake's unknown officer does not really bear out his contentions.
4   Kinglake

CHAPTER 22: *They will tell us we have neglected our regiments* (*pages* 269 *to* 282)

1   War Office Records, Public Record Office
2   Henderson
3   McNeil–Tulloch report
4   Higginson
5   McNeill-Tulloch report
6   When the Duke appeared in Sheffield after the war to unveil a war memorial he was greeted with cries of 'Who ran away from the Crimea?'
7   Portal

Index

293

Pennington, Pte. W. H., 44, 49, 109, 120, 200, 207–8, 213, 239, 241, 246, 256–7
Pera, 54
Phillips, Lt. E., 240, 245
Phoenix Park, Dublin, 60
Plumpton, Pte. M., 221
Plymouth, 78
Pollard, Pte., 228
Portal, Capt. R., 12, 77, 83, 124, 162–3, 206, 215, 244, 258, 262, 269, 272, 274, 276, 278–9
Portsmouth, 49
Potato famine, 32–4
Powell, Cpl. H., 255
Prendergast, Cornet L., 164–5, 190, 256
Punch, 145, 158

Quebec, 208
Queen's Regulations, 262

Radziwill, Prince, 236
Raglan, Fitzroy James Henry Somerset, first Baron, 15; character and career, 28–30, 31, 39, 42, 46; snubs Lucan, 57; put off Bashi-Bazouks, 58; ignores Turks' advice, 60; letter from Lucan, 61; attitude to Lucan, 62; at Varna, 63–4; gives Cardigan his head, 65–7; fails to support Beatson, 68; letter about Dobrudja, 71; second thoughts on Cardigan, 72; sends Light Brigade to Yeni-Bazaar, 72; dislikes unconventional dress, 74; fails to lead army, 76–7, 81; decision on 5th Dragoon Guards, 86; no commander, 88; orders for Crimea, 89; blame for conditions, 90; view of cavalry commanders, 91–2; reaction to Lucan's protest, 93; helps Mrs. Duberly, 94–5; en route to Crimea 98–9; lands in Crimea, 101, 102–4; dislike for French, 104; at Bulganak, 107–11; at Alma, 112–22; men's views of, 123–4; after battle, 126, 127; wish to follow up, 127–8; opinion of French, 128; 'bandbox' decision, 128–9; wish to pursue, 129; wish

to use Greys, 129–30; fails to understand cavalry, 130; decisions on Sebastopol, 130–1; at Mackenzie s Farm, 131–3; criticism of Lucan, 135, 136; Nolan's criticism of, 136; reaches Balaclava, 137; dispositions, 138, 139; headquarters, 142; dislikes Russell, 142, 143; distrust of cavalry, 143, 144; letter to Cardigan, 146, 147, 149; instructions concerning Balaclava, 150, 151, 152, 153, 154; gives Cardigan permission to sleep on yacht, 155, 156; orders redoubts built, 157–8; dislikes Dundas, 159; favouritism to Cardigan, 161; orders dangerous patrol, 162–3; warned of attack, 165; dislike of spies, 167; at Battle of Balaclava, 169 et seq.; orders infantry forward, 172; message to Cathcart, 172; arrives on battlefield, 174; his view of battle, 175; first order, 176; second order, 177–8; fear for guns, 192; third order, 193–4; fails to instruct aide, 195; fourth order, 196–7, 198, 201–5, 209, 210; watching start of charge, 214; Turks' bitterness against, 234, 252; accuses Cardigan and Lucan, 253, 256, 258; exonerated by Kinglake, 259; faced by Lucan, 261–2; visits cavalry, 264; blamed by men, 265, 266; despatch, 266–7, 269; lives in comfort, 270; reaction to Lucan's letter, 271; men's attitude to, 272; field marshal, 272, 274; attacked, 274–5, 277, 278; blamed by cavalry, 279–80
Regiments:
Cavalry involved at Balaclava:
Light Brigade:
4th Light Dragoons, 28, 42, 45, 50, 75, 77–8, 83, 86, 91, 104, 105–6, 107, 114, 141, 165, 169, 170, 199, 205, 206–9, 213, 223, 228–9, 231–2, 235, 237, 240, 242–3, 246, 248–9
13th Light Dragoons, 46, 49, 64, 66,